Lisa A. Baglione is Assistant Professor of Political Science, St. Joseph's University.

To Agree or Not to Agree

To Agree or Not to Agree

Leadership, Bargaining, and Arms Control

Lisa A. Baglione

Ann Arbor
The University of Michigan Press

Copyright © by the University of Michigan 1999
All rights reserved
Published in the United States of America by
The University of Michigan Press
Manufactured in the United States of America
♾ Printed on acid-free paper

2002   2001   2000   1999   4   3   2   1

No part of this publication may be reproduced, stored in a retrieval system, or transmitted in any form or by any means, electronic, mechanical, or otherwise, without the written permission of the publisher.

A CIP catalog record for this book is available from the British Library.

Library of Congress Cataloging-in-Publication Data

Baglione, Lisa A., 1962–
    To agree or not to agree : leadership, bargaining, and arms control / Lisa A. Baglione.
    p. cm.
    Includes bibliographical references and index.
    ISBN 0-472-10930-8 (cloth : acid-free paper)
    1. Nuclear arms control. 2. United States—Foreign relations—1945–1989. 3. World politics—1945–   I. Title.
JZ5665 .B37 1998
327.1'747'0973—dc21   98-25388
                                                                  CIP

To my mother,
for her unfailing support,
and
in memory of my father,
who encouraged me to follow
my heart's desires

It [leadership] is among the most challenging of human activities, stirring ambition, exciting admiration, arousing fear or pity (to one's taste), inspiring the dramatists since literature began, ignored by almost nobody in all of human history—until the coming of American political science.
—*Richard Neustadt*

Contents

List of Tables	xi
List of Figures	xiii
Preface	xv
Chapter 1. Leadership, Bargaining, and Arms Control	1
Chapter 2. Conflicting Strategies and Inconclusive Discussions: Khrushchev, Eisenhower, and the Test Ban Talks	21
Chapter 3. From Deadlock to Mutual Compromise: Khrushchev, Kennedy, and the Limited Test Ban Treaty	45
Chapter 4. The Search for Unilateral Advantage: Impasse at the Intermediate-range Nuclear Forces Talks	65
Chapter 5. Concluding the Intermediate-range Nuclear Forces Treaty: Gorbachev and New Thinking Break the Deadlock	85
Chapter 6. Finishing START and Achieving Unilateral Reductions: Bargaining and Leadership at the End of the Cold War	111
Chapter 7. Superpower Arms Control and Joint Decision Making in International Relations	133
Notes	151
Bibliography	191
Index	207

Tables

1.	State's Intentions and Conflict Resolution Strategies	4
2.	Value of Arms Control Agreements	8
3.	Determining Conflict Resolution Strategies	9
4.	Leader's Autonomy within the Domestic System	15
5.	The Nuclear Balance, 1956–60	22
6.	Public Concern with American Defense Policy	31
7.	Perceptions of Relative Power Positions and Superpower Peace Programs	32
8.	Projections of the ICBM Balance	35
9.	American Attitudes toward Testing and Arms Control	37
10.	Trial Heats of Possible 1984 Presidential Contests	73
11.	Issues and the 1984 Election	74
12.	The Superpower Strategic Balance, 1972–87	86
13.	Number of Soviet Officials Replaced, 1982–87	92
14.	Turnover at Party Congresses	93
15.	Impact of Iran–Contra on Reagan's Presidency	98
16.	The Strategic Balance, 1980–91	112
17.	Summary of Bargaining Strategies and Outcomes	135

Figures

1. Leadership Model — 16
2. Eisenhower's Second-Term Approval Ratings — 26
3. Kennedy's Approval Ratings — 50
4. Reagan's First-Term Approval Ratings — 72
5. Reagan's Second-Term Approval Ratings — 97
6. Bush's Approval Ratings — 121

Preface

After the collapse of the USSR, some scholars believed that traditional security issues, like arms control, would fade in importance in the post–Cold War era.[1] Recently, however, observers have come to recognize that this optimism was premature. In fact, the leakage of nuclear materials from the territory of the former Soviet Union, the Russian government's decision to sell reactors to Iran, its failure to ratify the START II treaty, and the Western decision to expand NATO suggest that Russian and American nuclear policies and their security relationship will continue to be of concern to students of international relations.

Despite more than 50 years of American–Soviet arms bargaining, however, we still do not fully comprehend why military rivals with fundamental differences in interests, domestic institutions, and values pursued negotiations to limit a principal source of their security and prestige. This book advances a framework for understanding that endeavor: the leadership model, developed from bargaining theory, constructivism, cooperation theory, and studies in comparative politics on the sources of power in the United States and the Soviet Union. From bargaining theory comes the insight that the key factors in determining strategy are the *alternatives* that a party has to arms control and the *value* that it places on a particular accord.[2] Constructivism suggests that both the alternatives and value depend on an assessment of security that is subjective and multidimensional.[3] Arms control was hardly ever a policy followed for its own sake, but rather was implemented as a means of promoting or maintaining security. So when a superpower considered weapons limitation, it also examined the other options that it could follow to achieve that goal. Moreover, as officials evaluated the worth of an accord, they weighed the motives of their opponent and considered the importance of military assets in guaranteeing the peace. Together, these elements defined a decision maker's *preferred strategy* at the table—whether to make concessions if they would be matched, accommodate a partner's concerns without expecting an adjustment in return, refuse to compromise, participate in negotiations only as part of a public relations campaign, or eschew talks altogether. Clearly, policy choice was a complex decision, and preferences were often contingent upon the expected effects on the opponent.

International concerns, however, were just one set of issues facing officials as they chose negotiating strategies. As specialists on interstate cooperation assert, bargaining is a two-level game, and elites had to consider international and domestic factors simultaneously when charting the national course.[4] In arms control deliberations, one individual above all was sensitive to internal pressures and therefore most interested in making the "correct" choice. That person was the national leader. Moreover, executives in the American and Soviet systems had differing degrees of flexibility throughout their tenures to pursue favorite policies. Scholars who study the executive's role in policy-making tell us that their room for maneuver depended on two variables: the *level of support* among constituents and the *timing* within the election or selection cycle.[5] When an executive was popular with those to whom he[6] was accountable and the date for choosing the leader was in the distance, he had the freedom to pursue the policy options that he favored. Conversely, when support was low and an election or selection was fast approaching, the executive tended to tailor his program to address the preferences of other powerful actors in the system. Thus, these factors—support and timing—interacted to determine a leader's *autonomy,* his ability to define policy independently in his system.

An executive's level of autonomy and preferred strategy together affected the national approach to arms control. When autonomy was low, leaders tended to doubt their ability to overcome the ideological and structural impediments to following anything other than a positional strategy at the table, regardless of their own preferences. Under those conditions, the chief governmental official engaged in *transactional* leadership, trying to please constituents and other powerful actors in the system in exchange for their support. A strong executive, however, could choose an approach depending on his assessment of the alternatives his state faced and the value of an arms control agreement. With traditional perceptions of the insignificant value of an arms control agreement, a leader would typically implement a strategy that would enhance the state's position relative to the opponent, regardless of his assessment of alternatives. Conversely, a highly autonomous executive who perceived an accord as valuable could elect to pursue an approach that he believed was beneficial for his state, regardless of its impact on the relative balance of power. Such leaders followed a *transformational* approach, contesting the missions of key domestic institutions as well as the closely held beliefs of elites and ordinary people.[7]

To test the validity of the leadership model against existing approaches, this book examines several cases of Soviet and American arms control decision making: (1) the test ban negotiations of 1958–60 that ended in failure, (2) the resumption of talks that produced the Limited Test Ban Treaty, (3) the breakdown of discussions on Intermediate-range Nuclear Forces (INF) from 1981–83, (4) the resurrection of negotiations and successful conclusion of an INF agreement from 1984–87, and (5) the steps taken as the USSR collapsed, including the completion of the START I agreement and the unilateral American and Soviet decisions to reduce strategic readiness and nuclear stockpiles.[8]

I chose the test ban and INF cases because those sets of negotiations allowed me to examine opposite outcomes of the bargaining process while keeping the historical context as similar as possible. During the periods 1958–63 and 1980–87, the Americans and Soviets were engaged in negotiations to institute a test ban and to reduce intermediate-range nuclear forces, respectively. Each set of discussions, then, provides for the analysis of an arms control failure (1960 and 1983) as well as a success (1963 and 1987). In addition to maintaining similarities in the cases across the test ban and INF issues, these two historical periods provide interesting comparisons. During both the test ban and the INF talks, many participants in the discussions felt that the United States and USSR were contesting for predominance in the international system. Moreover, throughout these periods, there was also diversity in the nature of the leaderships and their corresponding ideological or bureaucratic bases. These cases, then, provide challenging tests of the leadership model versus the alternative approaches and give the investigator insight into the impact of international- and domestic-level variables on interstate bargaining behavior and outcomes.

In addition, while the last pair, the "minicases" of 1991, are both examples of arms control success, they permit me to examine bargaining behavior in a period in which the international system was undergoing enormous upheaval (bipolarity was disintegrating) and the Soviet state was experiencing national and political revolutions. These cases also help me explore further the influence of the competing variables compared to that of autonomy and preferred strategy. Moreover, including these instances of arms bargaining allows for the examination of a greater variety of strategies; in 1991, the United States and the USSR both made decisions to reduce their arsenals unilaterally.

In each of the first four cases, I provide a discussion of the strongest competing explanation for that incident, derived from one of the existing schools of thought in international relations. In so doing, I am able to assess the ability of realism and the domestic politics approach to explain opposite outcomes at the table. I examine the realist account for the failure of the test ban talks and the success of INF, while exploring the quality of the domestic politics explanation for the completion of the test ban treaty and the walkout in 1983. For the post–Cold War instances of arms control, I show that both of the standard approaches are unable to explain the transformation of superpower arms control behavior in 1991. The leadership model, conversely, can provide solutions across all the varied cases, both during the Cold War and as it was ending.

Why Study Superpower Arms Control Today?

Continuing Theoretical and Methodological Concerns

Although analysts have devoted considerable attention to the study of superpower arms control, few existing works consider an extended period of time, analyze the behavior of both parties without a normative commitment to arms control, and test hypotheses drawn from the broader international relations literature.[9] While the single case studies often provide a rich story of a particular set of negotiations, they do not examine the arms control process in general or search for patterns in behavior. The tendency to focus on the decision-making process in only one country reinforces this problem. Because any bargaining process and its resolution depend on the interaction of two nations (at least), an examination of U.S. arms control behavior alone will necessarily be incomplete. Although some early works claimed to be studies of arms control in both systems, their language and basic assumptions about decision making revealed their grounding in the American one. In addition, several advocates of arms control negotiations have written excellent accounts of the process, but as supporters of the policy, they have tended to assume that all parties sought to reach an agreement and believed that accords were desirable. This book self-consciously attempts to avoid such problems and considers a wide range of motives for involvement in the talks.

In addition, students of arms bargaining have generally been uninterested in evaluating the power of different explanations across many cases. Arms control experts have only recently linked their analyses to the larger body of work in international relations. In this book, contemporary theoretical debates are central, and models of security decision making are developed from the contending paradigms in international relations. The realist model examines the impact of the distribution of capabilities in the system on a state's arms control behavior. Following from its logic, states should prefer independent action but consider agreements when they provide relative gains. Students who stress the primacy of domestic politics, on the other hand, insist that a country's stance at the table is the result of bargaining among bureaucrats and contenders for power at the top of the system. For the two sides to reach agreement, intrastate negotiations must produce positions in both countries that are mutually acceptable. In each of these existing explanations, structure is central for determining a state's bargaining position. The leadership model challenges the primacy of structure and examines the conditions under which the distribution of power has import and the times when individuals can take action to surmount structural barriers.

Continuing Empirical Relevance of Superpower Arms Bargaining

In today's world, where the USSR no longer exists and arms bargaining no longer grabs headlines, this focus on superpower arms control might appear somewhat dated. This study, however, sheds light on the end of the Cold War as well as on contemporary Russian-American relations and the general problem of joint action among adversaries in international relations.

With respect to the demise of the Cold War, comprehending precisely what occurred is important because politicians in both the American and Russian contexts use their interpretation of what happened to justify new policies and approaches. Central to the debate is an argument over how best to treat an opponent. Did the U.S. buildup of the 1980s compel the USSR to accept American terms on INF and START? Or did mounting economic problems and new conceptions of security change Soviet behavior? This study suggests that policymakers should be wary of approaches predicated on the assumption that "peace" always follows from increased "strength."

Moreover, the end of the Cold War has not meant the end of serious misunderstandings and disappointments in the Russian-American relationship. While some U.S. observers of the Soviet or Russian scene have recognized the key role that the leader has played, they have also, unfortunately, failed to comprehend the constraints on his power. This tendency not to conceive of both the domestic and foreign policy components of leadership has complicated the contemporary relationship. In the early 1990s, American confidence in Russia followed from the belief that President Yeltsin's commitments to reform and democracy would consistently underpin that country's policy. When Yeltsin authorized attacks on his parliament in 1993 and a breakaway region in 1995 and was less than enthusiastic about acting in concert with the West to restrain combatants in the Balkans, some American decision makers were confused and felt betrayed. Similarly, American behavior has puzzled Russian policymakers. Why is the United States unable to understand that Russia is building democracy and capitalism and will no longer be a threat? they ask themselves. They have watched with disappointment as the United States has not, in their view, pursued a consistent policy of partnership with Russia.

Furthermore, the end of the American-Soviet arms competition has not spelled the demise of arms races and proliferation. In fact, today, the potential for arms control has spread to new regions and types of armaments. Too many international actors still see nuclear weapons as the answer to their security problems because atomic firepower increases the destructive capability of an arsenal at a relatively moderate cost and enhances the prestige of its possessor. Moreover, regional rivalries continue to fuel security concerns and make nuclear proliferation seem like a "quick fix." Arms control, therefore, could be a policy option that additional actors—Israel and its Arab neighbors, Iraq and Iran; India and Pakistan; North and South Korea; and perhaps others—may want to consider in the future. Because conventional weapons are becoming increasingly deadly, the arms trade is booming, and stockpiles are growing throughout the world, weapons limitation is relevant not only as a means of managing nuclear weapons, but also as a way of controlling conventional ones.[10] Here again, the American-Soviet discussions are instructive since they are the principal, sustained experience of adversarial arms bargaining. The cases and the framework developed in this study, then, provide scholars with a laboratory for generating hypotheses about arms control and predicting the promises and pitfalls that await future participants in the endeavor.

Finally, while some would like to believe that a "new world order" exists, the post–Cold War era has actually been fraught with conflict, violence, and destruction.[11] The fall of communism did not bring about the "end of history" or the beginning of an era in world politics in which war was relegated to the trash heap along with communism. Along with this continuation of violence, however, comes the enduring opportunity for adversaries to resolve their differences at the bargaining table. And the record of superpower arms negotiations provides an excellent example of joint action among adversaries that might help practitioners and students of these new incidents of conflict to understand and ultimately resolve the problems at hand.

In the following chapters, I examine the superpower arms bargaining process and provide a model for understanding why the negotiations were alternatively frustrating and fruitful. In chapter 1, I examine the weaknesses of existing approaches and develop what I call the *leadership model,* with the help of students of negotiations, contemporary international relations theory, and the American and Soviet systems. This alternative framework follows from three central insights: (1) individuals, specifically national executives, occasionally have the opportunity to define bargaining strategy in negotiations; (2) an executive's preferred strategy follows from his assessments of the state's alternatives and commitment to arms control; and (3) whether the leader's preferred strategy becomes the national approach depends on his autonomy within the domestic system. Thus, the exercise of leadership—the executive's management of domestic politics while pursuing security policy goals—is central to this study.

In each of the next four chapters, I provide an account of Soviet and American arms control decision making that briefly highlights the empirical and theoretical inadequacies of one of the existing approaches and demonstrates the superiority of the leadership framework. Chapter 2 examines the realist and the leadership approaches in an investigation of the failed negotiations for the test ban. The difficulty that the two sides had in reaching an agreement in the late 1950s is of no surprise to the realists. The United States was clearly the stronger country, and verification technologies were underdeveloped. Thus, the United States should have been uninterested in tying its hands when it was ahead and Soviet compliance could not be guaranteed, and the USSR should have been opposed to limiting its freedom while it trailed in the arms race. The leadership model suggests that more than concerns about the balance of power affected the inability to reach an agreement. Chapter 3 then analyzes Soviet and American decision making for the test ban in the period 1961–63. Here, the explanations derived from the domestic politics and leadership approaches are juxtaposed. Domestic politics provides an interesting foil, because some analysts believe that leadership struggles in the USSR resulted in Soviet policy shifts, while others have argued that the ascendancy of liberals in the Kennedy administration opened the door for arms control in the United States. Domestic considerations alone, however, do not explain the most important changes in bargaining stances.

Chapters 4 and 5 investigate the negotiations for limiting Intermediate-range Nuclear Forces that occurred in the period 1981–83 and again in 1985–87. For these sets of talks, I compare the leadership model to the domestic politics explanation when examining the failure to settle from 1981 to 1983 and realism when explaining the return to the table and completion of an accord in 1987. In the first instance, domestic politics might appear to provide a suitable account of the failure—because of the election of a conservative American administration and the rise of some opponents to détente in the

USSR. Similarly, changes in the strategic and theater balance in favor of the United States might seem to explain why the Soviets gave in to long-standing American demands in 1987. The investigation of both cases, however, raises questions concerning the conventional wisdom and demonstrates that the bargaining process and the outcome depended instead on both domestic- and international-level concerns.

The final instances of arms control that this book investigates include two successes that occurred in 1991. In both cases, the leadership model equips the analyst with tools for understanding developments that seem inexplicable using the other approaches. In the last two and one-half years of the START talks, Gorbachev made some significant concessions and then appeared to reverse himself. Bush, at first, seemed wholly unimpressed with Gorbachev and what had already been achieved at the bargaining table. He even considered withdrawing from commitments his predecessor had made. In 1990 and 1991, however, the U.S. president made important concessions at the table and offered key economic enticements to Gorbachev to help seal the deal in the last months of negotiations. And then, only a few months after signing the START accord, both presidents announced major reductions in the size and readiness of their arsenals, without the benefit of any negotiations. While explaining bargaining behavior in START is a challenge for realism and the domestic politics paradigm, these incidents of self-adjustment in particular are beyond the scope of the existing approaches. Instead, the leadership model illustrates the causal power of autonomy and strategy, despite structural changes in world politics and the Soviet domestic system.

Chapter 7 analyzes the findings of the cases to draw conclusions about why and when the United States and USSR reached arms control agreements. Moreover, it uses insights from the leadership framework to examine the Strategic Arms Limitation Talks (SALT) of the late 1960s and 1970s. This examination provides a basis for understanding contemporary Russian and American international behavior and elucidates the sources of current Russian and American conduct. Finally, the discussion turns briefly to additional instances of bargaining between adversaries, including the potential for arms control in world hot spots and the negotiations to resolve conflict through joint action in Northern Ireland, the Middle East, and the Balkans.

The origins of this book are in the events of the second half of 1983, when a sense of danger seemed to pervade American–Soviet relations. At the end of August, the Soviets shot down a civilian airliner, killing 269 passengers. In October, the United States invaded Grenada in order to overthrow the government there. Most ominous, however, was the superpower confrontation over the deployment of American intermediate-range nuclear forces in West Germany. The Soviets had warned that if the Federal Republic agreed to accept those missiles, then the USSR would leave the bargaining table and would take countermeasures to threaten Western security. Just prior to the German legislature's vote on deployment, ABC television broadcast the TV movie *The Day After,* which portrayed life in the city of Lawrence, Kansas, the day after a Soviet nuclear attack. With the West German parliament's acceptance of the weapons and the USSR making good on its threats to order its ballistic missile submarines to patrol off the coast of the United States, nuclear conflict seemed very possible.[12]

During this very troubled time, I was an undergraduate not only contemplating the possibility of a superpower confrontation, but also trying to chart my future. Although I was working on a degree in Applied Mathematics–Economics, I was not overly enthusiastic about pursuing a career in either of those fields. Throughout 1983, the deepening freeze of the Cold War became increasingly relevant for me. That summer, I had toured Europe with my college chorus, but our visit to and performances in East Germany were canceled, a casualty of the growing chill in East-West relations. When I returned to school that fall for my senior year, I enrolled in a course on arms control and disarmament. That class and the events that occurred while I was taking it changed my life. A long-scheduled campus lecture by Georgi Arbatov, the director of the USA and Canada Institute in Moscow and adviser to the Kremlin, was canceled, the Soviets walked out of the negotiations on INF and refused to resume talking about strategic weapons, and the superpower relationship seemed to be at its worst state in 20 years. American–Soviet relations and the problem of managing nuclear arsenals both fascinated and frustrated me. There seemed to be many possible compromises that the two sides could have made to prevent this dangerous situation if they had desired. But why did the Soviets and the Americans choose not to agree in the fall of 1983? That question haunted me, particularly because the works of many students of arms control that I had been reading that semester seemed unable to explain this behavior. I decided that my future would be to study this puzzle.

This book is my attempt to make sense of the questions that first arose in my mind in 1983. It seeks to explain why the superpowers concluded particular arms control accords at specific times and failed to resolve their differences at the table at other moments. My argument is that superpowers reached agreements not because military decline, the balance of power, or institutional forces and bureaucratic bargaining compelled them toward arms control. Rather, the United States and USSR concluded accords when at least one leader actively sought compromises and another accepted the conditions offered or proposed additional concessions of his own. When domestic political conditions allowed them the freedom to make overtures to their adversaries, executives pursued settlements as a policy response to their perception of the alternatives to arms control and their assessment of the value of weapons limitation agreements.

The historical cases examined demonstrate that concerns about state survival were pervasive in the nuclear age. Generally, Soviet and American leaders conceived of military power as the essential element of security and were wary of negotiated agreements with the adversary. Therefore, discussions about limiting weapons production and deployment were slow-going and their accomplishments meager. Occasionally, however, leaders selected alternate paths based on different perceptions, and these choices offered hope for a negotiated settlement. When leaders had significant autonomy, were willing to use their prestige to build support for their policy, and adopted unconventional approaches to security and more positive images of their adversary, major agreements became possible. While the pursuit of such policies involved risk (at both the domestic and international levels), the cases show that leaders could sustain such approaches when their domestic political positions were relatively secure. Thus, the experience of superpower arms control suggests some hope for other instances of negotiations between adversaries. With the appropriate leadership, following from particular domestic political conditions and assessments of the international situation, negotiated resolutions are possible. Whether states pursue them depends on whether executives *on both sides* have autonomy and complementary bargaining strategies that are consistent with working constructively with an adversary.

There are several people without whose assistance this book would never have been completed. First, I would like to thank my teachers for their patience, support, and guidance over many years. I am especially indebted to Dan Caldwell, the professor who introduced me to arms control, disarmament, and political science when I was an undergraduate. I greatly appreciate the efforts of Peter Katzenstein, Myron Rush, and Judith Reppy, who worked with me on my doctoral dissertation, the basis of this book. They have each had an impact on my life that they cannot even imagine, and I feel extremely lucky to have worked with and learned from them. Although I never worked directly with him on this project, Ted Lowi deserves my heartfelt thanks. Not only has his scholarship had an important influence on my work, but his encouragement at the earliest stages of my academic career was vital. I am also indebted to Steve Jackson and Jack Moran of the Cornell-in-Washington Center, where I taught for two years.

My experience there was invaluable; by requiring me to teach students how to conduct social science research, they helped me improve my own understanding of the process.

I would also like to thank some colleagues for their help. In particular, members of my department at St. Joseph's University reinforced my determination to complete this book and provided me with firsthand insight into the bargaining process. Milica Zarkovic Bookman and F. Graham Lee deserve special commendation for their useful suggestions and moral support. I also owe a large debt of gratitude to Allison Peter Paul, who helped me navigate the literature on leadership and management. Finally, thanks are due to Anne Szewczyk and Rosann Jennings from St. Joseph's who prepared the graphics for the book.

Without the help of the anonymous reviewers of this manuscript and Malvern Lumsden, this book would be a far inferior product. I greatly appreciate their careful and constructive comments. In addition, Chuck Myers and Kevin Rennells at the University of Michigan Press were extremely helpful, sympathetic, and patient.

I also appreciatively acknowledge the financial support of Cornell University, the U.S. Arms Control and Disarmament Agency, the Institute for the Study of World Politics, the Cornell University Peace Studies Program, and St. Joseph's University. Each of these institutions provided funds that aided the completion of the manuscript.

A number of friends have been enormously supportive during this process. In particular, I want to thank Iris Papaioanou and Julie McDonald for their encouragement and concern.

I can honestly say that this book would not be appearing if it were not for the assistance, guidance, and reassurance of two very special individuals. Audie Klotz read several drafts of this work, provided copious comments, and cheered me on throughout this process. She is an intellectual inspiration and an invaluable friend, and my heartfelt thanks go out to her. My husband, Steve McGovern, has also been extraordinarily helpful. Steve and I met in graduate school, where he was also working on a Ph.D. in Government. When we were students, I always contended that Steve was an honorary member of my dissertation committee because he read and commented on so many drafts of my thesis. Since that time, Steve has continued to be a sympathetic, though exacting, critic. His attention to detail, understanding of politics, and forbearance with my mood swings while I worked on this manuscript have been amazing. I can never thank him enough for his help and affection during this process. I know that we are both equally relieved that the Elvis Costello lyric "every day I write the book" will no longer describe me and this arms control project!

Finally, I want to express my appreciation to my parents. Even though my mother thought that I was crazy to give up a good job and a secure career in "the real world" for unsure employment prospects in academia, her love sustained me through many of my most difficult days, particularly in graduate school. This book is dedicated to her and to my father, who unfortunately did not live long enough to see me graduate from college. Still, during our time together, he always encouraged me to pursue my dreams and seek excellence while also maintaining a balance between work and the "rest of life." While I have not always achieved that equilibrium, I value my father for, among other things, teaching me that only such a life is a full one.

CHAPTER 1

Leadership, Bargaining, and Arms Control

Thinking Theoretically about Arms Control

During much of the post–World War II period, the global rivalry between the United States and the Soviet Union dominated headlines, as the two states competed for allies, prestige, and military preeminence. Concerns about security were often foremost in the minds of American and Soviet leaders. Each nation could destroy the other, and analysts on both sides believed that some kind of confrontation was very possible, if not probable. Yet, despite fundamental differences in interests, domestic institutions, and ideologies underpinning each system, the United States and the Soviet Union conducted negotiations to limit nuclear weapons. Unlike any other previous rivals, the superpowers attempted to work together to manage the principal source of their security.

Superpower negotiations and the accords that occasionally resulted from them thus present a puzzle for international relations theorists. Under what conditions do adversaries engage in negotiations and conclude agreements that limit their military power? Why are these same opponents able to complete deals at some moments and not at others? Explanations that follow from two schools of thought in international relations provide interesting first-cut answers to these questions. Realists contend that states in decline seek arms control agreements only as a last resort to forestall their weakness, and domestic politics analysts argue that countries reach settlements when bargains struck between institutions within each nation produce proposals that make complementary demands on each state.[1] Both arguments actually hinge on structural variables: distribution of power in the international system or the balance of influence in the bureaucratic order or the highest levels of the executive branch. But an emphasis on structure exclusively is misleading and dangerous. The tendency is misleading because the historical record indicates that states have reacted differently to similar structural configurations and that neither organizational battles nor the liberal-conservative split among politicians is a satisfactory predictor of state policy. The danger of such assumptions is that a focus on the organization of the international or domestic system conceals responsibility for decision making, obstructs theoretical advancement, and impedes debate.

A glance at history raises questions about the realist claim that the international distribution of capabilities determines behavior in a universally predictable manner. For example, throughout the early 1950s, the Soviets refused to consider serious negotiations on disarmament; by 1955, however, the USSR and Western powers were involved in ongoing discussions in London.[2] Likewise, the Soviet approach to limiting European forces in the early 1980s was quite different from that of the late 1980s.[3] In both situations, the transformation of negotiating positions occurred without a significant corresponding change in the actual distribution of capabilities.[4]

There are also several difficulties with the domestic politics framework that typically is used to explain arms control. Many analysts employ a bureaucratic politics model, and some even graft ideological considerations onto their discussion of the decision-making process. Thus, policy outcomes result from the bargaining between actors whose positions come not necessarily from their office but from their political leanings.[5] Arms control is seen as a battle between liberal and conservative forces in the American context and a struggle between reformist and orthodox groups in the USSR; whichever group is stronger wins. If neither is dominant, the domestic actors involved in setting policy cut deals to arrive at a negotiating position that serves their organizational interests instead of national security.

The first problem with this conception is that the categories "liberal" and "conservative" are ambiguous. Several "conservative" politicians, for example, Richard M. Nixon and Dwight D. Eisenhower, have been advocates of arms control. Second, some politicians cannot be classified using the conventional categories. Was Khrushchev a member of the orthodox or the reformist forces? How should Paul Nitze be classified? Moreover, arms control opponents' influence over policy seems to vary in ways that do not correspond with the level of their criticism. For instance, despite significant opposition, Soviet and American administrations approved the partial test ban treaty.[6] Finally, such an analysis restricts the investigation to the highest decision-making level, poorly links these forces to the political process at large, ignores the overall dynamics of American and Soviet politics, and overlooks developments in the international system.

Apart from the aforementioned analytical difficulties, the existing approaches ultimately obscure responsibility for state actions.[7] If international system-level or domestic-level attributes determine outcomes, then no particular party, constituency, ideology, or individual is responsible for decisions. Policy flows from the situation; a country pursues an action because of its power position or because that particular policy was the one that resulted from the bargaining between several different organizations and officials. But often leaders have options and make real choices, and analysts should not classify these decisions as theoretically irrelevant. Furthermore, assigning responsibility is politically important, especially today when the United States and Russia are considering new security and domestic policies. Common sense tells most people that the identity of the executive has important implications for the security policies that a country will follow.

In light of the deficiencies of the existing frameworks, this chapter advances an alternative approach to the study of arms control. Turning to the work of bargaining theorists in psychology, labor relations, and international politics as well as to constructivism and comparative politics, I will develop the leadership model of adversarial bargaining. This approach puts a country's executive at the center of decision making for arms control, but it recognizes that a leader must balance international and domestic concerns to arrive at a national bargaining strategy. When he is strong domestically, he can pursue his preferred strategy at the table without fear of significant negative consequences at home. When his position is weak, however, a leader tends to pursue a default strategy of seeking from any agreement an improvement in his nation's power position relative to that of the adversary. To determine why this is, let us first turn to an analysis of the bargaining situation.

Sources of Bargaining Strategy

Bargaining as a Method of Conflict Resolution

Students of negotiations note that bargaining is only one of three methods for resolving differences between parties.[8] While bargaining entails finding a solution through negotiations to which the parties can agree, the other two are policies in which one side either uses power to impose an outcome on the other or adjusts its own behavior to remove any difficulties.[9] Thus, some students of conflict resolution distinguish bargaining as the *interdependent approach,* while the other two are termed *independent strategies.*

To engage in bargaining, however, does not automatically mean that a party seeks a mutually beneficial outcome. Thus, a complete analysis of the phenomenon must take into account the motivations and goals with which actors become involved in the process. When considering whether to sit at the table, parties grapple with two central questions: is an agreement desirable, and what kind of agreement should be sought? In resolving the first issue when the subject under consideration is arms control, decision makers weigh the importance of mutual action in world politics, the risk of cheating, the domestic political implications of an agreement, and the time involved in negotiating any solution. The second is a query about the distribution of costs and benefits from the agreement, or in the language of international relations theory today, the question of relative or absolute gains. Parties that are concerned primarily with their position relative to their opponent choose a "positional" or relative gains approach. Others that are focused on their own situation select a "nonpositional" or absolute gains strategy (table 1).[10]

Taking these two factors into consideration, I advance four bargaining strategies to explain how states behave at the table—*predomination, cooperation, accommodation,* and *obfuscation.* While Robert Keohane's terms describing the international situation as harmonious, cooperative, and discordant inspired this scheme, I derived these labels to overcome the analytic imprecision of applying Keohane's ideas to the negotiating process. For instance, Keohane contends that harmony "refers to a situation in which actors' policies . . . *automatically* facilitate the attainment of others' goals."[11] Does harmony exist if two states reach an agreement because there was an obvious bargain to be struck, or does it refer to situations in which the parties take action, without the benefit of negotiations, that conform to the preferences of one another?

Keohane's definition of cooperation is similarly insufficient for understanding the outcome of talks. He maintains that cooperation requires separate actions that bring the parties "into conformity with one another through a process of negotiation," or cooperation exists "when actors adjust their behavior to the actual or anticipated preferences of others, through a process of pol-

TABLE 1. State's Intentions and Conflict Resolution Strategies

Type of Gains	Seek Formal Agreement?	
	Yes	No
Absolute	cooperation accommodation	self-adjustment
Relative	predomination cooperation accommodation	obfuscation dictate

icy coordination." While many other scholars have accepted this definition of cooperation, to understand the bargaining situation we need to sharpen this analytical category.[12] There is an important difference between a deal struck in which both sides make equivalent concessions and receive equivalent gains and one in which one party gives up more than the other does. Given the existing definition of cooperation, both instances qualify as the same phenomenon. Finally, Keohane contends that discord exists when a party refuses to adjust its policies either at all or far enough to reach agreements. But such a definition lumps together failures at the table that follow from the lack of overlap in proposals with those that resulted from at least one party's categorical rejection of negotiated settlements.

In three out of the four bargaining approaches developed here, a state desires a negotiated outcome, although whether a deal is ultimately struck depends on the other party and the extent of gains resulting from an accord. Predomination is a strategy for "winning"; states that engage in predomination seek an agreement that will provide them with greater benefits than their opponents will accrue. They approach the negotiations as part of the overall competition and pursue an unambiguous victory. Cooperation is a strategy of trying to reach a bargain that spreads the costs and benefits of the agreement equivalently. Such an approach is not necessarily one of absolute gains. A declining power could view cooperation as the best way of preserving its relative position. Nations that are playing a strategy of accommodation are willing to make greater concessions and receive fewer benefits than their partners at the negotiating table. Again, a state experiencing a collapse could seek to accommodate as the best of some bad alternatives for maintaining relative power. The fourth approach, obfuscation, is a strategy of participating in negotiations, but for "show" only. States that obfuscate have no desire to conclude an accord.

There are two additional policies that states could adopt that are outside of the bargaining framework. The first is a policy of *dictate,* the strategy of using power to force a solution on an opponent.[13] During much of the early period of the Cold War, both the United States and the Soviet Union perceived their arms development decisions as wholly independent. In a sense, then, each chose to dictate its position to the other. After the mid-1950s, the two sides occasionally decided to engage in bargaining. The strategy of dictate then became less palatable because of foreign (and sometimes domestic) pressures. Another option that the superpowers could have selected (and did choose toward the end of the Cold War) was the independent strategy of *self-adjusting.* Self-adjustment implied the lack of concern with the other side's behavior and situation. Under those conditions, a state preferred to settle the issue through its own actions, without arriving at a mutual solution. While an agreement was not considered necessary, states that self-adjusted appreciated restrictions on weapons development and implemented constraints on their own.

Thus, the nature of joint state action is more complex than usually acknowledged in the international relations literature. However, thinking analytically about the types of approaches does not explain how states select a strategy in a bargaining situation. In the next section, we begin examining that choice by identifying key international-level factors.

Interstate Bargaining and Arms Control

Bargaining theorists note that how parties proceed in negotiations depends on two variables: a party's *alternatives* to arms reduction for achieving a desired goal and its *commitment* to or *value* of the particular agreement.[14] While bargaining is an interdependent solution to a joint problem, students of the process remind us that those involved are not identical and that their interdependence could very likely be asymmetrical.[15] Thus, the options that a party to negotiations has affects its approach to interaction. To illustrate that point and to underscore the importance of alternatives, consider the example of a woman buying a car in order to get to work and accomplish her errands in a reasonable amount of time. If there is only one dealer, the buyer's options will be severely restricted, and she will most likely have to settle on the seller's terms. However, if there are many dealers or there is excellent public transportation—so that she might have the option of achieving her goal of mobility without buying a car—her position at the table is stronger. Thus the question of alternatives is also one of a bargainer's perception of the level of interdependence of the parties. Having few options makes the parties appear highly interdependent, while possessing many alternatives corresponds to the bargainer seeing herself as especially independent.[16]

Similarly, one's commitment to the elements of the deal is an influential determinant of strategy. Again, following through with the car-buying example, some of the issues at stake here include the quality, cost, and brand of the product. If the buyer truly wants to purchase a Toyota, then she is highly committed to a particular type of outcome, and that will encourage her to be less demanding in terms of price and extras from Toyota dealers. When the buyer is not committed to any specific deal, she can play sellers off against one another. Being indifferent to brand allows the buyer to pursue other issues (price and options) more aggressively. Thus, low commitment to a particular outcome means that the buyer is more flexible regarding other issues involved in the negotiations.

In understanding how the superpowers chose among strategies, the factors identified in this everyday example also operate. States considered both the alternatives that they had to arms control as well as the value of any particular agreement. Since arms control was typically not pursued for its own sake but rather to serve other security goals, we must keep in mind those other aims when assessing alternatives. They included improving the state's power position, stabilizing the arms race, channeling the competition into less dangerous types of weapons systems, preserving a force structure that was adequate for deterrence, enhancing understanding and communication among the superpowers, and impressing members of the world (and sometimes domestic) community.[17] Obviously, the states involved had other policies that they could pursue to achieve similar outcomes. Whether one of the superpowers could *implement* an alternative approach—such as continuing to build up its forces on its own—depended, for instance, on the resources (financial, technological, material, or moral) that that country had at its disposal. Thus, the superpowers faced changing levels of alternatives to weapons limitation over the course of the Cold War.

While determining options is relatively straightforward, identifying the perceived commitment to or value of a certain outcome is more complex. Again, the relevant question was the extent to which an accord would satisfy the goals mentioned earlier. To make such an evaluation depended on both the impact of the accord on force structure and the intentions of the enemy. Students of deterrence have long noted that the superpower security relationship hinged on both material and subjective factors.[18] Regarding the material, the most important element of security during much of the Cold War was military capability. But the centrality of military power was derivative of the Cold War. In fact, security is multidimensional, and phenomena other than military hardware could have been defined as fundamental.[19] In other words, security, in the abstract, encompasses not only the military component, but also political, economic, demographic, territorial, and natural assets. Threats can arise from ideas ("fundamentalism") or transnational processes (pollution) or hazards to the population (illicit drugs) and not simply from destructive power. Thus, when decision makers approached arms control, they did so with a potentially complex understanding of security. Obviously, they were negotiating about one very important danger, nuclear weapons and the prevention of nuclear war, but they *might* have seen other components of security as equally, or even more, important.[20] Thus, in thinking about bargaining and how states approached the negotiating table, alternative security concerns cannot be eliminated a priori from the decision-making calculus.

In addition, the value of the agreement incorporates an assessment of the adversary's motives. An arms control accord during the Cold War offered an element of danger because each side tended to believe that the other desired to do it harm.[21] The question became, then, just how much harm does this opponent seek to inflict? To understand better why that query is relevant in a bargaining situation, let's look again at another simple example.[22] A used-car buyer negotiates differently with her grandmother than she would with either a large dealership that has a reputation for honesty or a stereotypical used-car salesman. One's commitment to an agreement is, in fact, a function of a perception of the motives of the opponent. In terms of international relations, we can imagine that states would bargain differently with allies, businesslike opponents, and implacably hostile ones. The reason for this difference follows from the uncertainty and absence of full information that exist in any bargaining situation. The fear of being exploited under these circumstances increases with the hostility of the opponent. Thus, one's interest in negotiated outcomes that necessarily force a party to live with uncertainty diminishes along with one's confidence in the goodwill of the bargaining partner.

Regarding the superpower relationship during the Cold War, neither side defined the other as an ally. Throughout the era, however, perceptions of the opponent changed, varying from a rival with whom one could do business to a state that was an unrelenting enemy. Moreover, military power was generally the most important element of security. Thus, bargaining to reduce or restrict nuclear weapons was a policy that typically had a low value. A partner conceived to be implacably hostile did not inspire much faith in weapons limitation agreements. Under those conditions, the fear that the enemy was concluding a particular accord in order to take advantage of the situation was real. When the negotiating partner was more businesslike, a more favorable commitment to arms control became possible if military force was not seen as the essential element of security. In that case, arms control was highly valued since there were other important security issues and the risk to security an agreement could impose was therefore less severe (table 2).

This disaggregation of the factors involved in determining the commitment to arms control shows, however, that decision makers during the Cold War typ-

TABLE 2. Value of Arms Control Agreements

Military Power is Key Guarantor of Security	Nature of the Adversary	
	Implacably Hostile	Businesslike
Yes	low	low
No	low	high

TABLE 3. Determining Conflict Resolution Strategies

Alternatives to Arms Reduction	Value of Agreement	
	High	Low
High	cooperate	predominate obfuscate dictate
Low	accommodate self-adjust	cooperate obfuscate

ically were skeptical of the value of arms control. Since the military component of security was often primary, and therefore arms control frequently was a suspect policy, this contention is not surprising. Linking this notion of value with the concept of alternatives to arms control leads us to some predictions about strategy (table 3). Under the conditions of the Cold War, the superpowers were most likely going to seek some type of relative gains strategy—predomination, cooperation, or obfuscation. Precisely which one depended on the alternatives available. If a state had multiple means for pursuing its security objectives, predomination was the strategy. Then, the only way that an agreement would be worthwhile was if the state were to win something from the interaction. When both the value of and the alternatives to weapons limitation were low, the state would pursue cooperation. Because of the state's limited ability to effect on its own a positive change in its security situation, making equivalent concessions to achieve an agreement that would serve its position was deemed acceptable. Note, however, that when the value of an agreement was low, a party could also obfuscate, regardless of its options. In this case, the state engaged in negotiations for the public relations effect. When analyzing Cold War negotiations, we should never exclude the possibility of obfuscation.

During the less-frequent periods when arms control was highly valued, states' bargaining strategies would vary between cooperation and accommodation. Under these conditions, a party placed a high value on an agreement and therefore was willing to make some concessions to achieve that desired outcome. The greater the policy alternatives that a state had, the lower the extent of uncompensated concessions it would fathom. Thus, when an accord was highly valued, bargaining strategies varied from cooperation, when a state had many alternatives, to accommodation, when a state had few options to an accord but prized a negotiated outcome.

Finally, at times when one or more of the superpowers rejected the notion of interdependently resolving arms problems, the states were eschewing bargaining for the two other means of dealing with conflict: dictate and self-adjustment. These policies followed when at least one state had no interest in a formal accord and had the ability either to compel an outcome that promoted its power position (dictate) or to address a concern on its own (self-adjustment). In the case of dictate, a state typically refused to participate in negotiations on principle. No mutually arrived at solution was acceptable. Agreements were thus scorned, and alternatives were high. Self-adjustment, on the other hand, followed when states valued arms reductions, had few other policy options, and were indifferent to changes in the relative balance. Self-adjusting states prized weapons limitation and restricted their arsenals in order to enhance their security.

Throughout much of this discussion so far, I have used the words *parties, participants, countries,* and *states* to refer to those involved in the bargaining process. What the foregoing discussion highlights, however, is that perception matters—perception of both the alternatives to and the value of an agreement. Once we focus on perception, then we must ask who is making this assessment and what other criteria, if any, are influencing this evaluation. To answer these questions, we now turn to the domestic political settings in which arms bargaining occurs.

Domestic Politics and International Bargaining

In an important 1988 *International Organization* article, Robert Putnam argued that international negotiations should be modeled as two interconnected and simultaneously played "games." The first one occurred at the international level and consisted of negotiating an accord at the bargaining table. The second, at the domestic level, incorporated the challenge of convincing a sufficient number of players at home of the wisdom of the accord in order to assure ratification of that agreement. While other scholars had noted the interplay between international and domestic considerations previously, Putnam was the first to treat the interaction systematically.[23]

In providing such a model, however, Putnam and some of his followers paid less attention to domestic politics and its impact on the international negotiations than they should have. There was a tendency to focus on the interaction of bureaucratic elites but to ignore the larger political process that links officials to constituents. Perhaps one reason for overlooking the role that constituents could play was the language that some two-level games analysts used. Instead of employing "leader" or "executive" to refer to the person in charge of the negotiating process, some of the authors used the concept of "chief of government" or "COG" throughout their discussion.[24] Such terminology, especially the acronym, obscured the identities of the decision makers and the political relationships within which they were embedded. Putnam and others contended that the term *leader* was too imprecise because policy-making was a group process.[25] True, but was there often one person who ultimately made the decisions? And on what basis did that *particular* individual make those *specific* choices? Moreover, the acronym COG conjured up the image of the principal decision maker as a cog in the wheel. Even if unintentional, this term masked the unique role of individuals in negotiations.

Like other work in international relations, the two-level games literature failed to take individuals seriously as actors in international relations. Instead, several of these theorists identified states or the important groups within them as the central figures in the bargaining process, without examining closely enough the dynamics of power within the parties to negotiations.[26] If they had done so, they would have seen that individuals mattered and that the flow of power within the system in which they operated had a very important impact on the kind of decisions that people in authority made.

Executive–Constituent Relations in the United States and USSR

Identifying leaders as central players in the arms control decision-making process is not simply a reformulation of a single-actor approach that posits a unified state behind some "great man." Executives make decisions about policy within the context of their domestic political system and while thinking about the international ramifications of their actions.

Executive Autonomy and Arms Control in the American Context
The American Constitution gives the president the power to make treaties with the advice and consent of the Senate and the approval of two-thirds of its members.[27] Congress as a whole is responsible for providing and maintaining the armed forces, and the president is the commander-in-chief. While control over policy-making is divided legally, one institution has tended to dominate at any given time period. In the period of the Cold War, the presidency was the leading institution, although authority in the system was still fragmented.[28] Thus, presidential power was the "power to persuade" members of Congress, bureaucrats, and the people that his program was the best for the country.[29] The most important of these groups for the president was the public, and the president was both manipulated and manipulator. Because the people determine who

sits in the executive office, a president had to be responsive to their needs. But the president could also shape public opinion. Using the media, the executive could appeal, over the heads of the Congress and interest groups, to the public for support. Thus, the executive-constituent relationship was double-edged; the link to people provided both constraints and opportunities for the president.[30]

Scholars have found that presidents were aware of their vulnerability to their constituents and tended to be especially responsive to public desires at certain points in their terms.[31] Students of the electoral cycle argued that presidents had considerable power over policy in the first two or three years of their first term. Generally, there was a honeymoon period for the president, during which the public was highly supportive of the executive (even if he did not win his election by an overwhelming margin). This was an auspicious time for the president to pursue initiatives because he was newly elected and popular. In the early days of his tenure, however, the executive typically was not able to take advantage of his constituents' goodwill, as inexperience in foreign affairs or problems assembling the foreign policy team could stymie presidential initiatives.[32]

Starting in the third or fourth year, however, presidents generally became concerned about the upcoming election. The level of anxiety varied according to the popularity of the leader. When he was in good shape in the polls, he could proceed along, knowing that voters would send him back to the White House. When his lead was small or nonexistent, however, a president typically adjusted his policies to incorporate the concerns of the electorate into his negotiating position. In terms of bargaining behavior, a relatively weak president would experience pressure from an upcoming election and would need to alter his negotiating position to the public will.

If the executive was reelected, he then had the best opportunities for pursuing his arms control agenda. He returned to office with a second mandate, four years of experience, and no pressure to face the voters again. This autonomy was ephemeral, however, lasting only as long as the president was not a lame duck. Thus, the early years of the second term of a popular president were the most propitious for arms control. Even if the opposition dominated Congress, a well-liked president could use his personal appeal and the prestige of his office to entreat citizens to support him. If the people did not spurn him, legislators had difficulty resisting his policy. Conversely, when he was unpopular, the Senate, with the power to ratify treaties and to authorize defense spending, and the House, with the power of the purse, had an easier time rejecting presidential initiatives. Sometimes, the level of support among constituents was moderate and the number of the president's supporters in the Senate and House was uncertain. This was a period when the president's overall support level was mixed; his ability to sway citizens and others was thus uncertain.

Executive Autonomy and Arms Control in the Soviet Context
Interestingly, the autonomy of the Soviet executive varied in a similar way. The primary differences were that the general secretary's constituents were not the people of the USSR, but rather the members of the Party Congress and Central Committee. "Selections" occurred about every five years (at the Party Congresses), and officials could gain or lose their posts at Central Committee plenums.

During the post-Stalin period and up to the last years of the regime, the Party controlled policy-making, although the Soviet Constitution designated the Supreme Soviet as the highest authority in the land. While the Party rules provided for collective leadership, often one man rose to become "first among equals." So, while power was formally dispersed, it could become concentrated in the hands of a single individual.[33] General secretaries did not achieve such power at the outset of their terms because they were taking over another person's (Party) organization. While some Party officials obviously supported the new leader in the contest to become general secretary, their support could be tentative or mixed. Since other members of the Politburo recognized the limits of the new leader's power base, decisions early in the term were made by consensus among this "superelite."

Over time, however, the Party leader was in the position to tip the balance of domestic power in his favor. As general secretary and head of the Secretariat, he had the authority to control appointments throughout the Party. This power over personnel allowed him to dismiss those with whom he disagreed on policy grounds or those whose loyalty he suspected. Essential for an ambitious general secretary was control of the Central Committee, since its members were his "selectors" as well as the people who ultimately had to agree to policy initiatives. Upon packing a Central Committee with supporters, the general secretary was in the position to control policy. Those who disagreed with the Party leader could not challenge him without risking the loss of their position. A general secretary with strong support throughout the apparatus could be sure of his ability to remove any renegades.[34]

Unfortunately for the Party leader, his control over the selectors and therefore over policy did not remain constant. If a general secretary did not continue to shore up his support throughout the apparatus or to remove possible challengers at the top of the system, he was leaving himself open to an erosion of power. Once this support dissipated, the general secretary had to work to build coalitions among the leadership in support of his preferred approaches to policy, particularly by reaching out to powerful groups—provincial Party officials, the military, and military industrialists. Nevertheless, the general secretary had the formal authority to pursue a controversial policy. Whether he would remain in position long after he pursued one, however, was questionable. This risk of removal loomed, particularly after Khrushchev's ouster, for any general secretary who had not amassed significant power and considered ignoring the wishes of key institutional actors in the Soviet state.

In Soviet politics, Communist Party officials—especially those on the Central Committee as well as the military-security forces and the military industrialists—were the most important constituencies with which any Party leader had to contend.[35] Of course, the Soviet leader was formally in charge of each of these groups, but they could be formidable foes—as Malenkov, Khrushchev, and Gorbachev all found out. These institutions were ideologically and organizationally opposed to a relaxation of tensions, a reduction in defense spending, or an increase in interactions between Soviets and Westerners. Consequently, these organizations were likely to undervalue arms control, except as a propaganda tool to convince the public of the peaceful intentions of the USSR.

The blocking power of these organs—in both foreign and domestic politics—convinced Gorbachev after about two years of frustration that to achieve his goals, he had to change the institutional basis of his power. His plans to make the Soviet people an electorate were approved at the 19th Party Conference in June 1988. There, Gorbachev proposed the creation of a new superlegislature called the Congress of People's Deputies (CPD). Two-thirds of its members would be elected in secret, competitive elections, and the chair of the Congress would become the Soviet head of state. While the Congress would be a large body of 2,250 representatives meeting infrequently throughout the year, it would delegate its power to a subset of its members, called the Supreme Soviet, that would operate as a real legislature, advancing bills, holding committee hearings, and enacting legislation. Elections for this body were held in early 1989, and the CPD held its first session in May. Thereafter, Soviet politics and the nature of executive autonomy changed. The Soviet leader was dependent on both the people and the Party because of its continued hold on coercive power. In 1990, Gorbachev took steps to free himself from Party influence, such as eliminating Article 6 of the Soviet Constitution, which established the Party as the "leading force," creating the state bodies of president and Presidential Council and changing the size and composition of the Politburo. Still, these moves made Gorbachev dependent on two conflicting constituencies, the people who became increasingly change oriented and traditionalists who dominated the CPD and the Communist Party of the Soviet Union (CPSU).[36]

In sum, in both the American and Soviet contexts, executives were not always free to pursue the policies that they might have personally preferred. Their autonomy was based on the level of their support among their constituents and the timing within the election or selection cycle (table 4). "Favorable" times were those when the executive's position was relatively secure. In the United States, such periods typically included the first through third years of a president's term as well as most of the second term. For a general secretary, propitious times were those after which he had succeeded in filling the Party apparatus with supporters. "Unfavorable" times in both systems were those just prior to an election or selection, when the leader was particularly concerned about appealing to powerful groups in both systems, institutions that typically opposed arms control.

Timing and support interacted to determine an executive's freedom of action. When autonomy was high, leaders had the best opportunity to pursue the strategy in international negotiations that they derived from their own evaluation of the alternatives to and value of an agreement. In other words, at such times leaders were relatively invulnerable because they could count on the support of their constituents and there was not an upcoming election to worry about. Under these conditions, leaders had the option to choose the strategy they believed to be best. When autonomy was low, executives did not have that luxury. The nature of the Cold War, with its assumptions about the hostility of the opponent and importance of military power, in essence caused the executive to accede to the preferences of others in the system, regardless of his predilection (fig. 1).

When autonomy was moderate, the direction that leaders would take was not as immediately obvious. The safe strategy would be to accommodate the wishes of key domestic power centers. With moderate autonomy, however, a leader could hope to pursue a different approach and win over constituents to

TABLE 4. Leader's Autonomy within the Domestic System

Level of Support Among Constituents and Other State Organs	Timing	
	Favorable	Unfavorable
Low or mixed	moderate	low
Significant	high	moderate

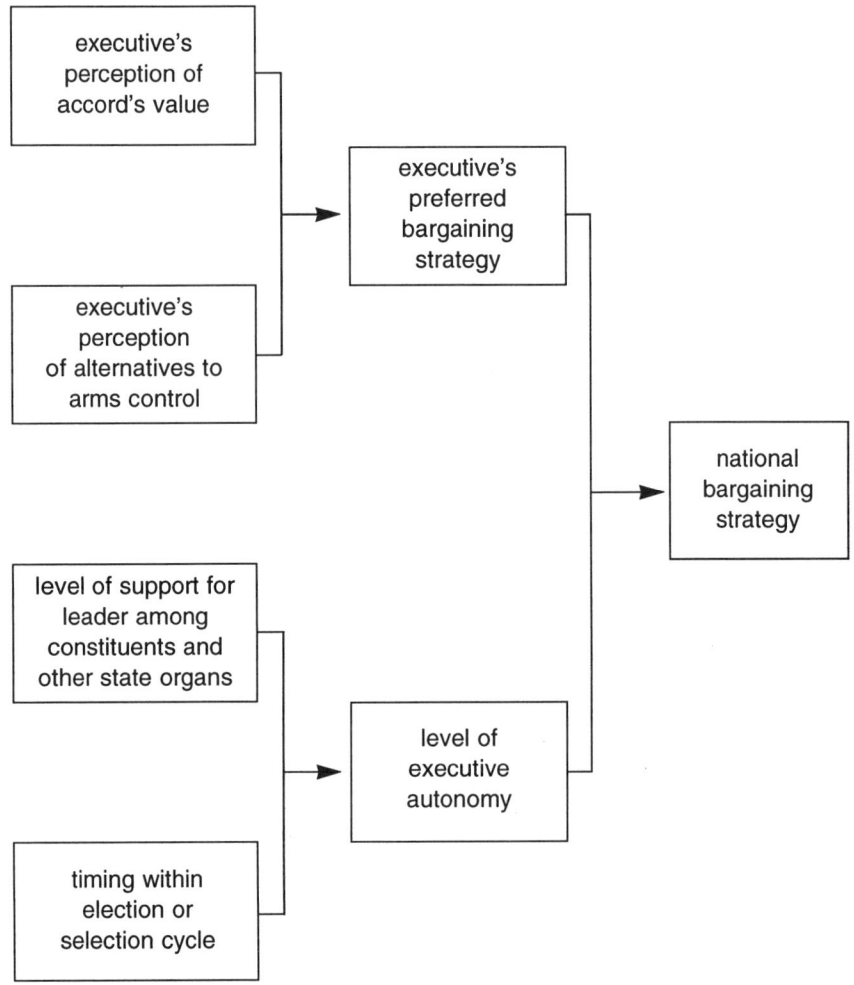

Fig. 1. Leadership model

his line of thinking. Embarking on such a strategy with some autonomy was risky because domestic opponents to such views would have power to challenge the leader. So what would an executive do in situations of moderate autonomy? This study conceives of leaders as individuals who balance domestic and international priorities and seek to shape the security posture of their nation.[37] Thus, leaders would allow their perception of the alternatives to and value of agreement to determine their strategy, but they would be cognizant of the risk involved in embarking on an innovative approach.

To implement such a strategy successfully required significant political acumen and an atypical vision of international politics. It demanded, in fact, *transformational* leadership, an endeavor in which an executive attempted to provide new meaning to his constituents regarding the value of arms control, by reconceptualizing the nature of security and the image of the opponent. The default strategy, on the other hand, allowed for the practice of leadership and politics as usual, in which executives engaged in *transactional leadership*. This leadership style consisted of a swap of valued goods, with leaders striking deals, implicitly or explicitly, with constituents. An example of transactional leadership would be an executive's appeal for support for his policy and a promise to direct funds to various key regions or societal groups in return. The transaction thus was completed when both heads of government and constituents delivered on their ends of the bargain. If either side reneged, then the exchange broke down, and, potentially, a new leader could emerge.[38]

The conclusion that the executive was a very important player in arms control decision making follows from this discussion of the American and Soviet systems, but the analysis also shows that neither the U.S. president nor the Soviet general secretary controlled policy all the time. Power in the system was fluid, and an executive had to be mindful of this flow. Regarding arms control policy, a leader had a preferred bargaining strategy that was based on his assessment of alternatives to and the value of an agreement. Sometimes these concerns were in line with those of others in the system; at other times, they were not. When the executive's preferred strategy failed to coincide with the default, relative-gains-oriented one, a leader faced a decision: should he compromise his beliefs to maintain his office? Generally, when executives were weak domestically, they decided to bend to the concerns of other key domestic actors. Such an approach would both safeguard their current position and potentially help build their future power. In effect, such a leader was engaging in transactional leadership, giving constituents their desired strategy in return for continued and, it was hoped, increased support.

When the executive had some autonomy, however, he was in the position to ensure that the national approach at the bargaining table corresponded to his preferred strategy. In other words, it was a time when the flow of power could work to his advantage, and the leader's assessment of the alternatives to and value of arms control could define state strategy. A strong leader, with an approach different from the norm, could implement his preferred policy. Then, using his significant political capital, he could try to transform arms control policy. If his autonomy were only moderate, however, the executive faced a real dilemma. Should he conform to the wishes of others, or should he risk trying to recast the debate and alter security policy? The second option required him to engage in transformative leadership, reaching out to new groups to build a power base that would help him resist the opposition of formerly privileged factions, if he hoped to implement his strategy successfully and maintain his position.

Leadership and Arms Control Decision Making

A close examination of the literature on interstate bargaining shows that to understand superpower arms control, analysts must take into account both international- and domestic-level factors.[39] Negotiated weapons limitation involved American and Soviet interaction, and any agreement had to be ratified in each state. Thus, the process intrinsically combined external and internal politics.

Central to the pursuit of arms control was the national leader, who was responsible for conducting the negotiations abroad and securing ratification at home. In guiding the national policy, the executive assessed his domestic position and the state's alternatives and commitment to arms control. The determinants of the leader's standing at home at any particular point in his tenure were his level of support among his constituents and the timing of any such measurement in the election or selection cycle. The higher his popularity and the farther away an election or selection, the more autonomous was a leader.

When an executive had strength domestically, he was in the position to put his mark on security policy, including arms control. At these times, his assessment of the international situation had an important impact on national strategy. His perception of the alternatives to an accord and his commitment to a particular agreement determined his preferred approach at the bargaining table. Traditionally, during the Cold War, leaders placed a low value on agreements and were very unwilling to make compromises, particularly unmatched ones.

The stimulus for judging accords undesirable came not only from an assessment of the state's alternatives and commitment. Domestic factors also compelled that evaluation. Because the strongest institutional actors in both systems favored the development of the national arsenal and were suspicious of arms control, the easiest approach for an executive to justify to the home audience was one that undervalued negotiated outcomes. Moreover, the general understanding among constituents was that the superpowers were locked in a deadly struggle and each side had to take independent action to enhance its own security. Leaders without autonomy could not effectively challenge that conventional wisdom. Thus, weak executives typically pursued transactional strategies that sought to enhance the power position of the state compared to its opponent *and* to provide benefits to important institutional actors.

But viewing the negotiating process and outcome as a transaction was not the only possible conception a leader, strong or weak, could have. Executives could also reinterpret the nature of the opponent's intentions, the meaning of national security, and their own alternatives. Such leaders then could engage in transformational strategies that redefined security and the superpower relationship. While transactional approaches could be pursued at any time in the leader's tenure, an executive could confidently put forward transformational ones only when he was significantly autonomous, because these strategies were contrary to the prevailing definitions of national security, the ideological stance and bureaucratic interests of the most powerful institutional actors, and the public understanding of the relationship between the superpowers.

In the following five chapters, the explanatory power of the leadership model will be tested against that of two other approaches—realism and domestic politics—to superpower arms control. In each instance, we will see that the leadership model better predicts the strategy that the United States and the Soviet Union followed at the negotiating table. The executive-constituent link accounts for changes in the bargaining approach, as less autonomous leaders were compelled to incorporate concerns of others into the national position and autonomous ones shifted that strategy to their preferred position. Executives who were independent from the outset were able to pursue the policy that followed from their assessment of the international situation. Thus, a model that incorporates factors from both the domestic and international arenas provides a better account than frameworks that focus simply on the distribution of power in the international system or the bureaucratic bargaining and ideological infighting within an administration.

CHAPTER 2

Conflicting Strategies and Inconclusive Discussions: Khrushchev, Eisenhower, and the Test Ban Talks

From 1945 to 1960, the superpowers conducted 258 atmospheric tests of nuclear devices as they sought to enhance the power and destructive capability of their arsenals.[1] Scientific evidence began to mount during that time, however, that these experiments were harming the health of the world's people. In 1957, several prominent individuals, including Jawaharlal Nehru, Albert Schweitzer, and Pope Pius XII, called for an end to nuclear testing as world public opinion was similarly turning against the policy of open-air explosions.[2] During this period, the United States and the USSR began negotiations for a test ban. The talks, however, were unproductive, and the tests and the contamination continued.[3]

To members of the realist school, the failure of this effort to stop nuclear testing is unsurprising. Technology had not advanced far enough to provide guaranteed verification of any agreement. In addition, superpower military capabilities were unbalanced, and their experience in exploding devices was unequal (table 5). The Soviet Union, as the inferior power, should have wanted to continue testing in order to improve its weapons. The only kind of agreement that the USSR should have considered was one that would have allowed it to continue these experiments, either by legally sanctioning specific kinds of tests or by providing inadequate methods for monitoring compliance that would have permitted the Soviets to subvert the ban illicitly. The United States, on the other hand, should have rejected any of these arrangements. As the superior power, the Americans should not have approved of a treaty that would have helped the Soviets catch up.

But the realist explanation is problematic for several reasons, and the test ban negotiations provide a more interesting case for analysis than one might ex-

TABLE 5. The Nuclear Balance, 1956–60

A. *Strategic Nuclear Weapons Arsenals*

	U.S.		USSR	
Year	Launchers	Warheads	Launchers	Warheads
1956	1,480	2,123	22	84
1957	1,605	2,460	28	102
1958	1,620	2,610	56	186
1959	1,551	2,496	108	283
1960	1,559	3,127	183	354

B. *Experience with Nuclear Tests, 1960*

	U.S.	USSR	U.K.	France	Total
Atmospheric	174	84	21	3	282
Underground	22	2	0	0	24
Total	196	86	21	3	306

Source: For part A: Stockholm International Peace Research Institute, *SIPRI Yearbook 1990: World Armaments and Disarmament* (New York: Oxford University Press, 1990), 23. Launchers include land-based missiles, bombers, and submarine-based missiles. For part B: Stockholm International Peace Research Institute, *SIPRI Yearbook 1995: World Armaments and Disarmament* (New York: Oxford University Press, 1995), table 18A.2, 722.

pect a priori. An examination of the decision-making process in the United States and USSR shows that the states were not united on security policy, and differences were resolved in each context in a way that reflected the preferences of one key individual, the executive. Strategic rationality and the primacy of the military component of power also did not operate as expected. The Soviets did not carefully guard their power potential as an inferior power should (observing a moratorium during the negotiations and cutting back their ground forces by a third), and the United States began to be as concerned about the tenability of its political position as its military strength. Finally, the case highlights the feedback between domestic and international politics; international crises (like the U-2 incident) had domestic political implications, which then affected a leader's ability to act in world affairs.

Understanding the behavior of both the United States and the Soviet Union requires the analyst to look at the leaders involved, their perceptions of the value of and alternatives to agreement, and their autonomy at home. In the USSR, Khrushchev was highly autonomous at the outset of the talks. He had recently demoted key rivals from their positions within the Presidium[4] and Secretariat and was clearly the leading member of the Soviet hierarchy. Given his domestic strength, he could bring the Soviet negotiating position in line with his own views of the international system. The first secretary[5] noted the key importance of military (especially nuclear) power and contended that the United States, under Eisenhower, was a businesslike adversary. Thus, for Khrushchev, arms control had only a low value. Still, the Soviet leader understood that informational asymmetries and the nuclear revolution provided the USSR with many alternatives to arms reductions. Khrushchev then engaged in negotiations but followed a strategy of predomination. He only wanted an agreement that would provide the USSR with unequivocal gains.

Like his Soviet counterpart, Eisenhower had significant domestic strength during most of the period under consideration. As a popular, second-term president, he was in position to embark on the policy he deemed best for the country. At that particular time, Eisenhower was skeptical of the value of an agreement with the Soviets, but he also recognized that the United States had few alternatives to negotiations. Thus, at the end of the decade, the president was willing to cooperate at the table.

While the two strategies—predomination and cooperation—were not complementary, the talks ultimately did not fail because of stumbling blocks at the bargaining table. Instead, the U-2 incident derailed negotiations. The test ban would have to wait for another year, a new leader, and different perceptions of the value of and alternatives to arms control agreements.

Assessing Autonomy and Strategy during the Test Ban Talks

In the late 1950s, both Khrushchev and Eisenhower had the domestic strength to take the lead in security policy. Khrushchev had recently defeated many of his rivals in the Party apparatus, replacing them with younger and politically weaker officials, and had restructured the administrative structure of the system and taken over the position of chairman of the Council of Ministers—the premiership. Eisenhower was also relatively strong. He had significant public approval, and as a second-term president, he was not concerned about reelection. He did, however, face a rather recalcitrant Congress.

Executive Autonomy: Khrushchev

After Stalin's death in March 1953, no single figure immediately dominated Soviet politics. Over the next five years, however, Khrushchev managed to eliminate all rivals and reach the pinnacle of power. In January 1955, he forced

Georgi Malenkov out of his position as chairman of the Council of Ministers. During the next two years, the first secretary intensified his attack on Malenkov, the cult of Stalin, and Stalin's excesses against the Party. In criticizing the former leader, Khrushchev also attempted to brand some of his rivals as Stalinist and therefore dangerous. The first secretary's assault prompted his adversaries to band together in an attempt to oust him from the Party leadership. But the Party leader foiled his opponents' plans by hastily convening an expanded session of the Central Committee in 1957. The plenum reversed the Presidium decision removing Khrushchev and instead voted to expel the "Anti-Party Group" (including Malenkov, Molotov, and Kaganovich) from the highest policy-making body. The first secretary achieved this victory with the help of Marshal Zhukov, but just four months later, Khrushchev drove the military leader to retire in disgrace. Over the next year, major shake-ups throughout the government and the Party continued as many high-ranking officials were dismissed and replaced with others lacking their prestige or experience.[6]

Starting in 1957, veteran Kremlin watchers could discern a cult of Khrushchev, as the press and officials began glorifying the first secretary. For example, the 1957 edition of the *Great Soviet Encyclopedia* claimed that the first secretary had played crucial roles on the front during World War II at the battle of Stalingrad, when Khrushchev actually had served as first secretary of Ukraine. In the spring of 1958, General Voroshilov nominated him to head the government, to become chairman of the USSR Council of Ministers. Within five years, Khrushchev received the official designations that were conferred on Stalin after more than fifteen, and his personal power continued to grow throughout the end of the decade. At the Extraordinary 21st Party Congress in January 1959, the first secretary was hailed as a "theoretical genius." This kind of praise signaled that Khrushchev was certainly *first* among equals.[7]

While timing and support combined to provide Khrushchev considerable autonomy in the late 1950s, he was never an absolute ruler in the same way that Stalin was, and he had to be mindful of maintaining the support of others in the leadership. Thus, Khrushchev could not simply rely on brute force and intimidation of his opponents to conserve his power position. After Stalin's death, the members of the leadership had renounced the use of terror as a political weapon to be wielded against one another. Khrushchev's support among his constituents, then, rested on his ability to keep them satisfied with his leadership, by keeping the patronage flowing as well as by pursuing policies that they could back. To accomplish these goals, Khrushchev provided his constituents with an interesting policy mix and set of promises. After 1957, he argued that the USSR could match and surpass American military and economic strength by developing nuclear forces—to the detriment of conventional ones—and transferring some funds from defense to the domestic budget.[8] Khrushchev argued, putting a new spin on Marxist-Leninist foreign policy, that changes in the nature of the American leadership, along with the superiority of the socialist system, made a new approach possible. Moreover, because Eisenhower was a "reasonable" person who could restrain the "mad men" within the capitalist ruling circles, the USSR no longer had to worry about the Americans launching some sort of preventive strike or initiating nuclear war. The president, according to Khrushchev, understood and was deterred by the destructive power of atomic and hydrogen weapons.[9]

The U-2 incident, when the USSR shot down an American spy plane over Soviet airspace in May 1960 and then the United States lied to the world regarding the nature of the mission, was an important event here. It raised questions about Khrushchev's policy toward the United States and his overall leadership in foreign affairs. These questions helped weaken the leader's support somewhat. In response, the first secretary did not back away from his theoretical innovation, but he admitted that he had been wrong about Eisenhower. Thus, Khrushchev was able to buy time for himself and for his policies while rebuilding the confidence in this approach among members of the Party elite.[10]

Executive Autonomy: Eisenhower

Determining autonomy in the American system is a relatively easier task. The analyst can look at the point in the electoral cycle in which the negotiations took place as well as the president's popularity and relationship with Congress. During these test ban talks—1958 to 1960—the president was in his second term and therefore not concerned about reelection, although he did have to worry about the onset of the lame-duck phase at some point at the end of his term. Inadequate policy leadership could bring on that stage sooner, while success could postpone it.

Regarding support level, Eisenhower was in relatively good shape throughout much of this period. In the 1956 election, he defeated his challenger convincingly; the final tally was in Ike's favor, 35.6 million versus 25.7 million votes, with the Democrat, Adlai Stevenson, winning only seven southern states in the electoral college. In his second term, Eisenhower's popularity ratings were always above 50 percent (with a low point of 52 percent), and through most of 1959 and 1960, 60 percent or more of those asked said they approved of his leadership (fig. 2). Unfortunately for the president, neither congressional Democrats—the majority party in both houses—nor Republicans were an easy

Fig. 2. Eisenhower's second-term approval ratings (percentage who approve). (Data from George H. Gallup, *The Gallup Poll: Public Opinion 1935–1971*, vols. 2 and 3 [New York: Random House, 1972].)

sell for his policies. The Democrats generally wanted to spend more money and combat the Soviets more aggressively by pursuing the arms race; they opposed Eisenhower's fiscal conservatism. Republicans, on the other hand, were often more isolationist than their standard-bearer. Thus, Eisenhower had a mixed support level, with strong public approval and a rather recalcitrant legislative branch with which to deal. The leadership model would predict, then, that the president had moderate autonomy, at least until June 1960. The breakdown of the Paris summit at that point, along with the onset of the presidential campaign, eroded his authority. By the summer, Eisenhower's ability to take on such a controversial issue as nuclear testing policy had diminished.[11]

Khrushchev and the Strategy of Predomination

At the end of the 1950s, Khrushchev charted a new foreign policy course, which consisted of trying to intimidate the West into capitulating to Soviet demands. From his perspective, the technology of the era—not only missile systems and nuclear weapons but also inadequate verification technology—along with the historically inevitable forward march of socialism provided the USSR with many options for pursuing Soviet security on its own.[12] During this time, Khrushchev also indicated that he believed the United States to be a businesslike opponent. The reason that American bellicosity had waned, according to the first secretary, was the USSR's possession of nuclear weapons. For Khrushchev, nuclear weapons—and particularly intercontinental missile capability—were the great equalizer, making the Americans vulnerable to a devastating attack in a way they had never been before.[13] Therefore, sober officials in the United States recognized this vulnerability and became realistic in their policy toward the USSR. Because destructive capability was what had convinced some Americans to change their ways, Khrushchev was highly impressed with the importance of military power. Thus, given this combination of bargaining variables, Khrushchev approached negotiations with a preferred strategy of predomination.

Throughout the late 1950s, Khrushchev exploited informational asymmetries to his advantage. Although a policy of deception was begun in 1955, the Soviets began stressing their military progress in earnest after the launch of Sputnik 1 in October 1957. Most audaciously, Khrushchev contended back in 1959 at the 21st Party Congress that "there are now tremendous forces capable of rebuffing the imperialist aggressors and *defeating them* if they would unleash a world war." At that Congress, the Soviets even made presumptuous claims about Soviet economic power. The new Seven Year Plan stated that the

USSR's economy would outdistance that of the United States by 1980 and that "Soviet superiority in the rate of production increase will create a real basis for overtaking and surpassing the present U.S. per capita output within approximately five years after 1965." Others echoed Khrushchev's confidence. At the Supreme Soviet meeting in January 1960, Defense Minister Malinovsky told the world that the USSR possessed ICBMs, although it had not yet successfully tested any.[14]

These boasts were not simply directed at the West, but also had a domestic audience. The first secretary was attempting to hold constant and even reduce expenditures for defense in order to devote more resources to improvements of the domestic economy and living standards. To make such budgetary allocations, however, Khrushchev had to convince a skeptical Soviet elite, which was ideologically and bureaucratically in favor of the military competition between the two different social systems. Prior to Khrushchev, the Soviets had maintained that negotiations with the West were dangerous, since the intractably hostile imperialist powers would always try to exploit the talks for their own benefit.

Beginning with his speech at the 20th Party Congress, the first secretary consistently claimed that the existence of a "world camp of socialism" and the "forces of peace" undermined the traditional Leninist line. There, Khrushchev contended the growth of the power of the socialist camp meant that "war was no longer fatally inevitable" because the imperialists were deterred. Later, Khrushchev developed the argument that the increases in Soviet and socialist camp power had induced a split in the bourgeoisie, causing some members of the American leadership to become "realistic" or "reasonable" while others remained "mad men." The realistic politicians hoped to resolve the differences between East and West peacefully. Khrushchev's innovation about the split in the ruling class of the imperialist powers opened the way for his policy of negotiations, since bargaining with realistic individuals made sense. Under the old formulation, all capitalist leaders were madmen, and discussions with them would be pointless.[15] Thus, for over a year after the 21st Party Congress in January 1959, Khrushchev's assertion that Eisenhower was a "reasonable" leader and "not one of those military men who rely only on guns for the settlement of knotty problems and who would like to settle all problems by force of arms" underscored the Soviet approach to the test ban talks with the United States.[16]

Others in the Presidium were skeptical that a division within the ruling class of the United States, or any other capitalist state, had occurred.[17] They kept relatively silent on the issue, while American behavior appeared to confirm Khrushchev's argument. The U-2 incident and Eisenhower's decision to claim responsibility for authorizing the overflights, however, undercut Khrushchev's theory as well as his policy. Thereafter, skeptics revealed their doubts about a policy of negotiation founded on the notion that "realists" could exist in the capitalist system. In the aftermath of the U-2 debacle, Khrushchev pulled back from negotiations in an effort to satisfy critics and to safeguard his domestic position.[18]

Thus, during the period of the test ban negotiations, Khrushchev preferred a strategy of predomination. He arrived at that approach in an interesting way, however. Although he remained committed to the importance of military power, unlike Stalin, he believed that the United States could be a businesslike adversary, and so negotiations could be worthwhile. The first secretary also maintained that arms control was only one of the many options that the USSR could pursue to enhance its security. This constellation of variables meant that Khrushchev would like to have achieved an accord if he could conclude one that would improve the Soviet situation relative to that of the United States. The U-2 incident, however, undermined perceptions in the Party of Khrushchev's political acumen. Given these autonomy concerns, he thus became less interested in reaching any agreement.

Eisenhower and the Strategy of Cooperation

American arms control policy at the end of the president's tenure contrasted sharply with earlier administration positions. At the outset of his term, Eisenhower and his advisers estimated that the threat facing the United States stemmed mainly from Soviet military power and that the USSR was a consistently aggressive adversary. Eisenhower and his secretary of state, John Foster Dulles, shared a "moral revulsion" of the USSR, a commitment to preventing the Soviets from making substantial military gains relative to the leader of the Western alliance, and a desire to prevent the United States from reverting to isolationism.[19] The USSR endangered the United States because of the potential damage it could inflict and because American policymakers feared that Soviet superiority would have devastating psychological effects on the European resolve to defend itself. Believing that the best way to redress American security problems was through the development of its nuclear arsenal, the administration initially contended that, despite some spending constraints, the United States had multiple alternatives to arms control for promoting its security. In fact, American officials believed that the United States had to act independently to develop weapons to match the Soviet threat.[20]

Throughout the first term and into the second, then, the leadership model would expect the president to seek to predominate in any negotiations. The president consistently rejected any formulas to slow the arms race that would require the United States to make concessions or take on risks that the USSR could pull ahead in the competition. In mid-1955, for example, the president rebuffed what became known as the USSR's May 10th Plan for breaking the deadlock in the disarmament negotiations. Instead of working with these tabled proposals to reach a compromise, the president advanced a completely different program, Open Skies, which reversed the momentum at the bargaining table. And at a critical moment in the London Disarmament Talks in the summer of 1957, Eisenhower refused to untie the test ban from the American disarmament package.[21]

But the image of the United States in world politics worsened after the Soviets scored two major sets of propaganda victories in the second half of 1957. In August, the Soviets completed the first successful test of an intercontinental ballistic missile (ICBM), and by October, they had launched a satellite into earth orbit. These achievements demonstrated to the world that the USSR was ahead of the United States in the missile race. Moreover, the Soviet advance meant that U.S. vulnerability to Soviet nuclear weapons would increase dramatically when their missiles began rolling off assembly lines. The U.S. and world public reacted strongly to this news. The tendency of the majority of Americans and other world citizens to perceive that the USSR was the rising (and even superior) superpower would remain relatively stable throughout the decade.[22]

A second set of victories revolved around the development of the Soviet reputation as the advocate of peace and disarmament. In September 1957, the USSR began a public relations offensive which, over time, succeeded in creating a widespread impression that it was the "disarmament superpower," while the United States was an obstacle to peace. At that time, the USSR proposed that all members of the UN General Assembly participate in disarmament negotiations. The United States opposed the measure, arguing that such a large group would be incapable of adequately addressing the problem and pushed through its plan for a much smaller forum. The Soviets responded that they would not take part in the American scheme for discussions because it excluded nonnuclear nations.[23]

Continuing on this course, the Soviets made another offer, suggesting that the United Kingdom, United States, and USSR begin a two- to three-year test moratorium on January 1, 1958. Eisenhower rejected the proposal because he said that the United States did not want to suspend tests without also reducing nuclear stockpiles. The countries of the Third World were skeptical of Eisenhower's explanation, believing instead that the United States was uncon-

TABLE 6. Public Concern with American Defense Policy

A. Are you satisfied with the present defense policies of the United States? (poll taken November 7–12, 1957)

Satisfied	New Look Needed	No opinion
26%	53%	21%

B. Identify the most important problem facing the United States (may name more than one problem)[a]

	Most Common Responses			
Dates of Poll	Economy (%)	Peace/Defense (%)	Sputnik/Space (%)	Integration (%)
May 17–22, 1957	21	40	—	—
Aug.–Sept. 1957	22	40	—	10
Jan. 2–7, 1958	18	39	11	—
Mar. 6–11, 1958	40	17	7	—
Sept. 10–15, 1958	19	42	—	11
Feb. 4–9, 1959	26	38	—	10
Apr. 2–7, 1959	24	44	—	7

C. In the last year would you say that respect for the United States in this country has increased or decreased? (published November 30, 1960)

Increased	Decreased	Stayed Same	No Opinion
22%	45%	23%	10%

Source: George W. Gallup, *Gallup Poll: Public Opinion 1935–1971*, vol. 2 (New York: Random House, 1972), 1526; George W. Gallup. *Gallup Poll: Public Opinion 1935–1971*, vol. 3 (New York: Random House, 1972), 1691.

[a]Findings reported here under "Economy" were sometimes recorded as "economy" and other times as "cost of living," "unemployment," etc. Similarly, under the category "Peace/Defense," survey reports sometimes listed "preventing war," "dealing with Russia," "atomic control," and "national defense," separately. Where disaggregated, I have added the numbers together.

cerned about the threat of fallout to their populations and unwilling to give them a voice in the disarmament talks (see tables 6 and 7).[24]

Soon thereafter, Eisenhower began to believe that the American position on testing was having an adverse effect on U.S. security.[25] The perception of U.S. intransigence on disarmament was complicating American diplomatic efforts around the globe, especially among third world countries. The president and Secretary of State Dulles came to believe that the United States needed to take action to bolster its image as a peaceful country, and Dulles thought that a change in the American test ban position was the best remedy. Intelligence reports indicated that when they ended their series of experiments in March, the

TABLE 7. Perceptions of Relative Power Positions and Superpower Peace Programs

A. Americans were asked: Do you think Russia is moving ahead of the United States in the development of missiles and long-distance rockets? (October 10–15, 1957)

Yes	No	Don't Know
49%	32%	19%

B. Citizens of several nations were asked: Who is ahead in the Cold War—Russia or the West? (January 8, 1958)

Place of Survey	% naming Russia	% naming the West	% No Opinion
All respondents	48	22	30
Johannesburg	69	13	18
Washington–Chicago	67	13	20
Copenhagen	57	14	29
Paris	55	16	29
Helsinki	47	12	41
London	47	28	25
Athens	44	11	45
New Delhi	34	41	25

C. Citizens of several nations were asked: Which country will be the strongest 10 years from now—Russia or the United States? (January 8, 1958)

Place of Survey	% naming Russia	% naming U.S.	Other	Undecided
New Delhi	39	11	36	14
Great Britain	36	27	16	21
Paris	29	17	8	46
Milan–Rome	28	37	8	27
Stockholm	25	40	6	29
Helsinki	24	31	8	37
Copenhagen	23	30	4	43
Melbourne	19	36	21	24
United States	14	73	1	12
Athens	11	21	5	63

D. Citizens of several nations were asked: Which country will be the leading nation in science by 1970? (February 10, 1960)

Place of Survey	% naming Russia	% naming U.S.	Other	Undecided
France	59	18	14	9
Great Britain	48	17	21	14
India	46	8	7	39
Holland	43	22	9	26
Uruguay	42	27	16	15

continued

TABLE 7.—Continued

Place of Survey	% naming Russia	% naming U.S.	Other	Undecided
Switzerland	40	34	19	7
Norway	38	22	9	31
West Germany	36	29	14	21
Greece	27	29	27	17
United States	16	70	2	12

E. Citizens of several nations were asked: Which is doing more to keep peace—Russia or the West? (January 8, 1958)

Place of Survey	% naming Russia	% naming the West	% No Opinion
Washington–Chicago	3	79	18
Helsinki	17	35	48
New Delhi	54	18	28

Source: George W. Gallup, *Gallup Poll: Public Opinion 1935–1971*, vol. 2 (New York: Random House, 1972), 1521, 1534.

Soviets were planning to announce a test cessation. With the U.S. series scheduled to begin in April and last through September, Dulles argued that the Soviet plan had the makings of another public relations disaster.

> During all of that time we will be under heavy attack worldwide. The Soviets will cite their test suspension and their call for a summit meeting while we continue to test. The effect can only be highly adverse on us with regard to enjoying the confidence of the Free World as the champion of peace. We held this confidence through the previous [Geneva] Summit meeting [in 1955]. For the last two and a half years we have been losing it. There will be very serious losses to us in respect to our allies and the neutrals if this pattern of events occurs.[26]

To avert catastrophe, the secretary of state suggested that the president issue an order vowing to refrain from testing for the remainder of his term. Aware of the inevitable criticism from the American people and Congress that such a move would elicit, Dulles maintained that the United States "desperately" needed "some important gesture in order to gain effect on world opinion."[27]

Although there were several powerful members of the administration who were opposed to Dulles's position, the secretary of state urged the president to discount the myopic view of the test ban foes. While the "Defense [Department] was approaching the problem in terms of winning a war," Dulles explained that the United States must

> think in terms of *all means* of conducting the international struggle. He [Dulles] said that we are increasingly being given a militaristic and bellicose aspect toward world opinion, and we are losing the struggle for world opinion.... [W]e are open to the charge of not being completely sincere, since we have in fact put impossible conditions on disarmament.[28]

While the president disagreed that the United States had made arms control impossible, he accepted the secretary's analysis of the country's image problem. Eisenhower was torn, however, because he also concurred with the Atomic Energy Commission's and Defense Department's contention that "the abolition of tests would probably *hurt us comparatively in a military sense.*" Projections of the future U.S. relative power positions were bleak, and several members of the administration wanted to retain a free hand to conduct experiments (see table 8). But unlike these test ban foes, the president recognized that "we need some basis of hope for our own people and for world opinion. As matters now stand we are bearing the onus of having turned down an agreement [at the London Disarmament Negotiations in 1957] calling for inspection."[29] So, while he was not ready to call off the scheduled tests, Eisenhower "was inclined to think that we must accept a suspension of testing," despite the possibly negative effects of a ban on the military balance. In fact, the president had a much more nuanced view of power than some of his advisers possessed, understanding that the United States could not effectively pursue its security without paying attention to politics. To address American political weakness, Eisenhower decided to move forward with the talks to halt testing. The U.S. position became that "our standing in the world is at a point where there is real danger to us in being adjudged militaristic. That danger can have consequences as serious as the foregoing of some nuclear weapons knowledge."[30]

Thus, at the end of 1957 and in 1958, the president changed his perception of the key component of power as well as his assessment of American alternatives. No longer was military strength alone sufficient to guarantee American safety. The United States had to worry about losing the battle for public opinion. Because of the continued belief that the USSR was an extremely dangerous state, this shift had no appreciable impact on the administration's preference for arms control in the abstract; it was still a policy option to be considered circumspectly. But the political beating that the United States was taking around the world had an important influence on Eisenhower's evaluation of American

TABLE 8. Projections of the ICBM Balance

	1959	1960	1961	1962	1963
Estimates in 1957:					
U.S.	0	30	70	130	130
USSR	100	500	1,000	1,500	2,000
Estimates in January 1959:					
U.S.	10	30	80–100	100–300	
USSR	10	100	100–300	500	

Source: Desmond Ball, *Politics and Force Levels: The Strategic Missile Program of the Kennedy Administration* (Berkeley and Los Angeles: University of California Press, 1980), 7, 8.

alternatives. To address the perception that the United States was not interested in disarmament, was in decline, and was dangerously bellicose, Eisenhower contended that the United States had to accept that its alternatives to arms control were limited. In fact, according to the president, the United States had few options other than some kind of Soviet-American weapons limitation endeavor in order to address its reputation problem. Only the serious American pursuit of a test ban could prove to the world that the United States was neither bellicose nor afraid of the USSR. Eisenhower's shift in his assessment of alternatives made cooperation—approximately equal concessions from both sides—his approach to the table. Although the president was still wary enough of the USSR and arms control in theory so as not to be willing to accommodate, Eisenhower understood that American options for improving the U.S. power position on its own were limited. Only mutual concessions appeared to resolve its problems at a fair price. Moreover, Eisenhower knew that his attempts had to be sincere; the United States already had enough of an image problem. He would not risk playing the game of or subjecting the United States to charges of obfuscation. The president, then, maintained his commitment to cooperation at the table until his autonomy eroded in the summer of 1960.

In sum, the leadership model would expect that the talks would result in failure because there would be no way to satisfy the Soviet desire to predominate when the United States sought to cooperate. Moreover, given these strategies, the model would predict that the Soviets would put forth proposals that would serve their interests, while the Americans would advance ones that attempted to take into account the concerns of both sides. The ability of the two states to maintain their approaches would be of short duration, since Eisenhower's second term would be over at the end of 1960. Thus, autonomy

36   To Agree or Not to Agree

would also have an impact on the prospects for agreement as 1960 approached and proceeded.

Executive Leadership and the Test Ban Negotiations, 1958–60

Three days after Khrushchev became premier in the spring of 1958, the Supreme Soviet passed a resolution promising that the USSR would not test nuclear weapons as long as other nations abstained from testing. Since the USSR had recently finished its test series and the United States was about to begin one of its own, this pledge was designed for maximum Soviet propaganda benefit. The resolution did its job; the Soviet move was hailed throughout much of the world.[31]

This public relations success concerned Eisenhower, but not enough to call off planned American tests. The president began, however, to look for ways to meet the Soviet challenge. According to Eisenhower, the United States could engage in test ban talks safely if it could share nuclear technology with its allies and if an adequate control system could be implemented to make sure that every party to an agreement abided by it. The president first sought to overcome these barriers by having Congress enact legislation to authorize the dissemination of nuclear know-how to its West European partners.[32] Second, he asked a group of American scientists to investigate the problem of test ban verification. They concluded that an effective control system for detecting and identifying illicit tests—except some small underground explosions—could be developed. The system that they envisioned, however, was highly intrusive and consisted of approximately 70 control posts, mobile access teams, and overflights of suspicious areas. Before any agreement was possible, then, the Soviets would have to consent to such a system.[33]

Learning that verification was scientifically possible, Eisenhower seriously began to consider a test ban—one that would require compromises from both the United States and the USSR—at a time when the American popular concern about testing and pressure on the administration had receded significantly (see table 9). In the aftermath of Sputnik, ordinary people and elites were more likely to be worried about the American strategic position than to be lobbying for an arms control measure. Some in the administration tried to warn Eisenhower that the reaction to a test ban in the polls and in Congress would be adverse.[34] By February, 49 percent of Americans favored a mutual two- to three-year moratorium, and in May, only 29 percent believed that the United States should stop testing completely.[35] The president became an advocate of the mutual cessation of tests in August when public support for the ban dipped

TABLE 9. American Attitudes toward Testing and Arms Control[a] (in percentages)

	April 1957	January 1958	April 1958
Do you think testing and fallout are dangerous?			
Yes	52	—	46
No	28	—	27
Can't say	22	—	27
If all nations agreed to stop testing, should the United States stop?			
Yes	63	49	29
No	27	36	60
No opinion	10	15	11

Source: George W. Gallup, *Gallup Poll: Public Opinion 1935–1971*, vol. 2 (New York: Random House, 1972), 1487–88, 1541, 1553, 1552.

[a]There was a slight variation in the questions posed. For instance, in April 1957, respondents were asked, "Do you think there is a real danger from fallout?" In April 1958, the query was, "Do you think continued testing will likely result in a threat to the health of future generations?"

even lower. While acknowledging that this policy was not at that point a popular one, either among the public or within his administration, Eisenhower nonetheless decided to pursue it. The president believed, however, that the United States had to pursue the test ban to redress its declining political appeal around the world. Because Eisenhower's domestic position was strong, he was able to act on his principles.[36]

To enlist the Soviets in the verification project, Eisenhower proposed that a gathering of experts from the East and the West be convened in Geneva, Switzerland, during the summer of 1958 for the purpose of developing a mutually acceptable control system. Initially, the Soviets refused to participate (since a verifiable ban would not allow them to test surreptitiously and thereby achieve military gains), but then Khrushchev changed his mind and promised to send a delegation. Yet even as the date of the opening of the technical talks approached, Soviet rhetoric remained consistent with the strategy of predomination. Khrushchev was still hostile to the notion of verification, and the USSR announced that it would participate in the discussions only if the United States vowed that the purpose of the negotiations was to halt nuclear testing immediately. Moreover, by June 28, the Soviet delegates had not requested visas for the July 1 meeting.[37]

Despite these ominous signs, scientists from the USSR did participate constructively in this conference. Ultimately, the delegates from both East and West concluded that a test ban was verifiable, and they established what became known as the "Geneva System," a control plan consisting of posts on the territory of nuclear and potentially nuclear powers. At each of these stations, an international team of scientists would monitor seismic activity. If the specialists detected any irregularities in the incidence and magnitude of earth tremors, they could initiate and conduct inspections of suspicious areas. American scientists were confident that they could develop a system of human and technological monitors that could catch any cheating. Since the Soviets agreed to give the inspectors the necessary access, the United States believed that the Geneva system was workable. This information—that the United States could certainly identify any Soviet tests—was the news that Eisenhower needed to move forward with the test ban talks. The Soviets also agreed to proceed with the negotiations, and the talks on a cessation of nuclear weapons tests were set to open in Geneva in October.[38]

The Geneva Conference on the Discontinuance of Nuclear Tests

Once the negotiations got under way, however, Soviet behavior revealed that the USSR was not interested in working with the United States to find a formula for a verifiable test ban. First, the Soviets were trying to ensure that their government would supervise the work of any control team on the territory of the USSR. Second, the Soviets continued to explode nuclear devices after the talks began, even though they had promised to observe a test moratorium as a sign of goodwill. Third, at the end of the year, the Soviets stepped up the pressure on the West in other areas of foreign policy. Khrushchev demanded that the situation in Berlin be addressed to his satisfaction, and the Soviets began bragging about their military prowess.[39]

While Soviet behavior was certainly troubling, more bad news for Eisenhower resulted from American efforts to ensure that it could identify any illegal tests. At the end of 1958, American scientists' confidence in the Geneva system plummeted. Data from the HARDTACK II test series indicated that the control system would not be able to detect all underground nuclear experiments. In the hope of resolving these problems and establishing a better control system, the American negotiating team suggested that the states take part in a joint seismology research project. The Soviet negotiators dismissed the American concerns as fabrications and declined to participate in any effort to improve the Geneva system.[40]

Eisenhower then called for a review of American test ban policy in the wake of these findings. He was angry that the scientists had agreed to the Geneva system before running the tests needed to determine its adequacy and thereby exposing the United States to worldwide criticism.[41] By the spring of 1959, however, the president had become convinced of the importance of halting testing and the imperative that the parties find some form of an agreement soon. The election was less than a year and a half away, and Eisenhower recognized that ratifying an agreement would be impossible once the campaign had begun. The president told his new secretary of state, Christian Herter, that he would be satisfied with an atmospheric ban, which might be easier to achieve. After a July National Security Council (NSC) meeting, Eisenhower set the achievement of a partial test ban as the U.S. goal, pulling back from the effort to reach a comprehensive treaty.[42]

In the meantime, despite an improvement in Soviet rhetoric toward the United States, there was no tangible difference in the content of Soviet proposals in Geneva.[43] The Soviets rejected American concerns about detecting underground tests and denied that more seismic research was necessary. When the USSR finally agreed to talk about controlling below-ground tests, they linked the discussion to another area of their concern, high-altitude testing. In the spring of 1959, the Soviets offered to discuss the problem of testing in space and at high altitudes, if the United States would limit the possible number of inspections per year. Eisenhower agreed to this offer, in the hopes of moving the control system forward. But while the two sides resolved the problem of monitoring testing in the upper atmosphere and outer space at the Technical Working Group I conference in mid-1959, they made little progress on the U.S. concerns with underground tests.[44] The Soviets had agreed, however, to discuss the requirements for below-ground monitoring at another meeting of scientific experts in December 1959. When the Second Technical Working Group conference convened, however, Soviet panelists indicated that they had not been authorized to make any compromises. The meeting was highly acrimonious and ended without a concluding report.[45]

Soviet behavior should not have surprised American negotiators. Although Khrushchev had recently visited the United States and had been positive about the potential for lasting peace, he had also given a speech at the United Nations that undermined all American attempts for negotiated arms *control,* again showing his desire for a decisive Soviet "win" from any agreement. Khrushchev proposed that both sides abolish all weapons within four years without any system for verification. Thus, the Soviet leader showed his commitment to his strategy of predomination in these efforts to secure a relative advantage for his side.[46]

Back in Washington at the annual year-end review of arms control policy, Eisenhower tried to find a way to make the cooperative strategy workable, given the new technical findings. He sought to address some Soviet concerns, without making unmatched concessions. The president resolved that the United States would offer a threshold ban—limiting underground tests above a certain level that scientists agreed was verifiable—and keep the atmospheric ban as a backup offer.[47] In accordance with the president's decision, the Americans proposed that a threshold test ban be instituted in phases. The first phase would ban all verifiable testing in the atmosphere, underwater, in outer space, and underground above a 4.75 reading on the Richter scale. In addition, the United States called for implementation of an international research program to improve detection and identification in order to lower the seismic threshold in subsequent phases. The Soviets accepted the phased proposal for the treaty on the condition that the United States approve a four- to five-year moratorium on underground tests below the threshold.[48] Eisenhower revealed to his advisers that he would be willing to refrain from testing for up to two years if the Soviets would sign an agreement, despite uncertainty about the ability to detect Soviet cheating. The president contended that committing to a controlled ban of testing would help the United States address its political problems without unacceptably disadvantaging the American military position in the long run.[49]

At the start of the new year and decade, the signs coming out of the Kremlin regarding Soviet-American relations and arms control were mixed. At the Supreme Soviet session in January 1960, the first secretary proposed that Soviet armed forces be cut by one-third. Even though the test ban negotiations seemed to be stuck, Khrushchev stressed the importance of the upcoming summit meeting between the heads of state of the World War II allies, hinting that a solution and even lasting détente was within reach. Then, as the summit date approached, there appeared to be a shift in the standard line. Khrushchev began stressing the role of imperialistic forces in American foreign policy. Also, a Soviet embassy official in Washington indicated to his American counterparts that the summit would not provide the breakthroughs hoped for in the negotiations; those would come only after Eisenhower's personal visit to the USSR.[50] Although the U.S. president refused the invitation, the two leaders were scheduled to meet with one another in the upcoming four-power (United States, Soviet Union, United Kingdom, and France) summit in Paris. There was a possibility that they could resolve remaining problems with the test ban there.[51]

These hopes were soon dashed. The downing of an American U-2 spy plane on Soviet soil and Eisenhower's handling of the affair ultimately meant the end of serious negotiations for a while. For many in the Soviet elite, the overflight of their territory indicated American bellicosity and recklessness and raised doubts about the first secretary's contentions that negotiations with capitalists, under certain conditions, could be worthwhile. Khrushchev, however, could have finessed this issue if Eisenhower had blamed the military or the CIA for undertaking the action. The Soviet leader had long argued that these were bastions of "mad men" and that the president had to battle them to pursue a sober line. Still, the first secretary was willing to go to Paris for the June summit to hear the American president out. When Eisenhower took full responsibility for ordering the mission, he undermined the foundations of Khrushchev's policy toward the United States. The president was not a "realist" at all; rather, he appeared to be one of the "militarists" in the American system. Khrushchev then stormed out of the gathering and declared that the summit was over.[52]

In the ensuing months, the two sides continued to meet in Geneva but made no real progress. The campaign for the U.S. presidency began in earnest, signaling the end of Eisenhower's ability to institute major policy innovations. The timing then was unfavorable, and the president knew it. According to one of his advisers, the president realized that "the stupid U-2 mess had ruined all his efforts . . . [and after it] he saw nothing worthwhile left for him to do now until the end of his presidency."[53]

After Paris, the two superpowers began fighting over issues in the test ban negotiations that would become central to their debates for the next two and a half years. Was on-site inspection really necessary for verification, and what should the composition of the control system staff be? The Soviets, in particular, showed little interest in the talks after the failed summit. Khrushchev had retreated from his stance that it was wise to negotiate with Eisenhower and was waiting for the outcome of the American elections before determining how to proceed.[54]

Accounting for the Breakdown: Contradictory Strategies Collide

Throughout these test ban negotiations, the Soviets were trying to circumvent control and achieve an agreement that would undeniably help their strategic position, while the Americans were seeking to conclude some form of a verifiable test ban. Ultimately, these two positions were irreconcilable, and the parties did not reach a deal. While traditional approaches to bargaining among adversaries might not find the negotiating failure very surprising, how and why the two superpowers reached these competing positions are interesting questions. For Khrushchev, the late 1950s were years of great domestic autonomy; he was in position to dominate the Soviet policy process. The first secretary understood that although the United States was more powerful militarily, it had no way of exactly verifying the extent of Soviet capabilities or the nature of Soviet intentions. These informational asymmetries offered the USSR enormous opportunities for acting on its own in the international system. By exaggerating Soviet military power and playing to American fears, Khrushchev hoped to be able to extract concessions from the United States without making any compromises. To achieve his goals, Khrushchev employed a strategy of predomination. Although his assessments would have been consistent with obfuscating at the table, there seems to be significant evidence to indicate that the Soviet leader wanted an agreement that would provide decisive advantages for the USSR. Such an accord—an uncontrolled test ban, for instance—would have allowed Khrushchev to argue the wisdom of his approach and build support for both himself and his policies. Moreover, if he had not been interested in a formal agreement, he could have continued with his grandiose proposals. The statements of the Soviet leadership regarding its "peacefulness" up until early 1958 had been quite effective in convincing the world that the USSR was seriously interested in disarmament. The move to accept real negotiations and even to acquiesce to the Geneva System seemed to indicate that Khrushchev wanted a treaty. Any accord, however, would have to assure Soviet advantage. Throughout the negotiations, then, the Soviets consistently offered proposals designed to enhance their relative power position, and this behavior appears to confirm the contention that Khrushchev was seeking to predominate.

The U-2 affair, however, had significant domestic implications for the first secretary. The infiltration of Soviet airspace and Eisenhower's support for this action contradicted the basis of Khrushchev's foreign and domestic policy. For several years, he had been arguing that there was a split in the American leadership and that "realists" predominated. As long as "sober men" were in charge, then the United States would not undertake bellicose moves against the USSR. Eisenhower, in Khrushchev's estimation, was a realist and was deterred by Soviet might. In making this argument, Khrushchev was able to justify not only the test ban negotiations, but also the cutting back of conventional forces by 1.2 million men and the transfer of resources to the domestic economy. These decisions were not extremely popular within the Soviet leadership. Although they were initially silent, in the aftermath of U-2, others voiced their criticisms. Khrushchev stepped back from the policy of negotiation and put the test ban on hold.[55]

In the United States, Eisenhower directed test ban policy to serve his understanding of American security interests. The president had moderate autonomy throughout most of the period because of his mixed level of support (strong among the public, unreliable among members of Congress) and the favorable timing within the election cycle during which most of the negotiations occurred. According to Eisenhower, by 1958, the poor global image of the United States was a significant threat to American security and a constraint on American security policy. To help remedy the U.S. reputation, the president was willing to consider a test ban, even though it could have a negative, short-run effect on the American military position. He asserted, however, that the conclusion of a verifiable agreement would help the overall U.S. stance because of its impact on the perception of the United States as a peace-loving power and self-assured state.

That Eisenhower engaged in a cooperative strategy at the table appears clear from both his deeds and his words in formerly classified documents. While the president could have implemented an approach solely designed for public relations and obfuscated, Eisenhower instead sought to make reasonable concessions and ask for feasible compromises from the Soviets in order to reach a verifiable test ban. Throughout the negotiations, American behavior was consistently cooperative, and the Soviets typically rebuffed it. The U.S. approach is incomprehensible according to a realist analysis, however. Why would the stronger power seek to make concessions to a weaker one?

The American position on the test ban in the late 1950s was also remarkable because the president's stance changed in opposition to public opinion and the preferences of many members of his administration. Prior to Sputnik, Americans tended to favor the test ban, but Eisenhower was opposed. Thereafter, he pursued a controlled moratorium when the public had become more concerned about the strategic balance. The president adopted this view because he believed that his domestic political position was safe and his approach was the correct one for preserving American security. With moderate autonomy (favorable timing and mixed support) and an ability to reach out to ordinary people if he needed, Eisenhower had confidence in his choice to lead, abandoning his serious pursuit of the test ban only after the U-2 incident. This episode, coming in the middle of his fourth year, brought on the lame-duck phase of Eisenhower's presidency. Thereafter, the president could not count on the support of constituents and other governmental officials for his security program. He was an outgoing president who had to leave policy innovation and arms control achievements to his successors.

Thus, the test ban case of the late 1950s shows the important role that leaders play in these negotiations. Each executive had his own particular assessment of the opponent, the most essential element of security, and the nation's alternatives for improving its security position. In the late 1950s, Khrushchev put his particular stamp on Soviet policy with his innovations in Leninist international relations theory. By arguing that war was not inevitable, that nuclear weapons could cause world annihilation, and that the capitalist ruling circles were not united, Khrushchev opened the door for arms control negotiations with the United States, as well as a relative shift in budgetary priorities and an alteration in the traditional Soviet preference for ground troops in favor of nuclear forces.

Eisenhower, on the other hand, perceived that the U.S. freedom of maneuver in the world system was somewhat limited because it was losing the battle for public opinion. He then instituted a cooperative strategy at the table, in which the United States would seek to work with the USSR to enhance peace. With such an approach, the president hoped to improve world opinion of American policy, thereby strengthening the U.S. political position while also constraining superpower military competition.

In addition, these negotiations revealed that there were times when an agreement was virtually impossible because of the competing strategies that nations played. Even without the U-2 debacle, the two sides would not have been able to conclude an agreement, as there was no way to achieve their goals simultaneously. The U-2 incident, however, highlights the feedback between international and domestic politics. World events can have an impact on the domestic political situation, which then forces a reformulation of security policy. After the U-2 event, Eisenhower was not capable of and Khrushchev was not interested in continuing effectively with the test ban talks. Eisenhower's ability to negotiate suffered because his autonomy declined enormously, and Khrushchev had to back away from the talks because the incident indicated that one of the assumptions upon which the policy had been founded (that Eisenhower was a "realist") was flawed. Thus, the test ban was effectively shelved for another time and for a new American leader.

CHAPTER 3

From Deadlock to Mutual Compromise: Khrushchev, Kennedy, and the Limited Test Ban Treaty

In March 1961 the superpowers resumed negotiations to ban nuclear testing.[1] After more than two years of talks, which were often marked by frustration, the parties negotiated intensively for ten days in July 1963 and arrived at a formula that prohibited tests in the atmosphere, at high altitudes, and underwater. Later in the year, the Limited Test Ban Treaty (LTBT) became law, as the legislatures of the countries ratified the agreement.

Domestic politics analysts would not be surprised that Khrushchev and Kennedy succeeded where Khrushchev and Eisenhower had failed, because they contend that the fate of arms control is closely linked with that of "reformist" and "liberal" politicians in the USSR and the United States, respectively. According to this type of analysis, when reformists or liberals (supporters of arms control) are in positions of power, a state is inclined to make compromises at the table. By contrast, when orthodox or conservative individuals have the most influence, the state is typically not interested in agreements. When neither group asserts dominant influence, then policy results from deals struck among domestic political actors and bureaucracies, and this internally negotiated strategy becomes the approach used at the international bargaining table. From this perspective, the achievement of a treaty in 1963 reflected the victory of the reformist faction in Soviet politics and the dominance of liberals in the United States.

More specifically, domestic politics analysts would argue that in the USSR, reformists and traditionalists had been battling over policy direction for several years. Khrushchev would often assert the reformist position, only to be thwarted by more traditional members of the leadership. In the spring of 1963, however, his main rival, Frol Kozlov, became very ill and had to leave the leadership. Because of Kozlov's exit, Khrushchev was able to push through the test ban treaty despite objections from other orthodox members of the leadership. In the United States, the argument is that in 1961 a "liberal" administration took office. Furthermore, in that year, the U.S. Congress created a new organization precisely for the purpose of promoting weapons limitation agreements, called the Arms Control and Disarmament Agency (ACDA). Thus, support for arms control was stronger than it had been under Eisenhower. By 1962, President Kennedy and his allies in ACDA, the State Department, and the Science Advisory Council struck a deal with opponents of the test ban in the military, intelligence community, and the Atomic Energy Commission (AEC). With the simultaneous improvement of the reformist position in Soviet politics, Khrushchev finally agreed with the U.S. offer in the summer of 1963.

While the domestic politics model provides a plausible interpretation, it does not capture the historical nuances of the case. Instead it exaggerates the degree of conflict within both systems and underestimates the role of the leader in shaping each nation's policies. Furthermore, the impetus for policy change often came from outside the bureaucratic process, as external shocks often convinced the executive to innovate. In addition, neither Khrushchev nor Kennedy was a strong advocate of arms control for its own sake. During this period, both were in relatively good positions domestically, so that their preferences on this issue could become state policy. And both perceived a modest value in arms control. For the Soviets, Khrushchev again contended that his country had many options besides negotiated agreements and continued with his policy of predomination at the table. The Cuban Missile Crisis, however, was a turning point that starkly demonstrated to Khrushchev the limits of unilateral Soviet action. Reconnaissance technology had improved, and the American determination to risk nuclear war linked the fates of the two superpowers more closely together than before. With this adjustment in his assessment of alternatives to arms control, Khrushchev thereafter shifted from a stance of predomination to cooperation that made agreement possible.

Kennedy, on the other hand, remained consistent in his pursuit of a cooperative strategy. For JFK, the value of an agreement was low, since he was convinced of the hostility of the USSR and the importance of military power, but the president also believed that his alternatives to a test ban were few. Not only did the United States have to consider the Soviet military challenge and the worldwide perception of the nuclear balance, but Kennedy also worried that the spread of nuclear know-how to other countries would aggravate the strategic situation. While the United States could undertake steps to build up its arsenal and show the world its prowess, the only way to slow proliferation would be to engage other states, especially the Soviets, in the project. JFK thus implemented a cooperative approach at the table. When the Soviets finally switched to a similar strategy, the two sides were able to arrive at a satisfactory formula and conclude the Limited Test Ban Treaty.

Assessing Autonomy and Strategy, 1961–63

The domestic politics models of decision making for the LTBT raise unanswered questions about the role of leadership in foreign policy, the values that inform arms control policy choices, and the links between domestic and international issues. With the leadership approach, autonomy provides a crucial link that explains when the executives take initiative on arms control and when they do not. Also, leaders' assessments of their commitment to agreements and alternatives to weapons limitation accords help us identify negotiating strategies that can account for the character of the discussions (productive or unprofitable) as well as the outcome.

Khrushchev's Autonomy, 1961–63

As we saw in chapter 2, after 1958, Khrushchev was the predominant force in Soviet politics. By that time, the first secretary had succeeded in removing his chief rivals from their positions of power and was named chairman of the Council of Ministers. As Party and government leader, Khrushchev visited the United States and the United Nations, arranged for a summit in Paris with the Western powers, and then canceled it when Eisenhower would not apologize for authorizing the U-2 mission.

Immediately after the breakdown of the summit in 1960, Khrushchev's policy failure caused him to adopt a less innovative approach. His rhetoric, not surprisingly, stressed more of the traditional, Stalinist themes, that "aggressive wars are inherent to imperialism and monopolistic capital" and that even "if war occurred, socialism would prevail."[2] Moreover, in mid-1961, the first secretary rescinded his decision to reduce Soviet ground forces by 1.2 million men. Because of an upcoming Party Congress and his apparent mistake in dealing with the United States, Khrushchev needed to respond to domestic concerns. But, in addition to bending to the wishes of others, the first secretary also went on an offensive at home to increase his support and his success at the congress. Using his control over the media, Khrushchev began aggressively developing his own cult of personality. During ceremonies commemorating the 20th anniversary of the start of World War II in 1961, the Khrushchev legend began to grow.

48   To Agree or Not to Agree

Not only was the first secretary commended for his role in organizing resistance to the Nazis in Ukraine, but he was credited with military-strategic brilliance in Ukraine and Stalingrad. Khrushchev was supposedly the most influential member of the Military Council, a body that made key strategic decisions on the war effort during World War II.[3]

This offensive continued into October, when at the Twenty-Second Party Congress, several speakers extolled Khrushchev for his theoretical genius and grasp of military affairs and attributed Soviet progress in economic and political matters to the first secretary's leadership. At the Party gathering, Khrushchev also demonstrated his personal power by bringing the dispute among communists out in the open, publicly attacking the Albanian Party by name and their Chinese sponsors by extension. October 1961 marked the beginning of open polemics within the communist system. Another sign of the first secretary's control was his ability to expel the so-called anti-Party group from the CPSU and the decision to remove Stalin's body from its place of honor in the Lenin mausoleum.[4]

After October 1961, favorable timing and significant support provided Khrushchev with a high level of autonomy that allowed him to make his preferred approach the national strategy. A year later, the first secretary's position was less certain. Because there was no Party Congress on the horizon, the timing in the selection cycle was favorable, but the Soviet defeat in the Cuban Missile Crisis cost Khrushchev some support and raised serious questions regarding his leadership.[5] Thus, from late 1962 on, the first secretary's autonomy was moderate (because of mixed support and favorable timing). Khrushchev, however, remained confident that he was strong enough to continue to control policy, and he decided to alter the Soviet bargaining strategy as a result of his experience during the crisis.

Kennedy's Autonomy, 1961–63

Throughout his tenure, John F. Kennedy was arguably more sensitive to his domestic political position than was any other postwar president. To help him manage his authority effectively, he asked Richard Neustadt of Harvard University to be one of his advisers. Neustadt had recently finished a book that criticized outgoing President Eisenhower for not understanding that presidential power was "the power to persuade" or realizing that the president can take his case to the people. Kennedy took Neustadt's lessons to heart and used this power to achieve his most desired goals.[6]

At the outset of his term, Kennedy had reason to be concerned about his

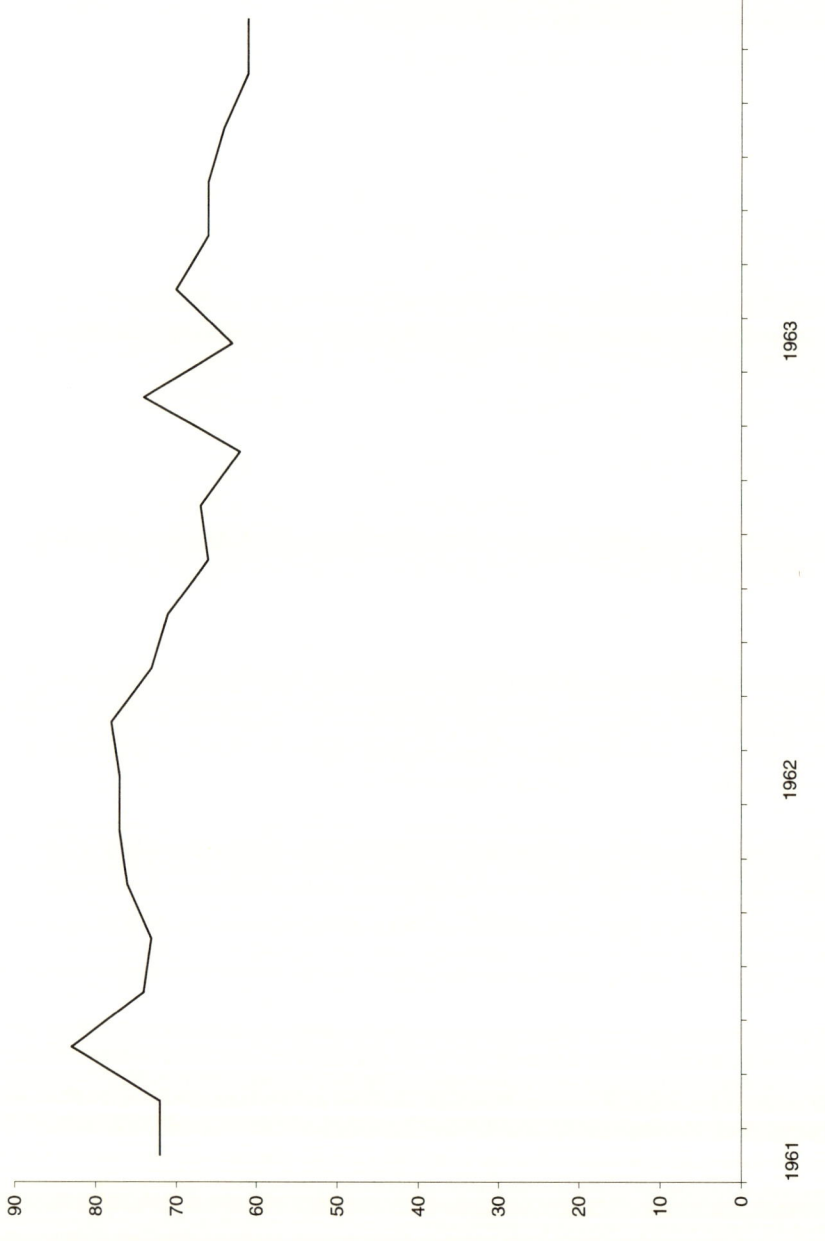

Fig. 3. Kennedy's approval ratings (percentage who approve). (Data from George H. Gallup, *The Gallup Poll: Public Opinion 1935–1971*, vol. 3 [New York: Random House, 1972].)

in the importance of military strength meant that the Soviet first secretary believed that arms control had limited value.

With respect to the second determinant of strategy, alternatives to arms control, the Soviet leader continued to perceive that the USSR had several other options to pursue. Again, informational asymmetries, nuclear missiles, and the apparent Soviet victory in the world battle for public opinion gave him room to maneuver independently.[11] Khrushchev believed that the closed nature of his society and the underdevelopment of reconnaissance technology still provided him with an advantage over the United States. Moreover, the first secretary was convinced that the American leadership was not used to being vulnerable to a nuclear strike and that Kennedy would ultimately back down to avoid any war. Finally, Khrushchev's confidence in the attractiveness of the Soviet economic model (compared to the capitalist one) remained strong throughout this period and gave him the edge in political battles.[12] Therefore, the first secretary continued to predominate in arms control negotiations, seeking only a formula that would clearly benefit the USSR at the expense of the United States.

The Soviet strategy changed in the aftermath of the missile crisis as Khrushchev learned that the basis for his assessment of multiple Soviet alternatives—the informational asymmetry and American fear of nuclear war—collapsed. American reconnaissance discovered the missiles in time to stop their full deployment and force their removal. Furthermore, Kennedy was willing to risk war with the Soviets, showing that he could not be so easily intimidated. Thus, the threat of nuclear annihilation had been palpable, and the recognition of the interdependence of the two nations' policies became unavoidable.[13] Khrushchev and other members of the Soviet leadership stressed the importance of compromise during the crisis and reminded critics (both abroad and at home) that the United States was a formidable foe with considerable nuclear capability.[14] With this adjustment, Khrushchev adopted a cooperative strategy at the bargaining table.

American Strategy toward the Test Ban Negotiations

Throughout his campaign for the presidency, John F. Kennedy made clear that he believed in the centrality of the military component of power. He argued repeatedly that the Eisenhower administration had allowed the U.S. position to slip dangerously and promised that he would seek to correct any imbalances. Despite learning upon taking office that U.S. military strength relative to the USSR was quite good, Kennedy still worked to keep his campaign promises. According to his national security adviser, McGeorge Bundy, the president considered superiority the "safest" possible "balance." Even the director of the newly constituted Arms Control and Disarmament Agency, William Foster, argued that military predominance was "an important factor in the deterrence of Soviet aggressions."[15]

Kennedy also perceived the Soviets as a highly menacing adversary. The president argued that the Soviets had "ambitions for world domination" and had to be convinced "that aggression and subversion will not be profitable routes to pursue these ends."[16] Given the importance he placed on military power and the magnitude of Soviet hostility he perceived, the president placed a relatively low value on arms control.

Regarding American alternatives to arms reduction, Kennedy conceived of arms control and the development of better weapons as intertwined approaches for improving American security. He asked for an increase in defense expenditures soon after taking office and began looking for possible disarmament measures to propose.[17] According to the president, "[d]iplomacy and defense are no longer distinct alternatives, one to be used when the other fails—both must complement each other."[18] The development of more and better weapons would help maintain and increase U.S. superiority, but disarmament measures could address other American security concerns. In addition, the president was concerned about nuclear proliferation and believed that it had to be stopped or at least slowed. The only way to try to control the spread of nuclear weapons was through negotiations with the Soviets (and others) and for the superpowers to be willing to take on some restrictions themselves. Thus, arms control was a necessary component of the administration's policy, and there were few alternatives to it.[19]

Given these views of both the alternatives to and value of an agreement, the leadership model would predict that Kennedy would cooperate at the test ban talks. The American president would be willing to make concessions if the Soviets matched these compromises but would not be interested in achieving a test ban agreement if it would require that the United States take on more onerous obligations than its partner.

The Leadership Model and the Limited Test Ban Treaty

In 1961, the Americans and Soviets, along with the British, resumed their negotiations for a test ban treaty. As we saw in chapter 2, for the previous year and a half, the parties had been engaged in talks, but the Soviets were following a strategy of predomination while the Americans were seeking a formula that would entail equivalent compromises. The two sides made little progress at the table, and the situation deteriorated as a result of the U-2 incident.

The inauguration of John F. Kennedy initially appeared to breathe new life into the talks. The Soviet press gave the president's first speeches balanced reviews, seeming to indicate that Khrushchev would consider working with the new American leader.[20] Also, Kennedy appeared to be serious about the negotiations. In the first months of his administration, the president asked his special adviser for disarmament, John McCloy, to conduct a detailed study of the past test ban negotiations. The disarmament adviser concluded that the United States could afford to make several concessions at the bargaining table.[21]

But once negotiations reopened, any expectations that an agreement could be easily reached were shattered. The United States again played a cooperative strategy, ready to work from the earlier accomplishments at the table, but the Soviets remained committed to predomination and reneged on previous positions. In fact, the chance of achieving an agreement was nonexistent in 1961 and 1962. Only in the sobering aftermath of the Cuban Missile Crisis did Khrushchev reconsider his assessment of Soviet alternatives to arms control and implement a cooperative strategy that finally allowed the two sides to find a mutually acceptable formula.

Deadlock and Recrimination at the Geneva Conference

When the Geneva Conference on the Discontinuance of Nuclear Weapons Tests reconvened in March 1961, the Soviet ambassador introduced two new demands: (1) instead of a single administrator, establish a three-person administrative council to oversee the proposed testing regime; and (2) include France in the negotiations. The Soviets sought the council in lieu of a single administrator because they argued that no one individual could be "neutral"; therefore, to protect the interests of all nations, each type of system—socialist, capitalist, and nonaligned—should have the right to veto administrative decisions. The Soviets also argued that the French had to be included in the talks since they could perform experiments for their allies, allowing the United States and Britain to subvert any test ban treaty. Because the parties to the negotiations had already agreed on the single administrator and the exclusion of France (the French did not want to participate), many in the West saw this motion as a sign of the Soviets' disinterest in reaching a test ban. Not only were the Soviets rescinding previously accepted positions, they were also making proposals that were either militarily advantageous (the administrative council) or a political boon (since the French would say no).[22] Such behavior confirmed the view that the USSR was seeking a conclusive victory over the West in the talks.

By contrast, the United States presented several concessions at the session, meeting the Soviets halfway with a proposal of a three-year moratorium and seismic research program, accepting the Soviet position on safeguards for experimental and peaceful explosions, offering a high-altitude test ban, reducing the number of control posts on Soviet territory by two, and accepting Soviet arguments that capitalist and communist representation on the control commission should be equal.[23] In April, the West formalized its position, incorporating these concessions into a draft treaty that banned all verifiable tests and included a three-year moratorium on those experiments that the parties presently could not monitor. The Soviets promptly rejected the offer.[24]

The prospects for an agreement worsened during the late spring and summer of 1961, as did American-Soviet relations in general. In April, the Kennedy administration aided Cuban émigrés in their botched attempt to overthrow the Castro regime. Although Khrushchev denounced this violation of Cuban sovereignty, the first secretary did not cancel an already scheduled superpower summit. The American administration took Khrushchev's commitment to go to Vienna as a positive sign that the Soviet leader was eager to work constructively with the United States, despite the American action in Cuba. But in Vienna, these hopes were dashed. There, the Party leader berated the president, reiterated the Soviet position on the administrative council, and threatened to relink the test ban negotiations with disarmament talks. At the end of the summit, the Soviets presented an *aide-mémoire* to the Americans in which they demanded a change in the status of Berlin and threatened to sign a peace treaty with the German Democratic Republic.[25] In response, the United States increased its forces in Europe. Escalating the situation further, the Soviets in July announced the expansion of their defense budget and the increase in troop strength.[26]

With the deterioration of the superpower relationship, Kennedy began to consider breaking the moratorium and authorizing a new test series. In the summer, he decided to observe the voluntary ban for a little while longer in order to demonstrate to the Soviets and the world the United States' sincere interest in achieving a test ban.[27] The Soviets, however, did not reciprocate the president's willingness to show good faith. Shortly thereafter, the USSR, along with its East German allies, began constructing the Berlin Wall. The Soviets then also started an ambitious series of nuclear tests, flouting the moratorium. Khrushchev justified the Soviet action as a necessary response to the U.S. force buildup in Europe and overall American bellicosity.[28]

While the president was willing to make matched concessions to the Soviets at the table, Kennedy also felt that the United States had to respond in kind to these aggressive steps. He announced that the United States had its own test series of underground experiments planned and asked the Soviet Union to join the United States in a ban on exploding nuclear weapons in the atmosphere. The Soviets rebuffed the offer, as the administration expected, but startled the United States and the world with the detonation of a 50-megaton device (equivalent to more than 3,000 Hiroshima-type bombs) for the culmination of their test series. The U.S. below-ground explosions were much smaller, about one-thousandth the size of this giant Soviet test, and American officials worried that a comparison in the destructiveness of these blasts would lead to the questioning of the power of the American arsenal.[29]

The president, therefore, authorized three additional measures. First, he asked the Atomic Energy Commission and its chair, Glenn Seaborg, to prepare a major series of atmospheric tests. Second, Kennedy formally asked the British for permission to use Christmas Island for such a series. And third, to combat any doubts about which superpower was superior, the president decided to reveal the truth about the strategic balance.[30] In a speech to the Business Council of Virginia, Deputy Secretary of Defense Roswell Gilpatric told the world that not only did the United States have more nuclear weapons than the Soviets, but the United States was so much stronger that it could absorb a first strike and still inflict unacceptable damage on the USSR.[31]

In retaliation, the Soviets responded with a move that strongly suggested their commitment to predomination. At the late fall 1961 negotiating session, the USSR reversed its position on several issues, withdrawing support from the comprehensive test ban treaty and the international system of verification. The Soviets also demanded that the talks be enlarged to include other countries and other disarmament issues. Although the United States reproved the Soviets for their reversal, it eventually acquiesced to their requirements.[32] The three power test ban negotiations then ended.

At the end of 1961 and into 1962, the Kennedy administration was trying to meet the Soviet challenge, while also looking for areas of compromise at the negotiating table. In response to this deterioration in the relationship and the tone of negotiations, Kennedy took other steps to enhance the American position. In February, the United Kingdom formally granted its authorization to use Christmas Island for a new round of above-ground tests if the Soviets would not agree to a controlled test ban.[33] Then the president began making preparations for the experiments while making one last offer for a controlled test ban that, if approved, would halt the upcoming series.[34] The USSR was not interested in accepting any proposal, however. In fact, the Soviets warned that they would reciprocate with their own series if the West proceeded with these experiments. Ignoring the threat, the United States went forward with its arrangements on Christmas Island.[35]

The record of this first year of negotiations, then, substantiates the claim that the Soviets desired a test ban agreement that served their military interests—allowing them to test without being detected, while preventing American experiments. The Americans, on the other hand, were sincerely interested in some form of mutual compromise. When the Americans could not convince the Soviets to act cooperatively, the president authorized the necessary steps to demonstrate that the United States would not be dominated.

The Expanded Negotiating Forum and the Worsening of Tensions

In 1962, arms control talks resumed in a new arena, the Eighteen Nation Disarmament Committee (ENDC). There, eight neutral nations and seven additional Western and Eastern countries joined the United States, Soviet Union, and United Kingdom for discussions on broader arms control issues. The Soviets, however, continued to try to achieve an outcome that would unambiguously favor their side. Despite agreeing to establish a separate realm under the auspices of the ENDC in which nuclear states could discuss testing—thereby resuming in some sense the negotiations begun in Geneva—the deadlock continued. The USSR proceeded with predomination, resisting any form of mandatory international control, and the United States continued with cooperation, trying to achieve an agreement that restricted testing and included effective verification procedures.[36]

Because of the lack of progress at the table, the United States prepared for atmospheric testing. The eight neutral nations on the panel tried to forestall the series with a plan that specified a controlled moratorium on above- and below-ground tests and provided for inspection by invitation of the country that had potentially violated the ban. While the Soviets were interested in the proposal, the Americans rejected that scheme. The United States categorically opposed any formula that allowed the suspect nation to determine when to authorize an examination of its test sites. The Americans had long argued that such an arrangement granted the accused offender the power to subvert control. Neither the Soviet nor the American reaction should have been surprising; each acted in a manner consistent with its approach to the table.[37]

Although the prospects for an agreement in this new forum appeared dismal, in the summer of 1962, the United States began to receive important technical information that would later help it offer an acceptable test ban proposal.

The findings of an American seismic research project called VELA indicated that unstaffed detection stations were more effective than originally estimated. VELA demonstrated that in policing any agreement, far fewer on-site inspections (OSIs) would be needed than initially thought. Moreover, the United States could have confidence that it could catch atmospheric tests with its sensors and would not have to rely on on-site inspection to detect those experiments. Because the president and others doubted the USSR's willingness to allow an adequate number of inspections to verify a comprehensive test ban, this discovery was important. It meant that some arrangement that prohibited tests was possible; if a ban were confined to atmospheric tests, the United States would not need to examine Soviet territory.[38] Because a limited ban "would prevent both the U.S. and the USSR from obtaining weapons effects information [needed to develop antimissile systems].... [and] would avoid the risk of undetected Soviet unilateral nuclear advances," it would require similar sacrifices from both sides.[39]

As a result of VELA, the president could offer the Soviets two different draft treaties. If the USSR would agree to on-site inspection in order to distinguish earthquakes from underground tests, the United States believed that the sides could complete a comprehensive test ban with a number of OSIs that was approaching acceptability for the Soviets. But, if the USSR still refused to allow international monitors on its territory, Americans now thought that they could verify compliance of a test ban in the air, water, and outer space without investigating Soviet lands.[40] Thus, in August 1962, the chief American negotiator, Arthur Dean, presented two draft agreements to those gathered in Geneva. The first was a comprehensive test ban (CTB) that outlawed all tests, provided for fewer on-site inspections than previous American offers, established a control commission consisting of representatives from the three types of countries, and required a less extensive network of detection stations. The second treaty proposed banning only tests in three of the four environments, that is, all tests that could be detected adequately with "national technical means."[41] The conditions embodied in both formulas reflected an American desire to take into account Soviet concerns, while also protecting American interests.

Revealing their indifference to compromise and fairness in any solution, the Soviets were unimpressed with these motions. They expressed their categorical opposition to the limited ban that "legalized" continued testing. On the comprehensive ban, the sides were far apart on the specifics of a control system, although the United States was willing to reduce the number of OSIs significantly. The Soviets would not even concede that inspection was necessary for verification, and therefore would not permit a satisfactory quantity of inspections or approve the procedures necessary to make any agreement workable.[42]

The Missile Crisis and Its Aftermath: Khrushchev Reconsiders His Bargaining Strategy

While the negotiators wrestled with the test ban, the president learned in mid-October that the Soviets were installing medium- and intermediate-range ballistic missiles in Cuba. After a week of strategy sessions, Kennedy revealed to the American public on October 22 that these missile sites existed and demanded that the Soviets remove them. The Cuban Missile Crisis lasted another six days, until the USSR agreed to withdraw the offensive weapons.[43]

Although those days in October 1962 are primarily remembered as a time when the Soviets and Americans considered nuclear war, the crisis also had serious long-term repercussions within the communist world and Soviet domestic politics. The Soviet failure to follow an aggressive path through to the end further damaged the Sino-Soviet relationship, as the Chinese complained bitterly about Khrushchev's decision to withdraw the missiles. Moreover, other members of the Soviet leadership were embarrassed by this episode and two years later, when Khrushchev was dismissed in a palace coup, they counted it among the first secretary's "hare-brained schemes." In the immediate aftermath of the crisis, however, the Soviet elite rallied around Khrushchev, relieved that nuclear war had not erupted.[44]

At the end of 1962, Khrushchev and the Soviet Union had apparently come through this brush with war relatively unscathed. The first secretary's pride might have been wounded and his attempt to improve the military balance might have failed, but Khrushchev maintained his positions as Party and government leader. Moreover, his experience on the brink of nuclear war caused a softening in the USSR's position on the test ban, as well as other issues. The crisis had shown the first secretary that his attempts to achieve improvements in Soviet security through unilateral actions of coercion had failed spectacularly. Although recent disclosures indicate that the Soviets were able to secure a secret arrangement with Kennedy to withdraw American missiles in Turkey as a result of the crisis, the Soviets were not allowed to reveal the deal at the time. Instead, they had to remove their weapons in apparent defeat.[45]

After this brush with nuclear confrontation, Khrushchev began to reconsider the Soviet options to arms control. In assessing alternatives, he came to recognize that he had been wrong about both his ability to deceive the West and

Kennedy's willingness to back down to avoid nuclear war. Moreover, the events highlighted the fact that the USSR and the United States were interdependent. If one leader had chosen war, both populations and the world would have been destroyed. In addition, the outcome of the crisis had severely damaged Sino-Soviet relations, revealing to Khrushchev that the USSR now had to face two powerful rivals, one in the West—the United States—and another in the East—the People's Republic of China (PRC).[46]

Thus, the crisis was essential for demonstrating to Khrushchev that the USSR's alternatives to arms control for improving the Soviet security position were limited. Deception, bluster, and the development of nuclear weapons would not ensure Soviet safety. After October 1962, the USSR had to contend with an emboldened yet sober adversary, the United States, that could either intentionally or accidentally begin a nuclear conflict and to consider the possibility of dealing with an assertive and hostile former ally, the PRC. This recognition of the failure of the early approach and the need to adopt joint solutions to security problems brought about a shift in Khrushchev's perception of alternatives in late 1962. He then altered his strategy at the table to one of cooperation. For the first time, the two sides would be playing complementary strategies, and there would be a real chance for reaching an agreement.

The first secretary's behavior reflected this change in strategy. In December 1962, Khrushchev sent a letter to Kennedy offering to accept some on-site inspection—about two or three inspections a year. This was the first serious concession that the Soviets had offered since the beginning of negotiations, and apparently Khrushchev had heard that his acquiescence to a few OSIs would be enough for the Americans. Kennedy, encouraged that the Soviets were finally accepting on-site inspection, responded positively but asked for considerably more—eight to ten—per year. The first secretary answered the president's letter, ignoring the call for more inspections and stressing that his smaller number would satisfy past U.S. demands that the Soviets agree to the principle of OSI. In the next few weeks, the disagreement over the number of inspections erupted into a major dispute as each side felt manipulated and betrayed by the other.[47]

After the brief promise of forward movement in late 1962, the two sides were at an impasse. The president, disheartened by the lack of progress, considered authorizing a new series of underground experiments.[48] In Moscow, however, there were some small signs of hope.[49] In April, these developments and the prodding of British Prime Minister Macmillan encouraged Kennedy to act. Kennedy wrote to Khrushchev suggesting that the parties hold high-level negotiations to discuss the ban. Khrushchev accepted and offered to host the talks in Moscow.[50]

The U.S. president recognized that the agreement was in reach, but it was far from assured. He was extremely aware of the vagaries of domestic politics, and he knew that treaty ratification required 67 senators. In the late spring, he could not be sure that two-thirds of his former Senate colleagues would support him. Kennedy then began an offensive with the American public, hoping to get the people behind the treaty so that the Senate could not resist. He started this effort with a commencement address at American University. There, the president suggested that a new era of U.S.–Soviet relations was possible and its achievement imperative and announced that high-level test ban negotiations would begin in Moscow in July. To indicate his seriousness, Kennedy revealed that former Ambassador to the USSR Averell Harriman would represent the United States at these discussions.[51]

The Soviets responded positively to Kennedy's speech, publishing it in the official press with favorable comments from the first secretary.[52] In a speech in East Berlin just two weeks prior to the arrival of the Harriman delegation, Khrushchev expressed for the first time Soviet interest in concluding a *limited* test ban treaty with the United States.[53] This was significant; the Soviets had never before accepted a partial ban without also insisting on an uncontrolled underground testing moratorium.

Harriman arrived in Moscow on July 15 for talks with Gromyko. Soon after the opening of these discussions, the Soviets indicated definitively that they would not allow any on-site inspection. Since the United States required OSI for a comprehensive ban, there was no longer any hope for a treaty prohibiting all tests. A partial ban then became the priority for the Americans, and the Soviets also retained their interest. As if to dispel any doubts on the part of his Western partners in the negotiations, Khrushchev publicly signaled his personal support for achieving an agreement on the limited ban.[54] After a total of 10 days of discussions, the countries were able to arrive at acceptable conditions and language. The foreign ministers signed the document in August.[55]

For Kennedy, achieving Soviet approval of an agreement was only part of the challenge. In addition, the president had to secure Senate consent. Even though the chances of winning a two-thirds majority in the upper chamber for an accord requiring the partial cessation of tests were higher than those of earning support for a comprehensive test ban, Kennedy was still concerned about achieving passage of the Limited Test Ban Treaty. Understanding that the ratification process was highly sensitive, Kennedy carefully controlled the flow of information about the talks that reached the American public and politicians while the negotiations were proceeding. The president feared that treaty opponents might leak news of possible provisions in order to poison the international and domestic atmosphere. To disarm the critics, he provided them with little informational ammunition. The results were few speculations about the treaty prior to the conclusion of the talks and commendations in the press for the U.S. effort after the agreement was reached.[56]

The president took his case to the public immediately after the treaty was initialed. In a national broadcast, President Kennedy framed the measure as a step toward curbing the arms race, thereby enhancing American security.[57] To solidify Senate approval of this measure, Kennedy invited backers and powerful skeptics to fly to Moscow for the signing ceremony. At the time, one of the president's advisers explained that "the purpose of the Senate delegation is to interest them as well as provide additional opportunities to direct public attention to the benefits of the test ban." Furthermore, Kennedy accepted the conditions that the Joint Chiefs of Staff attached to their backing of the treaty, including vigorous underground testing and weapons development programs. The president was trying to garner approval from all the key power bases—the public, the Senate, and the military—to ensure ratification of the treaty.[58]

Kennedy also worked to manipulate the ratification process to his advantage. He rushed the treaty to the Senate because, as he explained to Secretary Rusk, "we got [sic] to hit the country while the country's hot. That's the only thing that makes any impression to these goddamned Senators. . . . they'll move as the country moves. So, I think we've got to go to the country while . . . there's maximum interest."[59] In the Senate, then, Kennedy made sure that the Foreign Relations Committee took up the matter in an open forum before the closed hearings of the Preparedness Subcommittee of the Armed Forces Committee began. Because Foreign Relations was comprised of treaty supporters, the president expected less antagonistic questions and therefore a more favorable hearing, while the opponents on the Preparedness Subcommittee were expected to try to discredit the rationale for the LTBT. The president reasoned that "if they [the Joint Chiefs of Staff] go on record first in front of the Senate Foreign Relations Committee, then it's more difficult for them to [come out against the treaty later]. . . . [I]f we could get them on public, uh, record and publicize that to the nation, then whatever was leaked out of the . . . [Preparedness] Committee, uh, would have much less impact."[60]

The administration's campaign for the agreement had its desired effect. The Gallup organization measured public support at 4 to 1 in favor of the treaty, while a Harris poll found approval of the agreement to be 10 to 1. During the hearings, members of the Kennedy administration, including the Joint Chiefs, provided positive evaluations of the security benefits of the LTBT, stressing particularly the treaty's role in preventing proliferation, reducing radioactive pollution, promoting missile site survivability, and allowing continued Anti-Ballistic Missile (ABM) research. Those senators on the fence then agreed to vote for the treaty, and it passed by a vote of 80 to 19.[61]

Leadership and the LTBT: From Deadlock to Mutual Compromise

The case of the Limited Test Ban Treaty shows that domestic politics alone cannot explain the outcome of negotiations. While each leader had to operate within his political system and potentially was subject to constraints, considerable autonomy provided the executive with more influence than any of the other players. A leader who was personally powerful had a number of resources that he could use to help surmount the barriers to agreement in the system. Khrushchev created a personality cult that justified his having the last word on policy, and Kennedy utilized his link with the public and ability to shape the treaty ratification process to affect the outcome. Still, both the first secretary and the president had to work to build and maintain constituent support for their policies. As long as they kept that backing, both leaders could safely pursue the approach that they believed was best for their nation.

In arriving at a strategy, each leader's view of the opponent, perspective on the importance of military power, and assessment of security policy options had an impact. At the outset of the negotiations, Khrushchev held to his previous opinions, believing that when the United States was ruled by a "reasonable man" (which is what he deemed Kennedy), it was possible to work with that capitalist state. He also contended that military power was essential for providing the USSR with its security and obtaining a more compliant United States. Finally, he believed that nuclear weapons, missile technology, the closed nature of the Soviet state, and the dynamism of socialist economies provided the USSR with multiple options in the international arena. Because the Americans were now vulnerable, Kennedy feared nuclear attack, the United States could not definitively determine what the USSR was doing, and history was on the Soviet side, Khrushchev believed that he did not need to find a joint solution to the arms problem. In fact, there really was no nuclear "problem," but rather, opportunities resulted for the USSR because of the current state of weapons, delivery, and reconnaissance technologies.

The Cuban Missile Crisis changed Khrushchev's perception of his country's alternatives. The Soviet leader realized that he could no longer manipulate the international system to his advantage. Informational asymmetries were effectively gone, as the United States was able to discover what was happening in Cuba, and its satellites provided the United States with information on the true disposition of the balance of power. Moreover, the crisis also brought home the danger of nuclear war and the intertwining of the superpowers' fates. Thereafter, Khrushchev became willing to make some compromises to achieve an agreement. This change in the first secretary's assessment of the USSR's ability to act on its own led to the implementation of a cooperative strategy at the table.

Khrushchev eventually made the concessions necessary to achieve the LTBT. While the treaty was not a victory for the Soviet Union over the United States, it provided Khrushchev with some important benefits. First, the treaty allowed the USSR to garner worldwide approval for its peace policy without having to forfeit the goal of ever catching up with the United States, since testing was still possible. In fact, Khrushchev hoped that the treaty would slow the rate of change in the development of U.S. warheads. The agreement also helped maintain the Soviet power position relative to the People's Republic of China. By 1963, the relations between the two communist giants were clearly very strained, and the existence of the treaty complicated the Chinese task of achieving nuclear capability. Under the terms of the treaty, the Soviets could no longer legally help them with weapons development. In addition, the accord established a norm of no atmospheric testing, so that when the Chinese did make their first above-ground test, that development would likely be met with international condemnation.

The treaty also required the USSR to make some important concessions and therefore satisfied American requirements that it compel approximately equivalent concessions. Catching up with the United States in terms of warhead development was going to be more complicated because the treaty restricted testing environments. Moreover, the USSR could not hope to circumvent this accord with illicit experiments; they would be too easily detected. Finally, by agreeing only to the partial test ban, the Soviets were also assenting to the legitimacy of the American need for verification. Previously, they had scoffed at that requirement. Soviet acceptance of the principle of control was an important breakthrough that potentially indicated that future talks could also be productive.

From the outset of the negotiations, Kennedy was interested in cooperating with the USSR to achieve a test ban. Kennedy arrived at this approach not because of a particular attraction to arms control in the abstract, but because he believed that the U.S. ability to respond to the kinds of threats it faced required joint action in the international arena. According to the president, the American ability to offset threats could only partly be met through independent U.S. action. In addition, the United States needed to work with the USSR to slow the development and spread of nuclear weapons. Kennedy was not willing to make multiple, unmatched concessions to Soviet demands, however. Instead, he offered agreements to the Soviets that complicated the task of weapons development for both countries, while also responding firmly to Soviet aggression when necessary. In the end, his behavior at the table and, in particular, his handling of the Cuban Missile Crisis helped convince Khrushchev that the Soviet leader could not win any advantage from the young president. Throughout the process, Kennedy maintained his commitment to achieving some sort of agreement in which both sides took on obligations and sought a "middle-of-the-road" compromise between American and Soviet differences.

In sum, neither internal deals nor pressures compelled the United States and the Soviet Union to negotiate the Limited Test Ban Treaty. Instead, the leaders of both countries managed the policy process, and Kennedy especially did so with an eye toward building constituent support for his chosen approach. That strategy resulted from the leaders' unique understanding of the value of arms control and the alternatives to that policy. Initially the two sides were deadlocked, Khrushchev advanced no compromise, and Kennedy was not willing to disadvantage the U.S. position. The Cuban Missile Crisis caused Khrushchev to reevaluate his perception of Soviet options in the international system. Then, the first secretary changed his negotiating strategy from predomination to cooperation, and at last the leaders were willing to take on the obligations that made the LTBT a reality.

CHAPTER 4

The Search for Unilateral Advantage: Impasse at the Intermediate-range Nuclear Forces Talks

In the early 1980s, the Soviet Union and the United States conducted negotiations on the fate of Intermediate-range Nuclear Forces (INF). While the talks began under Jimmy Carter, Ronald Reagan ultimately was responsible for the position on the American side. From the outset of his stewardship over the negotiations, Reagan proposed the global elimination of all such Soviet and American weapons. The Soviet leadership, however, sought to confine the discussion to systems based in Europe, maintain their INF holdings in Asia, and count the relevant British and French forces as part of the American allotment. These two positions were fundamentally at odds, and the superpowers made virtually no progress in the first year or so of negotiations.

During this period, American and Soviet relations deteriorated, and the INF talks were as much a victim of the general condition of the relationship as a contributor to its degeneration. In the last year of these discussions, there were some muted American attempts to compromise, but still the talks broke down dramatically and ominously in November 1983. In response to the West German Bundestag's vote approving the basing of NATO missiles on the Federal Republic's soil, the Soviets walked out of the negotiations and vowed to take menacing countermeasures to the deployments. To many observers, late 1983 appeared to be a new nadir in American-Soviet relations, reminiscent of the deep freeze of the early 1950s.

The inability of the two states to conclude an agreement on INF at the beginning of the 1980s can be considered unsurprising. Domestic politics analysts would not expect the two sides to come to an agreement on INF in the first part of that decade because of the rise of conservative, anti–arms control forces in the USSR and United States.[1] In both contexts, it is possible to argue that the leaders of these factions prevailed in national politics, as Andropov challenged the policy of détente and succeeded Brezhnev, and Reagan won the 1980 American presidential contest, asserting that American foreign policy must be completely revamped. Moreover, ideological soul mates in various important bureaucratic positions were able to outmaneuver advocates of arms control and superpower cooperation.[2]

While there is some truth to this general outline, there are also some problems with the applicability of the domestic politics-style argument to this case. First, Andropov only took over the reins of Soviet politics in late November 1982. For the first year of serious negotiations, then, Brezhnev and the supposedly pro-détente forces were in control, but their approach to negotiations was not particularly cooperative. Although Andropov changed the style with which the Soviets pursued an INF agreement, appealing more overtly and adroitly to Western public opinion, the actual substance of the approach was not fundamentally different. The Soviets were not ready to accept U.S. deployments or bargain away existing holdings for hypothetical American missiles. Second, the battle of the anti– and pro–arms control forces in the U.S. administration was greatly exaggerated. The president appointed people throughout the executive branch who generally shared his view that the United States needed to rebuild its forces prior to making any kind of agreement and that any accord had to benefit the United States relative to the USSR. Moreover, whenever the administration considered concessions, the president played an important role in deciding whether to adopt them. In the first years, Reagan rejected compromises. Beginning in 1983, however, the president softened his stance, not because the "liberals" in the administration were winning any particular bureaucratic battle, but because he was concerned about the larger political process and the impact of the threatened Soviet walkout on the approaching American elections.

Finally, the domestic politics approach provides an inadequate understanding of the source of the shift in Soviet politics or the continuation in the American case. While Andropov certainly had his differences with his predecessor, as head of the KGB, he had been an important member of Brezhnev's foreign policy team throughout the 1970s. Both were supporters of the deployment of new intermediate-range nuclear missiles, and both were opponents to acquiescing to American demands for removing them. Moreover, the Republican president Richard Nixon—no dove on the American spectrum—was the author of détente and the SALT process, yet fellow Californian and Republican Reagan rejected the idea of détente and the policies associated with it. To understand these seeming puzzles, an analyst must recognize the importance of ability to exercise power. The president offered several programs that required the passage of legislation, but Kennedy was elected to the presidency by the slimmest margin ever. In addition, support for the president in the Senate (which would have to approve any treaty) was questionable. While Democrats outnumbered Republicans there, Southern Democrats often voted with the other party so that, effectively, there was a conservative majority in that key body. Strong popular support buoyed the president, as did his ability to use the media effectively to reach out to his constituents. Thus, throughout his tenure, the president could count on mixed support levels. Public opinion was solidly behind him, yet the legislative branch was a question mark (see fig. 3).

In terms of timing, Kennedy was a first-term president who could count on a honeymoon with the public for a certain period and did not have to become overly concerned with his own election for at least another three years. Thus, the timing was generally good throughout these negotiations. The president, then, had moderate autonomy, which meant that he could pursue his own agenda but that he had to be mindful of domestic consequences. Kennedy was well aware that to convince senators to ratify an arms control treaty with the Soviets, he would need to use his considerable power of persuasion with the public.[7]

Soviet Strategy toward the Test Ban Negotiations

As in the early 1950s, the first secretary remained wedded to his general notions about dealing with capitalists, the importance of military power, and the advantages that informational asymmetries and the laws of history gave to the USSR. With the inauguration of John F. Kennedy, Khrushchev believed that he again had a "realistic" opponent with whom to negotiate. An intelligence report recently unearthed by two scholars in the Moscow archives stated that "Kennedy, in principle, is in favor of talks with the Soviet Union, rejecting as 'too fatalistic' the opinion that 'you can't trust' the Soviet Union, that 'it doesn't observe treaties,' and so on."[8] After Kennedy's failure to send the necessary forces to ensure the success of the Bay of Pigs invasion, Khrushchev reportedly believed that Kennedy was weak and that the "young and inexperienced American president could be made to concede."[9] In addition, the first secretary was convinced that military power, and in particular Soviet nuclear power, had convinced the American president that "realism" was the correct way of dealing with the USSR. During the early 1960s, Khrushchev sponsored the creation and testing of super-size hydrogen bombs as well as the development of the strategic rocket forces.[10] Thus, Khrushchev's assessment of Kennedy and his belief the leader's perceptions of the international system in guiding arms control policy.

In effect, then, any examination of the domestic politics of arms control decision making that does not link the developments in the executive branch with the larger political process is incomplete. Moreover, such a discussion that asserts that internal concerns only drive security policy and ignores the influence of strategy will not provide a full account of the case.

A Newfound Western Concern with INF

In the 1970s, intermediate-range nuclear forces became an item of concern in the West and a source of pride in the East. After years of development, the USSR began basing SS-20s, new, mobile, intermediate-range missiles, with multiple independently targetable reentry vehicles (MIRVs), as a way of covering strategically important targets without violating already agreed upon restrictions on long-range launchers. The SS-20s were pointed at Western Europe (as well as East Asia), and NATO perceived these missiles to be a particular threat since they were far more capable than the systems that they replaced. While the older Soviet missiles carried only one warhead, each SS-20 had three highly accurate and independently targetable charges. Moreover, these rockets ran on solid fuel and could be launched more quickly than their predecessors.[3]

NATO leaders considered their options in the European theater as the Soviets began their SS-20 deployments. West German chancellor Helmut Schmidt, in particular, worried that these missiles, together with the codification of nuclear parity in the Strategic Arms Limitation Treaty (SALT), presented a distinct new threat to European security. In an important speech to the International Institute for Strategic Studies in London, Schmidt said that NATO depended on American nuclear superiority to deter the Warsaw Pact from invading and overrunning Europe with its more powerful conventional military machine. With the advent of the SS-20 and SALT, the United States lost both its theater and strategic advantage and, potentially, its willingness to come to the aid of Western Europe in case of a nuclear attack. To strengthen that commitment to European defense by more closely coupling the NATO and American arsenals, Schmidt advocated the basing of new American nuclear weapons in Europe. The argument was that if the Soviets attacked and destroyed these forward-based *American* missiles, even with conventional weapons, the United States would be less likely to ignore this attack as a strike against its own arsenal. Therefore, the United States would be more inclined to respond to Soviet aggression using its strategic weapons. In this way, the defense of Europe would be more closely "coupled" with that of the United States, and American missiles in Europe would strengthen deterrence and enhance the peace.[4]

The Schmidt speech created a stir on both sides of the Atlantic, and in less than a year, a consensus formed around the importance of the modernization of NATO nuclear systems, including the deployment of new American INF in Western Europe. But no NATO government felt completely comfortable with the notion of basing more American nuclear weapons on its territory: in the case of war, these missiles would make that homeland a target for Soviet nuclear weapons. Thus, Western European politicians suggested that NATO mandate both new deployments and arms control negotiations. In mid-December 1979, NATO reached what became known as the "dual track decision." One "track" consisted of INF modernization—the deployment of 464 American ground-launched cruise missiles (GLCMs) and 108 Pershing II missiles—while a second committed the United States to open arms control discussions with the Soviets on European INF. For many Europeans, the hope was that the successful completion of an agreement on INF would preclude some of the deployments.[5]

In November 1980, the United States and the USSR began these negotiations as scheduled, but they soon became irrelevant because a lame duck was presiding over the talks. Jimmy Carter lost the election, and there was no guarantee that Ronald Reagan would return to the table with the same position. The new administration then delayed the reopening of the negotiations until the end of 1981. Throughout the next two years, the superpowers made very little progress because their strategies were incompatible. Ultimately, the negotiations collapsed as the United States and NATO went forward with the planned deployments, and the Soviets left the table.[6]

Determining Autonomy and Strategy, 1981–83

In the Soviet Union in the early 1980s, Brezhnev and his generation were dying, and some members of the leadership were coming to realize that the nature of politics in the USSR had to change.[7] The weak physical condition of the leaders in conjunction with the dissension within the Party meant that the general secretary's autonomy was low. Thus, the Soviet leadership adopted an approach consistent with the preferences of the ideological traditionalists and military-industrial complex, which favored predomination at the table.

In the United States, Ronald Reagan was elected on a platform that challenged the consensus politics of Republicans and Democrats of the previous 12 years, rejecting the welfare state and détente with the Soviet Union.[8] At the outset of his term, Reagan had moderate autonomy. Timing was favorable, but support was only mixed; still, the president had the ability to put his own particular stamp on arms control policy. Reagan contended that the USSR was an implacably hostile enemy, that military power was the most important component of American strength, and that the United States had multiple options other than arms control for promoting its security. Thus, the United States implemented a strategy of predomination at the table. By 1983, however, the president's approval ratings had fallen, his party had suffered in the midterm elections, and considerations about the upcoming presidential contest loomed. Thus, the loss of autonomy compelled Reagan to respond to the concerns of the mainstream in the U.S. Congress and public. To try to dispel the impression that he was a warmonger, the president modified his bargaining approach to one of cooperation. Despite this change, the USSR remained committed to predomination. Given the incompatibility of superpower bargaining strategies, the first set of INF negotiations dramatically and ominously ended in failure.

Autonomy and Strategy in the USSR

Throughout the early 1980s, stagnation at the top of Soviet politics belied the turmoil underneath. At the beginning of the decade, the long-reigning party leader, Leonid Brezhnev, was physically sick and politically weakened.[9] His policies, particularly détente, were coming under attack. Although Brezhnev was able to cling to power until his death in November 1982, he could not control the succession. His rival and chief critic, Yuri Andropov, became the new general secretary. While Andropov gained power because of his promise to eliminate corruption and assert Soviet power, his autonomy was limited because he soon became very ill, too.

Despite the attempts of the Soviet press in the early 1980s to cover up or minimize concerns about the health of Soviet leaders, members of the elite and the general public were aware that their general secretaries were suffering from more than just the common cold.[10] In other words, throughout this time, Soviet officials knew that a Central Committee plenum to choose the new executive could be convened at any moment as a result of the death of the leader or a movement to unseat one that a high-placed cabal believed had become too infirm to rule. Timing within the selection cycle in the early 1980s, therefore, was unfavorable.

Support for the two general secretaries in power during the first set of INF negotiations was mixed. In domestic politics, there was one major cleavage that divided the elite into three broad groups. A large number of individuals supported the "Brezhnev way," which entailed "respect for cadres," or in other words, noninterference in their work and a blind eye to pervasive kickbacks and perquisites for the leadership. Others called for the end of corruption, the recognition of the serious problems that the USSR faced, and a new approach to both domestic and international politics. Still others waited on the sidelines to see which group would be victorious in order to preserve their position no matter the outcome in this battle of policies.[11]

On the issue of détente, there was more of a consensus, although some opposing opinions were apparent. The prevalent view of this policy was that strategic parity had made the USSR the military and political equal of the United States. Achieving this status allowed the USSR to pursue both negotiation and confrontation in its dealings with the West. Thus, as a result of détente, in the 1970s, the Soviets expanded trade somewhat, increased cultural contacts, and even engaged in arms control talks, while also building their military power and maintaining their support of revolutionaries throughout the world.[12] In the early 1980s, because of increased American bellicosity, some members of the Soviet leadership began arguing that the negotiation prong of détente should be scrapped, and the USSR should simply pursue confrontation. Both Brezhnev and Andropov, however, tried to appeal to those supporters of the primacy of military power while also arguing that negotiations were still relevant.[13]

In the early 1980s, then, the autonomy of the Soviet leader—Brezhnev and Andropov—was low. Because of their physical and (relative) political weakness, both leaders chose to defer in security policy to the preferences of the main institutional actors within Soviet politics. In this case, the safe policies were to resist the United States, both ideologically and militarily, and seek advantages for the relative Soviet position. Thus, the USSR charted a course of predomination at the negotiating table.

Ronald Reagan's Autonomy, 1981–83

In 1980, Ronald Reagan was elected over Jimmy Carter in a three-way contest. (John Anderson performed well as a third-party candidate.) The Reagan victory was not a ringing endorsement of the winning candidate and his policies, however. On the plus side for Reagan, the vote was decisively in his favor, the Republicans wrested control from the Democrats in the Senate, and many conservative House Democrats, along with their Republican colleagues, would vote with the president to hand him legislative victories. On the other hand, public opinion polls suggested that Reagan's election was more of a rejection of

Carter than a vote of confidence for the former California governor.[14] Moreover, the new president was not particularly popular with the electorate during his second and third years, although the American people responded with sympathy to Reagan in the aftermath of the assassination attempt (fig. 4). And after the midterm elections, Reagan faced both a House that was much more favorably disposed toward arms control and an activist (and highly popular) nuclear freeze movement that was challenging the president's arms control policy.[15] In effect, then, the support for the president was mixed.

In terms of timing, Reagan was in a good position during the first two years of the negotiations. He was a newly elected executive and had some time before he had to worry about facing the voters again. Good timing and mixed support provided Reagan with moderate autonomy in 1981 and 1982. After 1983, the president and his advisers became increasingly aware of the upcoming election and Reagan's vulnerabilities, especially on his stewardship of arms control.[16] Beginning in 1983, the drop in the president's support level to 37 percent (fig. 4) and early polls examining how Reagan would fare against possible Democratic challengers (table 10) made the upcoming election seem very close. Moreover, while foreign policy was not historically an issue that decided elections, Reagan's campaign staff had reason to wonder whether 1984 would be an atypical year. The public overwhelmingly supported a nuclear freeze, was frightened about the possibility of nuclear war, and tended to think the president's policies had increased the level of tension between the superpowers. These positions held fairly steady through 1983.[17] In addition, the American people were also not pleased with Reagan's economic stewardship (table 11). Thus, unfavorable timing and low levels of support meant that the president's autonomy was low in 1983. Reagan, then, became open to adopting a more constructive approach at the negotiating table, which was more in harmony with the position of majority of the House and the American public.

American Bargaining Strategy, 1981–83

The Reagan administration came into office in 1981 intent upon overturning the policy of détente that the United States had been following throughout the previous decade. In the estimation of Reagan and his advisers, previous attempts at détente or policies of seeking diplomatic solutions with totalitarian states were misguided because such powers pursue their expansionist impulses regardless of international agreements. In revamping American foreign policy, U.S. officials consistently identified the USSR as a menacing and evil adversary.[18]

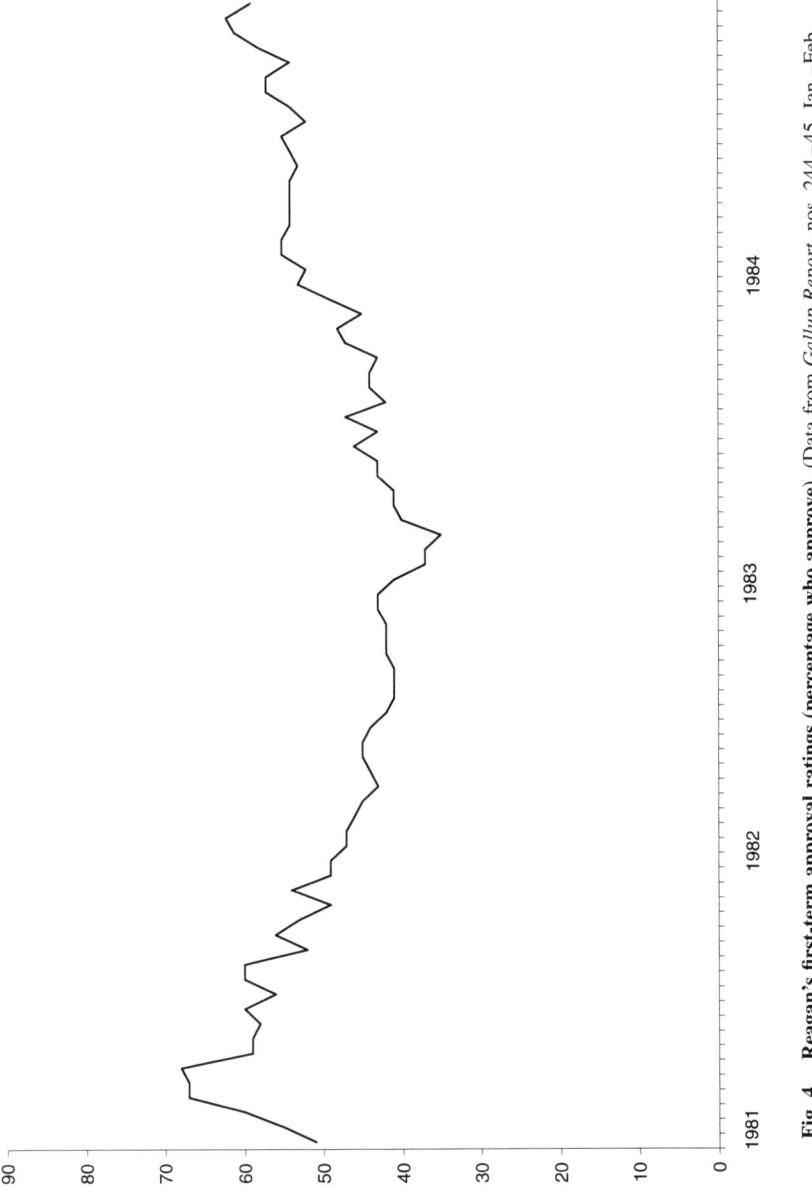

Fig. 4. Reagan's first-term approval ratings (percentage who approve). (Data from *Gallup Report*, nos. 244–45, Jan.–Feb. 1986, 23.)

TABLE 10. Trial Heats of Possible 1984 Presidential Contests

A. Reagan against Glenn

Registered voters were asked: "Suppose the 1984 presidential election were being held TODAY. If President Reagan were the Republican candidate and John Glenn were the Democratic candidate, which would you like to see win?"

		Reagan (%)	Glenn (%)	Other (%)	Undecided (%)
1982	Dec.	39	54	2	5
1983	Feb.	40	45	3	12
	Apr.–May	37	54	1	8
	June	38	53	1	8
	July–Aug.	41	45	2	12
	Aug.	40	46	2	12
	Sept.	42	48	2	8
	Oct.	42	49	2	7

B. Reagan against Mondale

Registered voters were asked: "Suppose the 1984 presidential election were being held TODAY. If President Reagan were the Republican candidate and Walter Mondale were the Democratic candidate, which would you like to see win?"

		Reagan (%)	Mondale (%)	Other (%)	Undecided (%)
1981	Oct.	54	37	1	8
1982	Apr.	46	46	1	7
	June	43	49	1	7
	Oct.	47	44	3	6
	Dec.	40	52	2	6
1983	Feb.	41	47	3	9
	Apr.–May	43	49	2	6
	May	42	47	4	7
	June	41	50	3	6
	July–Aug.	44	42	4	10
	Aug.	44	43	4	10
	Sept.	47	44	2	7
	Oct.	44	50	2	4
	Nov.	47	48	1	4
	Dec.	51	44	1	4
1984	Jan.	48	47	1	4
	Jan.	53	43	1	3
	Feb.	52	42	1	5
	Mar.	50	45	1	4
	Mar.	52	44	1	3

continued

TABLE 10.—Continued

	Reagan (%)	Mondale (%)	Other (%)	Undecided (%)
Apr.	54	41	1	4
Apr.	52	44	1	2
May	50	46	—	4
May	53	42	1	4
June	53	44	—	3

Source: For Glenn, *Gallup Report,* no. 218, November 1983, 28; for Mondale, *Gallup Report,* no. 226, July 1984, 15, and no. 230, November 1984, 5. (In *Gallup Report* no. 230, "Other" and "Undecided" were combined under one heading.)

Prescriptions for dealing with such a threat, according to the president and his aides, were based on their analysis of the "lessons of history," particularly the lessons of the 1930s and the 1970s. In those decades, members of the administration contended, two historical laws became evident. The first, derived particularly from the 1930s, was that totalitarian states were inherently aggressive and would seek advantages when democracies were weakly committed

TABLE 11. Issues and the 1984 Election

		A. Most Important Issues Facing the Country Today			
		Foreign Policy and Defense (%)	Unemployment (%)	Budget Deficit (%)	Cost of Living[a] (%)
1981	Jan.	6	8	—	73
	May	10	15	—	59
	Oct.	11	19	—	52
1982	Apr.	11	28	—	49
	June	14	38	5	26
	Aug.	10	45	5	23
	Oct.	6	62	4	18
1983	Apr.	16	54	5	18
	July	17	48	5	14
	Oct.	23	41	4	12
	Nov.	37	32	5	11
1984	Feb.	28	28	12	16
	Aug.	22	23	16	18
1985	Jan.	27	20	16	12

continued

TABLE 11.—Continued

B. Public Approval of Reagan's Soviet and Disarmament Policies

Individuals were asked to respond to the following statement: "Tell me whether you approve or disapprove of the way President Reagan is handling . . . relations with the Soviet Union and nuclear disarmament negotiations with the USSR."

Soviet Policy		Disarmament Policy	
Poll Date	% Approving	Poll Date	% Approving
1983 Jan.	41	1983 Aug.	39
Apr.	37	Oct.	45
Aug.	41	Nov.[b]	47
Oct.	44	1984 Nov.–Dec.	47
Nov.[b]	46		
1984 Feb.	43		
May	46		
Nov.–Dec.	52		

C. The Nuclear Freeze

Public reactions to a question regarding how people felt about an "immediate, verifiable freeze on the testing and production of nuclear weapons":

	Favor (%)	Oppose (%)	No Opinion (%)
November 1982	71	20	9
March 1983	70	21	9
1984	78	18	4

Source: For part A, *Gallup Report,* no. 198, March 1982, 27, no. 226, July 1984, 17, and no. 243, December 1985, 12–13; for part B, *Gallup Report,* no. 210, March 1983, 27, no. 234, March 1985, 10, no. 264, September 1987, 19–20; for part C, George H. Gallup, *The Gallup Poll: Public Opinion 1982* (Wilmington, DE: Scholarly Resources, Inc., 1983), 280; George H. Gallup, *The Gallup Poll: Public Opinion 1983* (Wilmington, DE: Scholarly Resources, Inc., 1984), 72; George Gallup, Jr., *The Gallup Poll: Public Opinion 1984* (Wilmington, DE: Scholarly Resources, Inc., 1985), 245.

[a]From April 1982 through October 1983, Gallup included "inflation" under the category "cost of living." At all other times, the pollsters considered "taxes" and "cost of living" together.

[b]These polls were taken November 18–21, 1983, prior to the Soviet walkout in Geneva.

to bold action or lacked capability. Often, in keeping with this scenario, the Reagan administration associated the USSR with Nazi Germany and the United States with Great Britain, with Carter playing the role of Chamberlain and Reagan that of Churchill.[19]

The second lesson was that totalitarian states only understood and responded to military power. American willingness to bargain with the USSR and to make concessions only emboldened the Soviets to ask for more. The United States thus had to reverse the policies of the 1970s when it concluded two strategic arms control agreements and, according to Reagan and others, neglected the development of its own nuclear arsenal.[20]

During the 1980 presidential campaign, Ronald Reagan called for the United States to abandon détente, which he viewed as a modern-day form of appeasement. Instead, he advocated "peace through strength." In his inaugural address, the president described the two components necessary to make his strategy work: power and will. Reagan vowed,

> We will maintain sufficient strength to prevail if need be, knowing that if we do so we have the best chance of never having to use that strength. . . . [And] above all we must realize that no arsenal or no weapon in the arsenals of the world is so formidable as the will and moral courage of free men and women.[21]

According to the president, the United States could turn itself around by acting on its own. The country had the economic, scientific, and moral capacity to rebuild both its power and its will. Reagan soon took the steps necessary to realize his plans for fortifying American strength by modernizing all three legs of the strategic triad, deploying intermediate-range nuclear forces, and investing in conventional armaments.

While such a strategy was expensive, the president did not hesitate in asking for sufficient funds to cover his military programs. According to defense analyst and former Reagan administration Defense Department official Lawrence Korb,

> by the end of his first term in office, real defense spending had increased 53 percent, an average of over 12 percent a year, a higher rate than during the war in Vietnam. In fact, real defense spending in 1985 was 13 percent higher than peak spending in the Vietnam War (1968). It is no exaggeration to say that in the Reagan years the Defense Department enjoyed a wartime build-up without a war. Defense outlays rose to 27 percent of the federal budget and 6.3 percent of GNP, their highest shares since the war in Vietnam.[22]

In effect, then, Reagan's articulation of "peace through strength" specified that military might was the central component of American power. While Reagan was trying to reduce the size and reach of government in other issue areas, the expansion of defense spending was unprecedented and serves as key evidence of the importance that the president placed on destructive capability. In addition, the approach also demanded that the United States reassert its independence in the planning of its military arsenal, recognizing that it had multiple options besides arms control agreements for improving its security. Concession making and restraint in the 1970s had led to the undermining of both American capability and Soviet confidence in the certainty of an American response to aggression. Therefore, the United States had to act on its own, eschewing arms control and joint endeavors, until its power position and its credibility were sufficiently rebuilt.[23]

Given Reagan's positions on the nature of the adversary, the importance of military power, and the many alternatives to joint action at U.S. disposal, the administration preferred a strategy of predomination. Before the United States would consider making any compromise, the American position had to be revitalized. If the Soviets wanted to make concessions to the United States, that was fine. But the United States would not conclude any agreement that did not entail substantial gains in its military position relative to the USSR.

The president would follow the strategy of predomination throughout 1981 and 1982. Thereafter, the deterioration of his autonomy forced a shift in approach. Beginning in 1983, with concerns about the upcoming election and his waning popularity at the forefront, the president decided to bend to the wishes of others. Reagan then adopted a cooperative stance at the table, but the Soviets did not reciprocate his newfound interest in equal concession making.

Impasse on INF: The Clash of Bargaining Strategies

While the INF talks officially opened for the first time in November 1980, the defeat of the sitting president made the developments there irrelevant. Both sides knew that the U.S. executive lacked the autonomy and authority to follow through on such sensitive issues.[24]

In January 1981, the United States inaugurated a new president, and the Soviets, the U.S. public, and the West Europeans waited to see how Reagan would react to the commitments that the previous administration had undertaken on arms control and theater nuclear weapons. Early on, the new administration hinted that it would like to discard the dual-track decision. In his visit to the Nuclear Planning Group in April 1981, Defense Secretary Weinberger declared his commitment to modernization but expressed disdain for arms control. Such a position disturbed European leaders, who pressured Reagan to set a date for the resumption of negotiations. After several months, the U.S. president promised that talks would reconvene in mid-November or December 1981—in effect, a year after they had first begun. The administration also noted that the "first track," the deployments, would be ready in late 1983.

Prior to the beginning of the negotiations, Reagan made public the opening American proposal in a speech to the National Press Club on November 18. The president advocated that intermediate-range nuclear missiles be eliminated from the face of the earth. This proposal became known as the "zero"—or, more accurately, the "global zero"—option. Soviet General Secretary Brezhnev publicly rejected the offer a few days later while visiting West Germany. Thus, when the INF discussions began in Geneva on November 30, 1981, the world knew the opening U.S. position and the negative Soviet reaction. With an examination of previous Soviet bargaining behavior, the U.S. administration could have predicted this Soviet response.[25] The USSR typically preferred to proceed with arms control incrementally and confidentially. Previous American attempts to suggest major changes in the arsenals and public announcements of its positions prior to negotiating sessions—like Carter's Comprehensive Proposal in 1977—had also met with rebuffs.[26] The United States, however, did not care about the Soviet reaction or about reaching an agreement with which the USSR could be happy. The goal of the administration was to achieve the elimination of all the Soviet missiles or to go forward with all the scheduled American deployments. In a strictly predominating fashion, any accord would have to be the "U.S. way" or no way at all.

At the first session, U.S. INF negotiator Paul Nitze tried to explain the logic of the American position to his negotiating partners, but the Soviets responded with a zero option of their own. They, too, were in no mood to take into account their opponent's concerns. At the outset of the talks, the USSR proposed that both sides maintain a moratorium on deployments throughout the negotiations and that the two sides eliminate, in stages, all intermediate- and shorter-range missiles from their European arsenals. Such a stance was clearly suited to the Soviet position, since the USSR was not planning to deploy any more weapons at this point, and the United States had only shorter-range systems. Moreover, the USSR also vowed that it would not sanction American INF deployments in Europe. Should the United States begin installing missiles, the Soviets promised to leave Geneva and to take countermeasures to restore what they considered to be the European balance.

While the United States held its position, the USSR opened the second round with a new proposal. Soviet negotiator Yuli Kvitsinsky suggested that the parties agree to a ceiling of 300 intermediate-range nuclear launchers in Europe for East and West. Including British and French INF in their count of the Western allotment, the Soviets argued that the United States would be required to *reduce* its aircraft in Europe to 49. In that way, American holdings combined with those of the French and British would total 300. Since none of the other Warsaw Pact states had INF launchers, the Soviets would be entitled to the whole 300. This offer was submitted as a draft treaty in May. Again, such a formula was designed to enhance the Soviet position at the expense of the American one. The United States had always maintained that British and French systems were not on the table, that aircraft should not be considered equivalent to missiles, and that the United States had to deploy its missiles in order to correct the theater *imbalance* that the SS-20 deployments had exacerbated. The Soviets, on the contrary, were insisting that to equalize the arsenals, the United States should not add any systems, but would need to subtract some instead.

During the late spring and early summer of 1982, the prospects for a negotiated resolution of the INF talks seemed highly unlikely. In July, however, Nitze decided on his own that he would like to investigate the extent of Soviet interest in bargaining. In what has become known as the "Walk in the Woods," Nitze invited Kvitsinsky to an afternoon outing at which the two men arrived at a possible settlement. The plan that resulted required compromises from the Americans and the Soviets. Both sides would be allowed the same number of missile launchers (a total of 75), but the United States would not deploy the Pershing II—a single-warhead ballistic missile that was fast (could reach Soviet territory in less than 10 minutes), highly accurate, and equipped with the new Maneuverable Re-entry Vehicle (MARV) technology. As compensation for holding only the nonballistic and slow-flying Tomahawk GLCMs, the United States would be permitted to keep more warheads than the Soviets. Seventy-five Tomahawks, at four warheads per missile, translated to a total of 300 American nuclear charges in Europe. The Soviets would have fewer warheads, 225 total, because each of their SS-20s carried three MIRVs. In addition, the Soviets would be required to limit Asian INF to 90 SS-20s, and both sides would be restricted to 150 aircraft in the European theater.[27]

This formula contained elements attractive to each side and corresponded with long sought-after principles. The Soviets would prevent the deployment of the Pershing II, which they considered a dangerous, first-strike weapon, and the United States would receive confirmation of its right not only to deploy missiles in Europe but to match exactly the number of Soviet launchers. Moreover, the Americans would earn the recognition that the United States was entitled to compensation in the form of extra warheads because the SS-20 was a ballistic missile that could deliver its charges far more quickly than could the GLCMs. In addition, bombers would be treated as a separate category of weapons, as the

United States had insisted. Finally, the U.S. position that British and French forces were nonnegotiable would be upheld.

Unfortunately for arms control advocates in 1982, Washington and Moscow did not perceive the benefits of the compromise reached in the grove in Geneva. Returning home, both negotiators found unreceptive audiences and were told to stop improvising and follow the positions formulated in the capitals. The reactions to the Walk-in-the-Woods plan very clearly demonstrated that the two leaderships were not interested in compromise. Although the American and Soviet negotiators found a solution that would address the stated concerns of both parties and achieve an equitable settlement that would strengthen stability, neither of the leaderships were interested in the deal. Instead, both sought relative gains for themselves, and thus this outline for an accord was discarded.[28]

Without the ability to search for compromise, the negotiators were stymied. Talks reopened in the fall, but there was no progress. After Brezhnev's death in November 1982, the Soviets more forcefully tried to woo Western European public opinion to prevent the deployments. The strategy was to court Europeans whose legislatures had to vote on accepting the missiles on their territory. If the Soviets could convince ordinary people that American INF were unnecessary or dangerous and that their installation would heighten the risk of a nuclear attack, then the hope was that these voters would pressure their representatives to reject these systems. In so doing, the Soviets would achieve their goal of preventing American deployments without having to make any concessions at the bargaining table. Such an approach was clever and still consistent with a strategy of predomination.

Thus, at the end of 1982 and into 1983, the Soviets tried to make their offers appear reasonable to West European publics while also threatening that if these proposals were not accepted, the danger of war would increase. In the first such effort, General Secretary Andropov proposed that the Soviets remove 81 intermediate-range missiles from Europe in order to reduce their arsenal to the size of the combined British and French missile forces—162. While the NATO publics and governments reacted favorably, the United States spurned Andropov's offer.

By early 1983, some in the Reagan administration were becoming concerned about American public reaction to the Soviet strategy. In January, Reagan's job approval rating was at the lowest of his term, and the American people strongly supported the freeze campaign.[29] The charge that the Reagan administration was bent on deployments while avoiding the second, arms control, track was becoming credible to increasingly larger portions of the population. To offset such a perception, the president approved the presentation of an "interim" proposal. While underscoring that the elimination of intermediate-range missiles from the European theater was the goal, Nitze revealed that the United States would now accept a treaty that allowed both sides to have an equivalent number of warheads in Europe and permitted the United States to deploy both cruise and ballistic missiles. Four days later, Soviet Foreign Minister Gromyko categorically rejected the American plan. Reportedly, the USSR recognized that domestic politics motivated this offer. Not exactly fans of Reagan, the Soviets preferred not to help him achieve his domestic political goals by accepting this formula.[30]

Talks were stalled when Andropov again sought to increase the pressure. In late August, the party leader reiterated his earlier proposal about reducing Soviet missile holdings to 162 in Europe and added the promise to liquidate and not redeploy the dismantled ones in Asia. Again, the United States rejected this formula.

With the West German vote on the deployment of the American Pershing IIs and GLCMs fast approaching, the Soviets repeated their pledge to leave the negotiations if the missiles were installed. In late October, Andropov offered another solution: the Soviets would reduce their INF arsenal to equal the number of British and French warheads, not launchers. While the West Europeans had single-warhead missiles, the Soviet SS-20s each carried three MIRVs. So the early Soviet calls to reduce to equal numbers of launchers allowed the USSR to retain an advantage in the number of nuclear charges. Still, the Americans insisted that this was insufficient; the United States had the right to deploy in Europe and needed to base its missiles there to correct the balance.

With that last interaction, the fate of the negotiations and the deployments was now in the hands of the West German Bundestag: would the legislators accept the American missiles? When the vote certified the installations, Soviet negotiator Kvitsinsky announced that the talks would not be continued.

Thus, in November 1983, the superpower arms control negotiations came to a deadlock that was rather predictable, based on the strategies the two sides were playing. At the opening of the talks two years before, each side was seeking to predominate, hoping for an agreement that would benefit itself more than its opponent. If no such formula could be found, each side was content to forgo an agreement and take whatever measures were necessary on its own to enhance its security. That the two sides were uninterested in achieving a mutually acceptable solution is starkly evident from their common rejection of the Walk-in-the-Woods formula. About six months after refusing to compromise, the U.S. president came under domestic pressure and then adjusted the American approach to one of cooperation. The Soviets, however, were still looking for a clear victory at the talks. Their commitment to predomination and the U.S. attempts to find some equitable bargain were necessarily unresolvable. Thus, the talks ended without the two sides reaching an agreement.

Talking Past Each Other, 1981–83

In the early 1980s, the superpower relationship was fraught with tension and danger. The popular press and media were filled with accounts of the threat of nuclear war, its horrific short-term impact as well as its ecology-altering, long-term consequences. In response, citizens in Western Europe and the United States joined peace movements in unprecedented numbers. Many other, less activist individuals were greatly concerned about the possibility of nuclear war and held their breath as the superpowers traded recriminations and threats.[31]

Despite all this concern, both superpowers showed minimal interest in negotiating a settlement on a rather minor element of their arsenals, intermediate-range nuclear forces.[32] While some may contend that this indifference was the result of the selections or elections of "conservatives" to lead the countries, the analysis of the first set of INF talks shows that that view is incomplete. In the Soviet case, there was significant continuity in the substance of arms control throughout this period, although a change in the style once Andropov took over in November 1982 was discernible. Moreover, there was general unity within the Soviet leadership on how to deal with the Americans on INF; Soviet officials preferred not to make any concessions and wait to see whether the United States would be able to install the weapons as planned.

In the United States, a shift in the country's Soviet policy began earlier under Carter in the aftermath of the Soviet invasion of Afghanistan. That change is probably most starkly demonstrated by the promulgation of Presidential Directive 59 (PD-59), which moved the United States toward a war-fighting stance.[33] In addition, the story of the Reagan administration's experience is not so much one of bureaucratic bargaining among conservative and liberal forces (although some infighting certainly occurred).[34] Rather, members of the administration were committed to a particular stance toward the USSR, "peace through strength," based on their assessment of the enemy, the importance of military power, and the alternatives to arms control that the United States possessed. Moreover, variation in administration policy did not result from the victory of a particular executive-branch group. Instead, concerns about the president's weakness drove a change in strategy, as the Reagan administration altered its course from one of predomination to one of cooperation on INF in early 1983. Interestingly, the administration was not so inclined on the more important—from the perspective of overall military power—Strategic Arms Reduction Talks (START), demonstrating that its interest in cooperation was purely for political purposes. Thus, Reagan advanced the Interim Proposal to try to allay fears of his bellicosity and strengthen his chances for reelection.

For much of the time, then, both the USSR and the United States were seeking to predominate at the table. This strategy was not so much a function of the constellation of competing domestic political groups as it was the result of infirmity at the pinnacle of Soviet power and the particular approach to arms control that Reagan brought to the table. From the time of the resumption of the talks until early 1983, the two countries were talking past each other. Each side sought gains from its opponent without taking into account the other's legitimate security concerns. The fate of the Walk-in-the-Woods formula and the lack of any evidence that a significant bureaucratic battle ensued on behalf of this proposal are excellent evidence of both sides' disinterest in any kind of agreement that would require real compromise.

In early 1983, with worries about its domestic political future at the forefront, the American administration backed off from its previous call for elimination of all these weapons and came up with a proposal that would have allowed both countries to keep some of their holdings or planned deployments. Still, the impasse could not be broken because the Soviets remained committed to predomination. Soviet stubbornness perhaps relieved the Americans, since they had adopted this position only under domestic political pressure.

Thus, in the early 1980s, the time was wrong for arms control. In the USSR, there was no leader with the power to be able to convince the others in the system of the benefits of compromise (or with the perception that concession making was warranted). In the United States, the executive was initially intent upon *not* making concessions and later became interested in compromising only if the Soviets would undertake similarly onerous measures. Thus, the two states were at an impasse, and the conclusion of the INF treaty would have to wait.

CHAPTER 5

Concluding the Intermediate-range Nuclear Forces Treaty: Gorbachev and New Thinking Break the Deadlock

In December 1987, just four years after the breakdown of one set of negotiations and the severe deterioration of the superpower relationship, the leaders of the Soviet Union and the United States signed the Intermediate-range Nuclear Forces (INF) Treaty at a summit meeting in Washington. Interestingly, the formula to which the superpowers agreed was very similar to the Reagan administration's opening position almost six years earlier. At that time, the United States had proposed the global elimination of all such Soviet and American forces, but the Soviet leadership had angrily rejected the offer. In 1987, however, the USSR dropped its objections to Reagan's "zero option" and even suggested that the superpowers eliminate all their shorter-range nuclear missiles, too. The INF Treaty codified this global, double-zero formula.

What happened in those six years to allow the superpowers to agree to a plan that was even more dramatic than the opening American position? One well-accepted answer to this question follows from a realist-type analysis. Adherents of that approach argue that by the mid-1980s, the United States had improved its power position by building up its strategic and theater nuclear forces and threatening to develop a space-based defense system. In reestablishing its power, the United States forced the Soviets to bargain, since the USSR recognized that its position was slipping and would continue to fall if the United States were to move forward with all its plans. The military balance, then, explains state behavior, and the INF Treaty is a classic case of a declining power (the USSR) trying to forestall the further deterioration of its position by agreeing to a formula that the superior power (the United States) presented.[1]

This account is problematic for several reasons. First, that the strategic balance shifted in favor of the United States during the 1980s is actually debatable

TABLE 12. The Superpower Strategic Balance, 1972–87

Year	U.S.		USSR		U.S.–USSR Ratio	
	L	W	L	W	L	W
1972	2167	7601	2207	2573	.9819	2.9541
1973	2133	8885	2339	2711	.9119	3.2774
1974	2106	9324	2423	2795	.8692	3.3360
1975	2106	9828	2515	3217	.8374	3.0550
1976	2092	10436	2545	3477	.8220	3.0014
1977	2092	10580	2562	4242	.8220	2.4941
1978	2086	10832	2557	5516	.8158	1.9637
1979	2086	10800	2548	6571	.8187	1.6436
1980	2022	10608	2545	7480	.7945	1.4182
1981	1966	10688	2593	8296	.7582	1.2883
1982	1921	10515	2545	8904	.7548	1.1809
1983	1905	10802	2543	9300	.7491	1.1615
1984	1943	11500	2540	9626	.7650	1.1947
1985	1965	11974	2538	10012	.7742	1.1960
1986	1957	12386	2506	10108	.7809	1.2254
1987	2001	13002	2535	10442	.7893	1.2452

Source: SIPRI Yearbook 1990: *World Armaments and Disarmament* (New York: Oxford University Press, 1990), 23. Launchers include ICBMs, long-range bombers, and submarines.

Note: L = Launchers, W = Warheads

(table 12). Using warheads as the criterion, the U.S. and Soviet arsenals were never more equal than in 1983, when the two sides were unable to find a compromise and the Soviets walked out of Geneva. Moreover, the statistics do not support a further claim of the realists that the Soviets decided to return to the bargaining table in 1984–85 because the United States had restored parity and was threatening superiority.

Second, even after the United States began its deployments, the shift in the theater balance was not so great as to warrant such dramatic changes in bargaining positions.[2] Third, that future deployments of a multibillion-dollar defensive system forced Soviet acquiescence also seems unlikely. While the Soviets were concerned about strategic defense, they also knew that they could institute cheap methods to match any American space defense program and that such a system would take decades to implement. Whether the United States could maintain the commitment to such a project—billions of dollars over many years—was also questionable.[3]

Probably the most important weakness of this account is that it fails to recognize that the choices that the USSR made regarding INF were very much a function of domestic political developments and the executive's *perceptions* of international-level factors. The leadership model, unlike the realist approach, identifies Gorbachev as a central character in this tale, one who does not simply manipulate factions but seeks to promote a political agenda, respond to international constraints and opportunities, and maintain and protect his own personal political position. Reagan also played an important role. He put his own mark on American security policy, and his approach followed not from some objective evaluation of the military balance, but from his personal assessments of the character of the adversary, the importance of might, and the capacity of the United States to undertake whatever actions were necessary to promote its security. But even Reagan, who was known for ideological clarity, was not immune to domestic political concerns. When his domestic position was threatened, the American president decided to bend to the preferences of others on arms control. Thus, the nature of the superpower interaction during the INF negotiations and the conclusion of the treaty were dependent upon both executive autonomy and bargaining strategy.

Getting Back to the Table, January 1984–January 1985

The second half of 1983 was an extremely tense period in American–Soviet relations, marked by the USSR's shooting down of a civilian airliner, the U.S. invasion of Grenada, increasingly hostile rhetoric coming out of the Soviet Union, and the Soviet walkout of the INF negotiations. Fears about nuclear war seemed prevalent, with the superpower relationship plummeting to one of its lowest points in 20 years. But soon after reaching the nadir, the United States and the USSR began to work their way back from this low point, with the United States taking the lead in the reconciliation.[4]

The INF talks fell apart a little less than a year before the 1984 American presidential election. As we saw in chapter 4, with concerns about autonomy at the forefront, in 1983 the president and his advisers felt that he had one important vulnerability—his foreign policy, particularly his approach to arms control. People feared that the president was too bellicose and could lead the United States into a nuclear war. To soften the candidate's image and to allay public fear, the administration began almost immediately in 1984 to look for ways to reopen negotiations, since the American electorate was uncomfortable with the heightened superpower tensions.[5] Starting with a January 16, 1984, address to the nation on the American–Soviet relationship, the president purposefully moderated his rhetoric and tried to sound more optimistic about world politics in general and relations with the USSR in particular. In that speech, Reagan even said that the United States "can now offer something in return" for Soviet compromises at the bargaining table.[6]

Democrats sensed Reagan's concern and attempted to weaken the president further by making arms control an issue in their favor in 1984. Republicans tried to distance themselves from the president's hard-line policy and to convince Reagan to be more considerate.[7] In June, the House authorized most of Reagan's requests on defense for fiscal 1985, but with conditions. It released the funds for only 15 MX missiles, not the 40 that the president desired, and attached stipulations to the authorization bill intended to compel the administration to restart negotiations. The Senate also took action to reduce the number of MX missiles procured, to prevent the deployment of antisatellite weapons, and to constrain the development of Reagan's Strategic Defense Initiative (SDI) program. Even congressional members of the president's own party challenged Reagan's stand on defense and arms control. To improve their appeal to voters back home, some GOP members of Congress established the Republican Mainstream Committee, which favored negotiations with the Soviets. As one staffer explained, "most congressmen don't want to be portrayed as anti–arms control and therefore anti-peace."[8] Even Senate Republican Leader Howard Baker revealed impatience with the president's policy toward the USSR. In a commencement speech at Dartmouth College, Baker prodded Reagan to meet with his Soviet counterpart, suggesting that "direct, regular, genuine, face-to-face, give-and-take communications between the two most powerful people on earth is an imperative of our perilous time."[9]

The president was not oblivious to the pressure, and he responded. In July 1984, he sanctioned meetings between American and Soviet officials aimed at resuming the Geneva talks.[10] After a summer vacation, the administration announced that it would like to discuss a test ban agreement with the USSR, and the president decided not to publicize alleged Soviet violations of past arms control agreements. In a speech at the opening of the UN General Assembly, Reagan tried to bridge the gap with the USSR on restarting negotiations by suggesting "umbrella" talks, in which all kinds of weaponry—intermediate-range, strategic, and defensive—would be the subjects of discussion. Such an arrangement would allow the Soviets to argue that they were not simply returning to the INF negotiations without the Americans making any substantive changes and would provide the USSR with a forum in which to complain about American plans for a space-based defense system. Perhaps the most obvious play to voters' concerns about the administration's disarmament policy was the White House's promise just days before the election that it would name an arms control "czar" to promote the conclusion of agreements.[11]

While the Reagan administration, under domestic pressure, appeared to be enthusiastic about resuming negotiations, the USSR, predictably, was not. Soviet politics was under the pall of having its third dying general secretary in office in three years. There was little apparent interest in resuming INF talks or proceeding effectively with the START discussions. Some commentators speculated that Soviet leaders were reluctant to help Reagan change his image from cold warrior to peace-loving statesman prior to the U.S. election. In September and October, Secretary Shultz and Foreign Minister Gromyko met a few times to discuss the resumption of disarmament talks but seemed to make little progress.[12]

After the American election, however, the foreign secretaries were able to resolve their differences. Gromyko and Shultz thereafter achieved a breakthrough and signed an agreement in January 1985, consistent with Reagan's UN offer, that committed the superpowers to resume arms control discussions in March. This time intermediate-range, strategic, and space weapons would all be on the table.[13]

While many people greeted the news of the return to the table with relief, others were not so sanguine about the possibility of agreement. The Soviets insisted that the negotiations in the three arenas were interconnected, meaning that there could be no treaty in one area without a resolution in all three. Moreover, the USSR had vowed that it would never sanction the abandonment of the ABM treaty and approve the development of the American plan for space-based defense, SDI, dubbed "Star Wars" in the U.S. media.[14] Reagan, on the other hand, promised that he would allow nothing to interfere with the progress of SDI and that the three sets of discussions were independent. With these substantial differences dividing the two sides, the prospects for the three-tier forum were very dreary.

Other factors also pointed to pessimism in January 1985. Reagan was returning with a mandate from the voters; his autonomy would allow him to pursue his favored strategy at the table. In 1985, that policy was one of predomination. As we will see in the following section, the president continued to believe that the USSR was the "evil empire," that military force was the most important component of power, and that the United States had many options besides arms control for improving its security situation.[15] Any agreement that the president would accept had to provide distinct advantages over the Soviets. In fact, U.S. positions reflected those goals, maintaining that SDI was completely off the table, ICBMs (the category of weapons that made up the bulk of Soviet strategic forces) should be drastically cut back, and INF should be eliminated globally. Each of these positions would favor the United States relative to the USSR.

In early 1985, the attitude toward arms control was not any more favorable

90   To Agree or Not to Agree

in the USSR, either. Leadership problems and internal decay still plagued the Soviets. The general secretary had been out of sight for several months, and this vacuum meant that arms control policy would follow the default preferences of the major institutional power bases in the USSR.[16] Therefore, the Soviet approach would continue to be one of predomination. Again, the sides were playing contradictory strategies, and the potential for agreement seemed null indeed.

These predictions turned out to be wrong. Over the course of the next few years, a new general secretary embarked on an effort to transform Soviet domestic and foreign policy. As he shored up support at home and began to try to solve his country's problems, the new Soviet leader became an advocate of a policy of, at first, cooperation and then accommodation. Once he had the domestic political strength, Gorbachev authorized the necessary concessions to make an INF treaty a reality. President Reagan accepted these concessions and moved forward with the general secretary to eliminate not only intermediate-range nuclear forces globally, but shorter-range ones, too.

Determinants of Soviet Bargaining Strategy, 1985–87

Autonomy in Soviet Politics

Mikhail Sergeevich Gorbachev became the last general secretary of the Central Committee of the CPSU in March 1985. Over the course of the next two years, he amassed moderate autonomy, which allowed him to pursue with care his preferred approach to the INF talks.

The conditions surrounding Gorbachev's selection have long been the subject of controversy. It was unique in both the speed in which the decision was made, the informality of the proceedings at the Central Committee plenum, and the nature of the media coverage of that event. Because of the rapidity—less than 24 hours passed between Chernenko's death and Gorbachev's selection—some Politburo members were excluded from the selection, and the full Central Committee was also not present.[17] Moreover, unlike most nominating speeches, Gromyko's seemed spontaneous, and the foreign minister actually attempted to convince the voters—the plenum attendees—that Gorbachev was the best man for the job. Gromyko avoided the typical formula that Gorbachev was the unanimous choice of the Politburo and instead personally endorsed the candidate. Finally, the speech was not published in *Pravda* as usual but only appeared in the Party journal *Kommunist* at the end of the month.[18]

Since then, Soviet watchers have learned from Yegor Ligachev, at the 19th

Party Congress, that the period after Chernenko's death was one of "anxious days." Ligachev remarked that "totally different decisions could have been made [at the plenum]. There was a real danger of that."[19] In his memoirs, he also maintained that Moscow city Party leader Grishin was trying to become general secretary; however, provincial Party first secretaries and members of the old guard on the Politburo "sided with the future."[20] Georgi Arbatov, American expert and a member of the Central Committee at that time, also told interviewers that there was a choice for general secretary. Moreover, Arbatov suggested that the delegates selected Gorbachev because they preferred his program of reform to the policy of continuation that his opponent espoused.[21] While Gorbachev himself asserted that he received unanimous support from the Politburo, his version does not necessarily negate those of the others.[22] In fact, Grishin and his supporters could easily have understood that they did not have the ability to prevent Gorbachev's selection. They would then be better off getting on the Gorbachev bandwagon than taking the fight to the Central Committee, where his support was strong.[23]

The importance of these details is in stressing that Gorbachev took over an organization that was divided between those who supported and those who opposed the continuation of the Brezhnevite approach. Obviously, the opponents of the old way were more influential and numerous because they succeeded in securing the position for their candidate, but the "change coalition" was a varied group of people, including, for example Ligachev, Andrei Gromyko, and future Politburo member Aleksandr Yakovlev.[24] In effect, then, once the general secretary became specific about his approach to reform, he was in danger of alienating some of his backers. Gorbachev thus had the daunting task of consolidating his position within the Party while maintaining the coherence of his disparate crew of supporters. Moreover, a Party Congress was on the horizon; the general secretary had to be circumspect because he was at a particularly vulnerable stage in the selection cycle. He was a new Party leader, and substantial mistakes could cost him his position. Thus, his support level (mixed) and timing (unfavorable) meant that Gorbachev had low autonomy in 1985.

Because of these constraints on his domestic authority, Gorbachev had to consider the realities of power as well as policy. According to Eduard Shevardnadze, Gorbachev's ally in this endeavor, "you cannot proceed rapidly and confidently toward a goal [in Soviet politics] without glancing over your shoulder at the people who are trying to thwart you. If you don't factor that in, you can lose everything."[25] Thus, in that first year, Gorbachev called for change, although he was generally short on specifics. He announced his support for perestroika, glasnost, democratization, and new thinking, but in talk-

TABLE 13. Number of Soviet Officials Replaced, 1982–87[a]

Type of Official	11/82–3/85	3/85–3/86	3/86–8/87
Deputy chairmen, USSR Council of Ministers	3 of 13	8 of 14	2 of 12
Other members, USSR Council of Ministers	25 of 82	30 of 82	23 of 81
First secretaries, republic Party CCs	4 of 14	4 of 14	2 of 14
First secretaries, party oblast committees, autonomous republics, and territories	48 of 150	46 of 150	38 of 150
Commanders of military districts and groups	12 of 20	6 of 20	14 of 20
Voting members, republic Party bureaus (removed)	37 of 164	47 of 163	41 of 163
Voting members, republic Party bureaus (changed job)	15 of 164	15 of 163	10 of 163

Source: Jerry Hough, "Gorbachev Consolidating Power," *Problems of Communism* 36, no. 4 (1987): 31, 34.

[a]Officials who died in their posts are included in the counts. If the occupant of a post changed twice or more, only one change was recorded.

ing about these policies, there was something in each of them that all members of his change coalition could support.[26]

Throughout that time, with the help of Yegor Ligachev, the official in charge of cadres policy, Gorbachev attempted to remake the Party and put together a team, by unseating those who were corrupt or could not learn to work in a new way and replacing them with those more suited—in both work style and attitude—to reform. The upheaval among the Soviet elite was dramatic (table 13). There were new additions to the Politburo, as well as important deletions.[27] The changes were not, however, simply confined to the summit of Soviet politics. Continuing with the transformation of the cadres that had begun in the Andropov years, individuals who had been involved in corruption were removed throughout the Party and government structures.[28]

The Party Congress of late February and March 1986 helped solidify Gorbachev's autonomy (table 14). At the 27th Party Congress, all those individuals who had lost their positions since the last one participated as "dead souls."[29] Thereafter, however, they were not part of these Party gatherings, and therefore Gorbachev's position was strengthened. After March 1986, Gorbachev's timing was favorable—he would not face another Congress for several years. Given the mixed level of support for the general secretary—the Party was still divided between "friends and foes of change," and even those reformers were split about exactly what he should do—Gorbachev had moderate autonomy, which he would maintain throughout the negotiations for INF. Although he continued to put pressure on the Party and remove those who refused

TABLE 14. Turnover at Party Congresses

Congress (and year)	Population of Interest within the Central Committee	Percentage Expelled
Khrushchev:		
20th (1956)	all members	38
22nd (1961)	all members	50
Brezhnev:		
23rd (1966)	all members	21
24th (1971)	all members	23
25th (1976)	all full members	11
26th (1981)	all full members	13
Gorbachev:		
27th (1986)	living, full members	40
	all full members	45
	candidate members	60

Source: Seweryn Bialer, *Stalin's Successors: Leadership, Stability, and Change in the Soviet Union* (New York: Cambridge University Press, 1980), 92; Thane Gustafson and Dawn Mann, "Gorbachev's First Year: Building Power and Authority," *Problems of Communism* 35, no. 3 (1986): 3; Jerry Hough, "Gorbachev Consolidating Power," *Problems of Communism* 36, no. 4 (1987): 28, 33.

to change, Gorbachev never achieved high levels of support. As he became more specific about the type of reform he envisioned, the general secretary had a more difficult time finding those within the Party who could support his plans. As a result, in 1987, the Soviet leader began to implement a program for including the population more directly into the political process, as a way of putting pressure on recalcitrant Party officials—even ones who were ostensibly part of the "change coalition."[30] While these actions would later make him less popular with segments of the Party elite, throughout 1987 his support was still relatively good (mixed), as was the timing. Thus, during the last two years of negotiations on INF, Gorbachev's autonomy remained fairly constant, at the moderate level.

A Different Approach to Bargaining: The Impact of New Thinking and Reykjavik

When Gorbachev and others first began mentioning "new political thinking," a slogan in foreign affairs to match the three domestic policy watchwords of perestroika, glasnost, and democratization, Western skeptics were quite doubtful that Gorbachev was calling for any kind of truly "new" or positive change in

Soviet external behavior. At the 27th Party Congress and after, however, the elements of new thinking were more clearly spelled out, and while critics could still doubt the sincerity of the Soviet leadership, they could not question the novelty of the approach for the USSR.[31]

New thinking asserted the interconnectedness of nations and individuals and raised questions about traditional approaches to security. New thinkers pointed, in particular, to the danger that nuclear weapons posed to people throughout the world. The superpower arms race not only increased the probability that any war would lead to the annihilation of humanity because of the destructive capability both countries possessed, but that the competition also contributed to the tensions between the states, thereby augmenting the likelihood of war. Accepting the findings of scientists who claimed that a superpower nuclear exchange would cause the destruction of the ecosystem, these analysts maintained that a Soviet-American conflict was intolerable because it would not only decimate the current population but also threaten the existence of future generations. In addition, the new thinkers noted that a "security dilemma" existed and that to pursue security effectively in contemporary conditions, states had to recognize that their policies had to be constructed to enhance universal, not national, security. The massive size of the American and Soviet arsenals, their complicated technologies, and the speed with which total annihilation could occur closely linked the fate of all the world's peoples. Therefore, decision makers needed new approaches to security that provided them with far greater flexibility and included a willingness to compromise.[32]

In effect, then, new thinking called for the transformation of the key variables that affected Soviet bargaining strategy. While suspicions of the Reagan administration remained strong—both Gorbachev's memoirs and contemporaneous statements suggest that he believed that the American president was extremely hostile and trying to take advantage of the USSR throughout 1985 and 1986—the Soviet leadership reconsidered its assessment of the importance of military power and the alternatives to arms reduction.[33] In fact, the new thinkers identified the traditional, single-minded pursuit of military might and nuclear weapons as a reason for Soviet security problems. Previous Soviet leaders had not understood the mutuality of security and how the buildup of weapons had frightened others (West Europeans, especially), thereby complicating their task. Instead, the new thinkers stressed that security had multiple components and the military element should not be privileged above others.[34]

The potential for total annihilation in nuclear war meant that the superpowers' fates were intertwined. Unitary action could not help to reduce the risk from accidental war. The superpowers had to work together to address that danger and the threat of ecological annihilation that would result from any nuclear conflict. Arms control and confidence building measures were, therefore, important steps that the two sides could take to help prevent disasters from occurring.[35]

Thus, after March 1986, when Gorbachev's domestic position was sufficiently secure, the general secretary began advancing a new approach to bargaining. The value of arms control was still low because, despite the importance he placed on political over military approaches to security, the new thinkers continued to perceive the unabated hostility of Reagan's United States. The key source of change in their approach resulted from the new thinkers' assertion that the superpowers were highly interdependent. For the first time in the 1980s, then, the Soviets were willing to cooperate at the bargaining table.

The culmination of this cooperative strategy was at the Reykjavik meeting in October 1986. There, the Soviets came prepared to bargain seriously on arms control, looking for mutual compromises that the two sides could accept. While there was ultimately no agreement reached at these talks, the discussions were important for their impact on the Soviet assessment of the United States. Gorbachev called Reykjavik a "breakthrough" in arms control and Soviet–American relations. For the first time, the general secretary could see the Americans—particularly Reagan and Shultz—engaged in a give-and-take. As a result of this meeting, the Soviet leader reevaluated his view of the United States and agreed that it was a businesslike opponent.[36] In addition, the changes in American politics at the end of 1986 and into 1987—the strengthening of pro–arms control forces in the Congress and within the administration—helped reinforce this view, particularly as the United States began to bargain effectively and sensitively. Thus, with this redefinition of the nature of the bargaining partner, Gorbachev sought to implement a strategy of accommodation at the table.

If Gorbachev were worried about whether he would be able to follow through with that approach given his moderate level of autonomy, developments in the USSR in 1987 helped encourage his decision to lead. At a Party plenum in January, the general secretary moved forward with plans for increased openness in society and more popular participation. Thereafter, glasnost, the policy of societal openness, moved into a new phase. Increasingly, the state and citizens were dealing honestly with their past and were able to discuss the present. In addition, the meeting specified a project of further democratization. The Party authorized the calling of a Conference to consider the creation of a new legislature that would consist of some freely elected members.[37] Gorbachev authorized this step to provide himself with more room for maneuver in Soviet politics. Despite the continued turnover within the apparatus (table

13), the Party was blocking Gorbachev's reform efforts, and he hoped to create a new power base (and empower new social groups as constituents) in order to proceed with change.[38]

Another, unlikely event gave him the opportunity to reinforce his position further. When West German teenager Matthias Rust successfully landed his small plane in Red Square—on Border Guard Day, no less—Gorbachev had the chance to shake up the military leadership.[39] The replacement of many officials who had opposed policy innovation provided Gorbachev with greater certainty that he could sustain accommodation with moderate autonomy.

Determinants of American Bargaining Strategy, 1985–87

Ronald Reagan was reelected in a landslide in 1984 and began his second term in an enviable domestic position. With his renewed political strength, the president reverted to a hostile approach toward the Soviets and moved away from compromise on arms control. But in late 1986, the president's autonomy began to decline seriously. The Republicans lost control of the Senate, and the public learned of the Iran-Contra affair. Suddenly, the president's approval ratings fell, he faced two unfriendly houses of Congress, and the end of his term seemed very close. The deterioration in Reagan's autonomy forced him to bring the administration's arms control policy in line with the preferences of the other power centers. Thus, the president and his advisers began to look for ways to cooperate with the Soviets.

Reagan's Autonomy: After 1986, the Teflon Wears Thin

Although Reagan was in a strong position during most of the first two years of his second term, November 1986 marked a turning point. Just two years before, Reagan had defeated Walter Mondale convincingly and returned to the White House in January 1985 as a highly popular president. But with the revelation that the president was involved in a secret plan to sell weapons to Iran (against official U.S. policy) in order to obtain the release of American hostages in the Middle East and that some of the profits from these sales were diverted to the Nicaraguan Contras (to whom military aid had been banned by Congress), Reagan's approval ratings dipped sharply. In about a 45-day period, the president's popularity fell by 16 percentage points, and he recovered from that slip only as he was leaving office, two years later (fig. 5).

Immediately following the disclosure of the scandal, commentators, policymakers, and Reagan loyalists began to raise concerns about the presi-

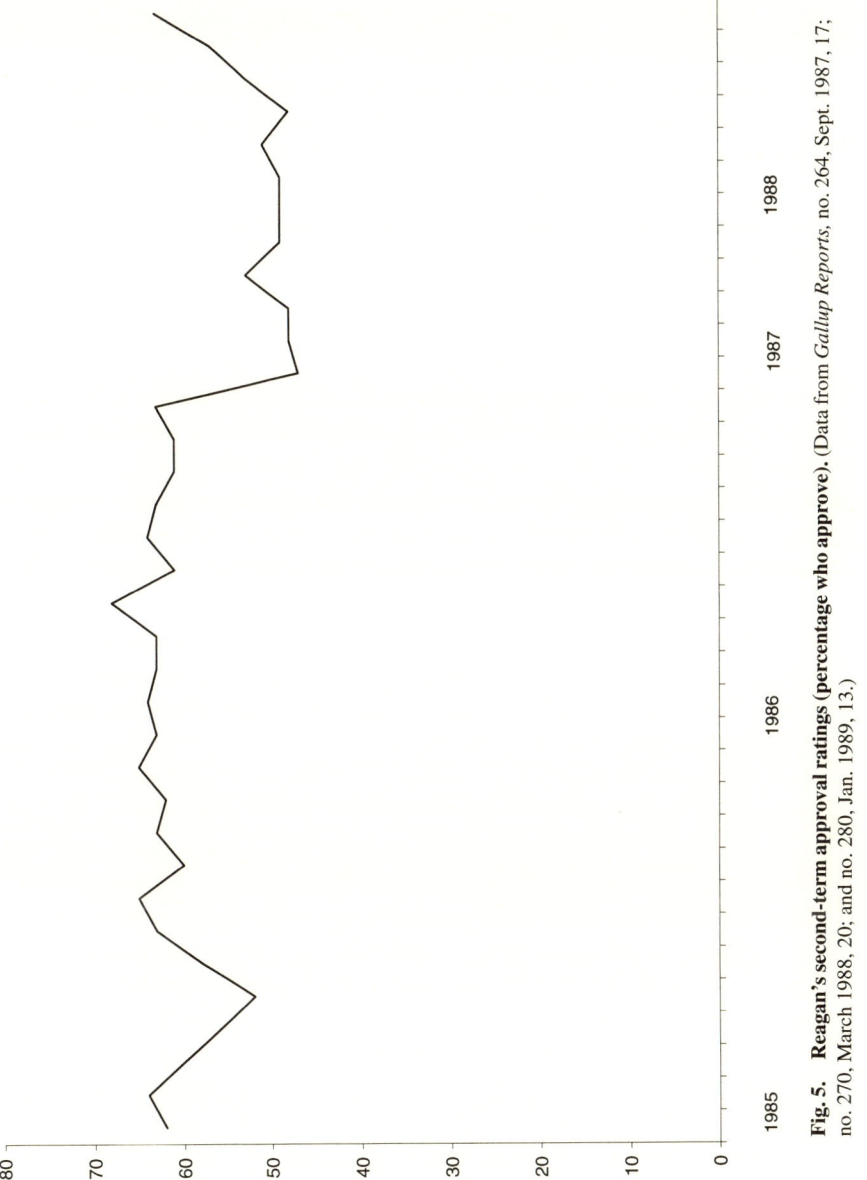

Fig. 5. Reagan's second-term approval ratings (percentage who approve). (Data from *Gallup Reports*, no. 264, Sept. 1987, 17; no. 270, March 1988, 20; and no. 280, Jan. 1989, 13.)

TABLE 15. Impact of Iran–Contra on Reagan's Presidency

Question: "Do you think the controversy over the Iran contra affair has made it very difficult for Ronald Reagan to be an effective president over the next two years?"

	Yes (%)	No (%)	No Opinion (%)
Dec. 1986	58	36	6
Jan. 1987	63	31	6
Apr. 1987	66	28	6

Source: Gallup Report, no. 260, May 1987, 14.

dent's effectiveness for the remainder of his term. The consensus was that Reagan's "Teflon coating" had finally begun to wear thin and that damage from this scandal was going to stick (table 15). The effects were particularly severe because Iran-Contra undermined confidence in the president's character, one of "the hallmarks of Mr. Reagan's personal popularity over the last six years."[40] The atmosphere in the White House was so gloomy in late 1986 that the administration reportedly welcomed any coverage, even bad press, as long as did not involve Iran-Contra.[41]

Complicating Reagan's task of regaining the initiative in the policy-making arena was the Republicans' loss of control of the Senate. Congressional Democrats communicated their intention of pressing for their own foreign policy priorities, particularly in promoting arms control and preventing SDI development and deployment. The new chair of the Senate Armed Services Committee, Sam Nunn, warned that failure to consult Congress on the interpretation of the ABM treaty would cause a "constitutional confrontation of profound dimensions" and promised to hold funding of SDI hostage to any administration activity on that matter.[42]

The president thus seemed to be weakened during the first months of 1987. Besides the challenges from an unsympathetic Congress dominated by the rival political party, Reagan's approval rating remained below 50 percent, and the public increasingly believed that Iran-Contra had damaged the presidency (fig. 5 and table 15). Along with this decline in his support levels, people were suggesting that the lame-duck phase had begun.[43] Thus, the president, with this significant loss of autonomy, adjusted his arms control stance to conform to the preferences of others in the system. The administration then cooperated with the Soviets, who were interested in making serious concessions in 1987. By the end of the year the two sides were able to conclude a treaty, as they were finally playing complementary strategies.

Choosing a Strategy: Continuing as Before and Then Conceding to Domestic Political Realities

From the outset of his second term, the president continued to place a low value on arms control. Reagan indicated that his hostility for the USSR had not abated, although his confidence in the American ability to prevent war had improved. Thus, Reagan and his advisers persisted in their adherence to "peace through strength." The position was based on the continued contention that the Soviets were an implacably hostile enemy that would exploit any weakness that the United States displayed. In particular, Reagan believed that the United States had to continue to strengthen its armed forces and maintain its commitment to combat Soviet aggression. He warned that "there must be no wavering by us, nor any doubts by others, that America will meet her responsibilities to remain free, secure, and at peace." Others underlined this determination not to be lulled by renewed Soviet interest in arms control in 1985. As Secretary of State Shultz explained to members of the Senate Foreign Relations Committee, "when the Soviets shift tactics, it is more often than not an adjustment to objective conditions without basic diversion from their long-term aims. . . . The Soviets can be counted upon periodically to do something, somewhere, that is abhorrent or inimical to our interests."[44]

In addition to this sustained assessment of the USSR, the administration remained committed to its contention that military force was the most essential component of U.S. security. Reagan and others maintained that only the renewal of American strategic and theater forces had compelled the Soviets to return to the negotiating table.[45] Moreover, administration plans to pursue the buildup of the U.S. arsenal provided unambiguous evidence of the centrality of military power in its approach.

During this second term, administration officials reiterated their concern with Soviet motives, the need to take active measures to prevent aggression, and the importance of power and will. According to the president, "the U.S. cannot afford illusions about the nature of the USSR. We cannot assume that their ideology and purpose will change. This implies enduring competition." Still, "American strength . . . caught Soviet attention" and made the improvement in American–Soviet relations possible. But the United States had to be wary of the USSR since the Soviets were always ready to strike.[46]

The president also continued to believe that superpower interdependence was very low and alternatives to negotiated agreements with the Soviets were many. Reagan stressed the importance of his country's taking steps on its own—such as building a space-based defensive system—to prevent nuclear war. That this development would have any impact on Soviet security was generally denied (although when pressed, the president promised to share this technology). Reagan preferred relying on good old American ingenuity rather than any kind of joint action with the USSR. Thus, alternatives and the value of arms control combined to keep the Reagan administration on a path of predomination at the negotiating table.

With the loss of autonomy at the end of 1986, the president no longer had the ability to sustain his approach at the table. Regarding arms control, other players in the system wanted to see an agreement on INF and an improvement in U.S.–Soviet relations. With reduced autonomy, Reagan then implemented a cooperative strategy. Luckily for him, Gorbachev was willing to give more than he received in return. In the end, then, the president did have an agreement that provided a conclusive victory for the American power position.

Getting to Yes on INF: Finally, Gorbachev Accommodates and Reagan Assents

From 1985 to 1987, the USSR and the United States would find a way to resolve the issue of intermediate nuclear forces. During this time, there was a progression in bargaining strategies that made way for the final agreement. In 1985, the new Soviet leader was circumspect and potentially vulnerable at home. While some elements of his proposals appeared conciliatory, the manner in which they were delivered—in public, for maximum exposure—raised questions regarding whether these were serious offers or motions put forward to gain optimum advantage for the USSR. After Gorbachev's position became more secure in March 1986, the Soviets began looking for mutual compromises; but the cooperative strategy yielded few concrete results. Despite these frustrations, at the end of 1986, Gorbachev came to believe that the United States was a businesslike partner and that accommodation was warranted. In 1987, he then pursued accommodation aggressively and made key concessions that enabled the signing of the accord.

The American president also altered his approach over the course of the negotiations, but these changes followed not from a reevaluation of the bargaining situation, but rather from the loss of domestic political autonomy. Reagan sought to predominate at the table from the reopening of the talks through the end of 1986, but then, after the erosion of domestic strength, in 1987 the president began to adopt a more conciliatory approach. Gorbachev, however, moved most of the way toward Reagan's position, precluding the necessity of the president's making equivalent concessions.

Continued Frustration in Geneva, March 1985–September 1986

The INF talks reopened as scheduled in March 1985, despite coming just days after General Secretary Chernenko's death. At the outset, the positions of the two sides were far apart. The Americans were insisting on the *global elimination* of intermediate-range missiles and the distinctness of the three sets of discussions, while the Soviets sought to limit INF in Europe only, argued that they deserved compensation for French and British forces, and vowed not to restrict any type of offensive arms, including theater weapons, until the United States accepted limits on SDI.

In the first session, the negotiators agreed to an American proposal to divide the umbrella talks into three working groups. The subdivision would allow experts in each of the fields—intermediate forces, strategic forces, and space weapons—to concentrate on one issue. Shortly thereafter, Gorbachev announced that the USSR would stop deploying SS-20s in Europe and eliminate those additional weapons that had been installed as a counter to American INF. The Soviet leader also proposed that both the United States and the USSR observe a freeze in offensive weapons and a moratorium on ABM development and research. Because the Soviets did not have a similar program under way, this suggestion was designed for their advantage. Not surprisingly, the Americans welcomed the proposed reduction of SS-20s, but they rejected the other offers.[47]

Throughout most of 1985, the story was similar. Gorbachev would stress the close link between strategic and space-based systems and call for cuts in both types of weapons. He would also suggest reducing the European INF arsenals. The Americans would reject these offers, contending, first, that they had a right to interpret the ABM treaty in any manner they pleased; second, that the United States needed to continue rebuilding its strategic forces; third, that British and French forces were nonnegotiable; and fourth, that only the elimination of INF worldwide was acceptable.[48]

During this first year of renewed talks, the general secretary sought the initiative. Then, if the Americans remained indifferent to its proposals, at least the USSR would win in the battle for world public opinion. To attract European sentiment, the Soviet leader announced that he was ready to deal with INF, regardless of the fate of strategic and space weapons, in a visit to France in early October 1985. He also told the admiring French that his country had unilaterally reduced the number of SS-20s to their 1983 level and pledged to phase out all SS-4s and SS-5s.[49] Since these missiles were far less capable than the SS-20s and the Soviets still held on to a huge lead in INF, Gorbachev's proposals seemed somewhat inconsequential, more on the order of Andropov's ploys of 1983 to exert West European pressure on the United States to be more forthcoming at the table.

The Americans generally greeted these offers with indifference. When the Soviets could not elicit movement in the U.S. position, Gorbachev again took center stage on January 15, 1986. Then, the general secretary presented a sweeping proposal for the eventual elimination of all nuclear weapons from the face of the earth by the year 2000. During the first phase, the superpowers would reduce the number of intermediate-range missiles in Europe to zero, and in the two subsequent phases, they would rid the world of all nuclear weapons. Because of the dramatic unveiling and the sensational goal (nuclear disarmament), reaction to the plan from those in the Western arms control and defense community was generally unenthusiastic. Reagan, however, was encouraged to see that the Soviet leader had incorporated the principle of eliminating all INF in this formula.[50]

In 1986, the Soviets moved away from these more utopian proposals and began to make concrete offers that appeared to be designed to take into account the mutual concerns of both states. At the Party Congress, Gorbachev emphasized that he would like to see the superpowers deal with INF first and resolve it before tackling the more complicated and interconnected issues of strategic offensive and defensive weapons. During the summer, Gorbachev announced new positions that were more concessionary. The Soviet leader said that he would accept the elimination of all Soviet and American intermediate-range missiles from *Europe* if the British and French would freeze their holdings. In addition, the Soviet leader pledged to liquidate and not deploy the European missiles in Asia. This proposal was somewhat promising. First, it unlinked the arenas of negotiation. If the Soviets were serious, it was an enormous concession on their part; with it, they were giving up significant bargaining leverage over SDI. Second, Gorbachev incorporated three key American positions in the offer: equality of superpower INF missile launchers in Europe, the number zero (but not globally), and concern with the Asian balance. Unfortunately, the Soviet leader also tied this deal to the British and French arsenals, which the United States had long maintained were *not* on the table. Moreover, he sought to keep existing Soviet forces in Asia. Still, this offer embodied small steps forward in the process. The United States, however, was not greatly impressed.[51]

In the first year and a half of the new talks, the USSR changed its position from one of predomination to one of cooperation. As Gorbachev attained more autonomy—through the permanent removal of opponents at the 27th Party Congress—he was able to articulate his new vision for international relations.

That approach was based on a new assessment of the alternatives to arms control (which were few because of the mutuality of security in the nuclear-missile age) and a recognition of the inadequacy of purely military solutions. Thus, the general secretary became willing to engage in mutual concession making with the United States. The United States, on the other hand, was not ready to respond in a similar fashion. Reagan returned to office domestically stronger than he had been throughout his first term (more popular and without concern about reelection) and convinced that his understanding of the Soviets and the bargaining situation was accurate. The United States, then, continued to play a strategy of predomination. The record of the negotiations shows that in 1986, the Soviets began to make proposals asking for both sides to compromise, while the Americans continued to seek unilateral advantages. Not surprisingly, the two states were unable to resolve their differences.

Reykjavik and After

Frustration over the state of the negotiations, as well as with that of the overall superpower relationship, brought the two leaders together for a hastily planned meeting in Reykjavik, Iceland, in October 1986. During the summer, the arrest of a Soviet spy in New York and the Soviet retaliation by bringing similar charges against an American citizen had caused new tension. In an attempt to mitigate any possible negative effects of this incident on the relationship, Gorbachev and Reagan agreed to meet in the early fall. Both men appeared to have a strong belief that an improvement in personal understanding and the development of a relationship between the two leaders would have a positive impact on superpower relations in general.[52]

While Reagan and his team came to Reykjavik to discuss the overall relationship, the Soviets arrived with a very specific arms control agenda. The proposal that Gorbachev put forward was designed to elicit important compromises from the United States, while also making key concessions to American concerns. The Soviets advanced a plan for each of the three arenas of negotiations in a package deal. On INF, they promised to eliminate superpower European INF, drop demands that the British and French freeze their holdings, and agree to conduct negotiations on Asian INF. Regarding strategic weapons, the USSR offered to institute 50 percent cuts across the board in strategic arms, with no weapons systems avoiding the ax. And for space systems, they proposed that the two sides commit to observing the ABM treaty for ten years, thereby allowing the Americans to conduct research on SDI as long as it could be performed in a laboratory.[53]

104   To Agree or Not to Agree

This plan—its specifics and its sweeping nature—took the Americans by surprise. While the U.S. team was heartened by the significant concessions that it contained (Soviet willingness to eliminate European INF regardless of British and French actions, to cut their ICBMs, and to allow the continuation of some SDI research), the administration deemed the proposal deficient. It did not provide the United States with total freedom in developing defensive systems, it would cut back American strength while also cutting Soviet forces, and it would not go far enough to achieve U.S. goals of the global elimination of INF. In short, Gorbachev's offer required both sides to make approximately equivalent concessions. This was not something that the Reagan administration was prepared to do. In fact, the United States tried to get the Soviets to unlink their proposals (to drop their insistence that any limits on INF and strategic weapons had to be matched by constraints on SDI) and to cut the number of intercontinental ballistic missiles by 50 percent. Both these measures would have enhanced American power relative to that of the USSR, since the United States was far more aggressively pursuing the development of missile defense and since the bulk of the Soviet strategic arsenal was on land-based missiles (while the United States relied far more heavily on bombers and submarines). Although the Soviets remained committed to the package, they did try to sweeten the offer during the talks by adding a promise to limit INF deployed in Asia to 100.[54]

The United States, however, was not interested in the whole plan. It wanted the package untied and rearranged; Reagan wanted to accept the pieces that best served American interests. Reykjavik, then, was dramatic evidence of the Soviet interest in cooperation and the American desire to predominate. The talks ended without agreement, and the two leaders were exhausted and frustrated. At times a settlement had seemed so close, yet the final concessions necessary for an accord—either the Soviets' moving completely to the American position or the Americans' meeting the Soviets halfway—never came. The outcome was disappointing to both sides, and observers worried about the long-term impact of this failure.[55]

Contrary to this anxiety, the meeting was an important turning point in the Soviet–American relationship. The interaction showed the Soviets that the Americans were serious about eliminating INF (that the global zero option was not simply a ploy designed to mask U.S. deployments) as well as reducing strategic arms. In so doing, the experience suggested that the Americans were a "businesslike" adversary.[56] Soon, Soviet perceptions of the domestic pressure that the U.S. president faced also helped reinforce this new assessment. There was a sense in 1987 that Reagan and the United States would be interested in actually bargaining at the table. This change in their assessment of the bargaining partner encouraged the Soviets to implement a policy of accommodation, agreeing to make some compromises that were unmatched in order to achieve an agreement. In addition, after January 1987, Gorbachev's plans for the transformation of the Soviet domestic system were proceeding. These efforts enhanced confidence in his ability to successfully pursue innovative foreign policies, too.

What had happened in the United States to promote this reevaluation? In November, Republicans lost control of the Senate for the first time in Reagan's tenure, and revelations about the Iran-Contra affair hit the news. Moreover, the Democrats, particularly those in the Senate, vowed to be less forthcoming with funding the president's defense program.[57] Public approval of Reagan dropped significantly, and pundits and ordinary people began to talk about the paralysis of the presidency (see fig. 5 and table 15). The president's domestic autonomy then eroded. To combat the deterioration of his popularity, those close to Reagan suggested that he shake up his administration and take steps to move forward on arms control by considering compromising with the USSR.[58]

Before the president could put forward a new plan, however, Gorbachev broke the ice. At the end of February 1987, just as the report of the Tower Commission investigating Iran-Contra was due to be published in the United States, the Soviet leader unlinked the discussions from the strategic and space talks for a second time.[59] Since Reykjavik, there had been little progress because the two sides perceived any forward movement in one area as dependent on agreement at the other tables. In February, Gorbachev was conceding once and for all to come to some conclusion on INF, regardless of the status of the space talks. The United States reacted favorably to the proposal, but American officials also stated that they would convert their Pershing II missiles to short-range Pershing IAs if the two states agreed to eliminate INF. The Soviets reacted angrily to the U.S. plan and called the U.S. commitment to the zero option a "bluff."[60]

Still, Gorbachev persisted. In a visit to Czechoslovakia in April, he suggested that the two sides eliminate shorter-range missiles (500–1,000 km) and freeze the number of operational tactical missiles in existence. During Shultz's trip to Moscow later that week, Gorbachev offered the European double-zero option, in which both alliances would eliminate all intermediate- and shorter-range missiles, except 100 INF that could be deployed outside the theater.[61]

Gorbachev's offer caught the NATO allies by surprise and was especially disturbing to the West Germans. Although Reagan had been an advocate of a nuclear-missile-free Europe, most of the allies had viewed these American weapons as essential for coupling the defense of their territory with that of the United States. In fact, the West Europeans, led by former German chancellor

Helmut Schmidt, had lobbied hard for American INF deployments on the Continent.[62] In addition, the West Germans owned some short-range Pershing IA launchers (for which the Americans supplied the warheads)—that they wanted to keep. Gorbachev's proposal required the elimination of these systems, too, and West Germany was initially unwilling to restrict this asset.[63]

While on balance, the Soviets were making the larger concessions—eliminating far more missiles and warheads and giving up systems that directly protected their homeland—this new offer required the West to compromise. To reach this agreement, the United States and West Germany would have to give up shorter-range systems, too.

In the summer of 1987, the Soviet leader took another dramatic step. In late July, he announced that the USSR would accept the *global* double-zero option. After seven years, the Soviets finally agreed to give up their missiles in Asia. A month later, West German Chancellor Kohl promised to remove the Pershing IAs once the treaty was in effect. The agreement looked close at hand, and the foreign ministers were engaged in final negotiations throughout the fall. These entailed resolving some verification issues and setting a date for the signing. But those last discussions were not easy; Gorbachev began to seek more assurances regarding the American SDI program. The general secretary had heard disapproval of his accommodation of American concerns from some other Soviet officials. Because he had only moderate autonomy, this criticism gave Gorbachev reason to be wary of more policy innovations and to see whether he could evoke some concessions in return.[64] When the Americans did not yield in return, the Soviet leader relented. He agreed to go to Washington in December and sign the INF treaty.[65] In coming to an agreement, Reagan, on the other hand, was moving toward the generally favorable position that most Americans and members of Congress had regarding the importance of improving U.S.– Soviet relations and reaching arms control agreements.[66] He was shifting, however, from the position of many members of his administration. As the prospects for the INF treaty became progressively brighter over the course of 1987, several officials became concerned. Secretary of Defense Weinberger frequently tried to undercut the more conciliatory administration positions. Likewise, arms control negotiator Ed Rowny complained about the "softness" of the new Reagan stance.[67] With each new significant Soviet concession in 1987, another American hard-liner seemed to announce his resignation. Richard Perle decided he would leave in March after the Soviets unlinked INF from the other elements of the umbrella talks and sanctioned the principle of on-site inspection. Following Gorbachev's announcement in late July that the Soviets would accept a worldwide ban on INF and not insist on keeping 100 missiles in Asia,

ACDA director Kenneth Adelman said he would resign. And in November, Frank Gaffney decided to leave his position at the Pentagon over his opposition to the verification provisions in the final treaty. Ronald Reagan's true believers were incredulous in 1987; if their champion were willing to reach an arms control agreement with the "evil empire," then they would rather leave the administration behind. The behavior of these officials seems to suggest that many of them had been supporting a strategy of obfuscation; they had opposed the completion of any accord. Even though Reagan was concluding a deal that was decisively in the U.S. favor, they still could not support this policy. Thus, they jumped ship.[68]

In the last year of the negotiations, then, a change in the Soviet approach to the table had an enormous impact on the outcome. After Reykjavik, Gorbachev contended that the United States would be a worthy partner at the table. He then changed his stance to one of accommodation. Developments in early 1987 and continuing through that year helped the general secretary feel confident in implementing such a revolutionary policy. (At no other time in nuclear arms control negotiations had either side been willing to make far greater concessions than the other.) Thus, beginning in February, Gorbachev reopened a constructive dialogue with the United States, and over the year, he made the necessary concessions throughout the last phase of talks.

At the same time, Reagan was reeling from domestic political troubles. In a way, Gorbachev threw him a lifeline, helping him divert attention from the scandal, rebuild public confidence in his leadership, and achieve a significant arms control treaty. The American president was able to conclude an agreement that addressed his major concerns—eliminating INF globally and enhancing the U.S. power position. He did, however, have to concede to remove the shorter-range missiles, but this compromise was a small one when compared with the advantages the United States had won in the treaty.

Concluding INF: Gorbachev Accrues Autonomy and Transforms Soviet Bargaining Strategy

The INF Treaty was an important success for arms control. The two sides agreed to eliminate a class of existing weapons, implement new and intrusive verification measures, and began a more positive phase of superpower relations.[69] Only four years before the signing of the treaty, the two sides were far apart on the issues at stake in the discussions, and the relationship was fraught with tension.

Some analysts believe that what brought the Soviets back to the table and convinced them to agree to American terms were the changes in the relative power positions of the two powers in the ensuing years. This explanation, however, cannot account for the timing of the return to the table, the character of the interaction, or the final agreement. First, the changes in the strategic or theater balance were not dramatic over the course of the years in question. Second, the *Americans* began wooing the Soviets back to the table prior to the supposed correction in their power position. Third, the Soviets became even more conciliatory in 1987 when the Senate was threatening the funding for many of the U.S. strategic and space programs. In other words, the USSR became more conciliatory precisely when the American commitment to SDI and the offensive buildup became less clear. Therefore, the future degeneration of the Soviet power position was also uncertain.[70] Finally, the agreement that the two sides reached required some compromises from the West. Although the Soviets conceded more, both sides had to reduce all their shorter-range nuclear missile holdings in Europe, too.

The Americans sought to return to the table during 1984 because of domestic political pressures. It was an election year, and early on, polls indicated that the president was vulnerable on the issue of peace. Moreover, the Soviets understood this pressure, as well as Reagan's opposition to compromise at the table. Thus, they were indifferent to returning to the table until they were sure of the outcome of the election. The strategic balance or theater balance had little to do with the motivations of both parties.

To understand why the two countries were able to reach an agreement in 1987 when the basic formula had been on the table for more than six years, it is important to focus on the leaders of the two countries, their domestic political positions, and their understandings of the bargaining situation. Gorbachev and Reagan were leaders who were balancing their domestic political obligations with their unique perceptions of international politics and the utility of arms control. The combination of these internal pressures and understandings of the external environment allowed them in 1987 to pursue policies that were complementary and permitted the conclusion of the INF Treaty.

During the first three years of his tenure, Gorbachev was working toward changing the internal and external behavior of the USSR. As he himself admits, he did not have a blueprint to implement, but he understood that reform was necessary. There were many people who supported change within the system— they had backed Gorbachev's candidacy as general secretary—but the leader knew that he needed to consolidate his position before embarking on serious reform, and support among his constituents for the specifics of his program might be tenuous.[71] Therefore, Gorbachev waited to release the details of "new thinking" and move forward with that approach until after the 27th Party Congress. Even after that gathering, the Soviet leader was sensitive to constraints on his autonomy. Though timing was favorable, the general secretary knew that his support was, at best, only mixed. With only moderate autonomy, he began to institute a new policy of cooperation at the INF negotiations, recognizing that he had to be careful regarding the extent of the concessions he would make.

In seeking to innovate in foreign policy, Gorbachev called into question the fundamentals of previous Soviet positions. New thinking rejected the primacy of military power, blaming, in fact, the reliance on military approaches to the detriment of political ones for the USSR's challenging position of the 1980s.[72] Perhaps even more important, Gorbachev concluded that the problem of security in the age of giant nuclear arsenals and advanced delivery technology was not so much the task of preventing intentional, coldly calculated attacks, but rather strengthening crisis stability and lowering the probability of accidental use of weapons. To make sure that the horror of nuclear war did not occur, the superpowers were obliged to work together and take steps to reduce tensions in the world. In essence, Gorbachev maintained that the United States and USSR were highly interdependent, and their fates were closely intertwined.

New thinking thus brought about a shift in bargaining strategy that Gorbachev instituted after the Party Congress. Thereafter, Soviet proposals on INF (as well as strategic and space weapons) were designed to evoke approximately equivalent concessions from the United States.

Although these Soviet steps were not enough to entice the Americans into settling, the failure of the cooperative strategy at Reykjavik did not cause Gorbachev to give up on bargaining with the United States. In fact, this episode of frustration helped Gorbachev understand that Reagan was serious about achieving agreements (although they might not agree on what kind of accord) and was a worthy opponent. Changes in U.S. politics at the end of 1986 helped reinforce that view. With Reagan under pressure at home to be more forthcoming on arms control, Gorbachev believed that the United States would behave in a businesslike manner. This change in assessment of the United States' intentions opened the way for Gorbachev to accommodate American concerns on INF. Continued turnover in the Soviet elite in 1987 and plans for structural changes in the system strengthened his conviction to take this risk and accommodate. In that last year, then, he made key concessions—giving in to longstanding American demands—that allowed for the achievement of the treaty.

Throughout the same period, there was no similar rethinking of the American approach. The president returned to office in January 1985 convinced that his assessment of the Soviets, the stress he placed on military power, and his preference for American independence in defense issues were correct. Thus, he remained personally committed to predomination throughout the period, and the proposals that his administration forwarded were consistent with codifying significant victories in the U.S. power position.

At the end of 1986, however, Reagan's autonomy eroded and forced him to respond to domestic political pressures. At the time, the American people, important U.S. senators, and many of his advisers, were pushing for some kind of arms control breakthrough. Just as he had done when under similar pressure in 1983, the president began to look for areas in which the two sides could cooperate. Luckily for Reagan, however, over the course of 1987, Gorbachev accommodated most of the Americans' basic goals on INF and the deal was struck.

Reagan's behavior in 1987 deserves further notice, however. First, his willingness to conclude the treaty over the objection of many of his advisers—dramatically demonstrated by their jumping ship as the agreement was nearing conclusion—suggests that the president had long been committed to predomination, not obfuscation (which those advisers appeared to favor). Second, it also showed that the president was not simply the head of a hard-line faction in American politics, but was a leader who made decisions based on his understanding of what was best for his domestic position and the American security position. Reagan was a true believer in the need to eliminate elements of the nuclear arsenal, and he achieved that goal over the protests of many security specialists.

Thus, this case once again highlights the importance of feedback between the domestic and international arenas. It also indicates that each leader tried to understand what made the other tick and used that assessment in determining the appropriate bargaining strategy. Furthermore, the executives in this case were very sensitive to their autonomy and the possible dire political consequences that they could face for overstepping their domestic authority. Each of these factors, then, contributed to the conclusion of the INF Treaty.

CHAPTER 6

Finishing START and Achieving Unilateral Reductions: Bargaining and Leadership at the End of the Cold War

1991 was a year of impressive achievements in arms control. In July, the United States and the Soviet Union signed the first START accord, and in the fall both states independently decided to reduce their readiness for war, eliminate tactical nuclear weapons, and accelerate reductions called for in the newly signed treaty. These developments were remarkable because of the *magnitude* of the restrictions involved in START—both sides agreed to slash their strategic arsenals by between a quarter to a third—and the *approach* taken in the autumn—both states self-adjusted, choosing to take steps without binding the other in a verifiable, legal commitment.

The completion of START I might initially appear to be consistent with the explanations of the competing approaches. Realists may maintain that in the case of START, the declining power—the USSR—made concessions to prevent the further erosion of its position in the world arena. In the realist formulation, a state is wary of concluding arms control agreements with an adversary and will do so under only two circumstances: (1) if the treaty improves its position relative to the opponent's, or (2) if the accord forestalls decline. Realists expect stronger nations to accept only those agreements that enhance their power and weaker states to agree to formulas that preserve their position or prevent it from worsening further.

The START accord, however, weakened the relative Soviet power position, as the agreement required deep cuts in the Soviet strategic arsenal, set sublimits on heavy missiles that would force the USSR to slash these weapons by half, and instituted provisions for counting nuclear charges that undervalued gravity bombs and air-launched cruise missiles relative to warheads. Each of these provisions affected the Soviet arsenal disproportionately. Since 1975, the USSR

TABLE 16. The Strategic Balance, 1980–91

Year	U.S. Warheads	USSR Warheads	Ratio U.S.–USSR
1980	10,608	7,480	1.418
1981	10,688	8,296	1.288
1982	10,515	8,904	1.181
1983	10,802	9,300	1.162
1984	11,500	9,626	1.195
1985	11,974	10,012	1.196
1986	12,386	10,103	1.226
1987	13,002	10,442	1.245
1988	13,000	10,834	1.200
1989	12,100	11,320	1.071
1990	11,966	10,880	1.100
1991 (pre-START)	12,316	10,880	1.132
1991 (post-START)	10,936	8,564	1.277

Source: Robert S. Norris et al., "Nuclear Weapons," in *SIPRI Yearbook 1991: World Armaments and Disarmament,* ed. Stockholm International Peace Research Institute (New York: Oxford University Press, 1991), 25; Regina Cowen Carp, "U.S.–Soviet Nuclear Arms Control," in *SIPRI Yearbook: World Armaments and Disarmament,* ed. Stockholm International Peace Research Institute (New York: Oxford University Press, 1991), 397.

had been investing enormous amounts of resources into defense in an effort to close the gap between the level of its strategic warheads and those of the United States. But just as they were approaching numerical equality in the late 1980s, the Soviets made all the necessary concessions to reduce their arsenal and to decrease capability further relative to the United States. The USSR had also carefully developed and protected its right to hold heavy missiles. The United States, on the other hand, had not invested in that area and would not suffer from that restriction. Finally, the counting rules also clearly favored the United States, which had devoted more resources toward its bomber force than had the USSR. In START, then, the Soviets agreed to give up hard-won and expensive gains (table 16).[1]

But were the Soviets better off establishing these mutual reductions in 1991 because their economy was deteriorating and unable to support continued defense spending? Underpinning this question is the notion that for Soviet leaders, military spending was one of several competing budgetary priorities and that overall economic problems would put pressure on defense allocations as well as on other spending considerations. But until the late 1980s, Soviet defense spending had not been sensitive to economic pressures, despite the fact that the country was experiencing serious difficulties. If structural concerns—economic combined with strategic—were primary, then the Soviets should have been interested in cutting back their strategic forces much earlier.[2]

Perhaps even more damaging to the realist explanation is American behavior. If the USSR were so obviously in decline and positional concerns were primary, why would the United States be interested in setting any limits on its ability to develop its own strategic arsenal in 1991? As the superior power and a relative-gains seeker, the United States should not have agreed to take on obligations restricting its options.

Proponents of the domestic politics model can also construct a plausible explanation for the START agreement. As we have seen, they typically contend that arms control policy results from the bargaining between domestic actors, whose positions come not from their office but from their political leanings. Arms control is seen as a struggle between reformist and orthodox members of the elite in the USSR and a battle between liberal and conservative forces in the American context; whichever group is stronger wins. If neither is dominant, then the parties involved in setting policy cut deals to arrive at a negotiating position that serves their ideological interests.

In the case of START, the focus would be on the transformation of Soviet politics and its impact on arms control policy. In the last year of talks, the Soviet position flip-flopped as traditionalists tried to assert power. In concluding the START agreement, Gorbachev and his reformist supporters regained control over the process and made the necessary concessions. Later, in the decisions to cut back tactical weapons, the Union president and the republican leaders agreed to huge reductions in the Soviet arsenal. These cuts advanced both the budgetary and institutional interests of the advocates of change.

But for domestic politics analysts, the question of the pulling and hauling between powerful institutional actors remains. In the Soviet case, Gorbachev innovated and provided significant concessions at the table from 1987 through 1990 despite considerable opposition from traditionalists. After the fact, the bastions of "old thinking"—the military and the Party organization—tried to force him to reverse these concessions in late 1990. And this fight over policy was not simply a backroom battle, but rather a struggle over control of the state. Moreover, while this contest was occurring, Gorbachev was still trying to rewrite the rules of the game by refashioning Soviet politics. This project did not proceed as the general secretary expected, however. In empowering individuals, he was not able to keep control over the process and maintain the support of alternative groupings. By the end of 1990, then, Gorbachev could depend on neither the old power centers nor the new ones for support. Precisely because the Soviet leader's base had crumbled, he was vulnerable to the attacks of the old thinkers. At that point, Gorbachev was left trying to please whichever group he thought was the stronger one in order to hold onto power. While Gorbachev's behavior in his last year might appear to confirm the domestic politics approach, key forces pressuring the Soviet leader were located outside the state structures. Moreover, Gorbachev's earlier control over the bargaining process is inexplicable without an understanding of autonomy and the links that an executive has to his constituents.

In the U.S. context, although there is evidence of bureaucratic infighting during the Reagan years, the tale of START decision making under George Bush is relatively free of internal wrangling.[3] In addition, the domestic politics approach has trouble accounting for the fact that Bush sought to toughen the American stance at the table in 1989. That is puzzling because George Bush was supposed to be the "moderate" or "pragmatist," and observers always characterized Ronald Reagan as the ideologue. By this logic, then, Bush should have been more interested in arms control than was his predecessor. Finally, if there were no bureaucratic or ideological battle being waged, why did President Bush become more conciliatory over the course of his term? Apparently, factors external to the decision-making process must have had an impact on his policy choice.

In explaining the superpowers' decisions to act unilaterally in the fall of 1991, the existing approaches are again at a loss. Realism cannot account for the move to limit war-making potential. Why would the superior power initiate such action, and why would the inferior power reciprocate when by refusing, it could win an improvement in its position? From the realist perspective, the behavior of both the United States and the Soviet Union in the fall of 1991 appears incomprehensible.

Domestic political developments, as students of arms control typically conceive of them, also cannot explain these unilateral decisions. The idea for the first American step came from George Bush while he was on vacation in Maine. There is little evidence of either a bureaucratic struggle or a debate between liberals and conservatives in the administration over these measures. Instead, there appears to have been a consensus within the administration in support of these moves to change American alert procedures and enact unilateral reductions. In the Soviet decision to reciprocate, domestic politics also did not affect this choice in ways that its adherents would expect. After the coup, the structure of power was almost completely changed. The communist party and the power ministries were discredited. In their place, republic leaders were essential players, and Gorbachev had to obtain their consent to change Union-level nuclear policy.

In sum, the standard explanations appear to have difficulty accounting for these instances of arms control at the end of the Cold War. The two states did not simply act as relative gains maximizers, as realists would predict; in the end, they were not strictly motivated by an improvement in their positions. Nor can bureaucratic politics or the competition between rival ideological factions within the executive branch account for the shifts in state behavior that occurred throughout the talks. Instead, leaders played principal parts. Their ability to manage the process over time, moreover, seems to have varied with their domestic political positions. And both executives evidently had their own particular understanding of the international situation and the appropriate approach for dealing with their rival. Whether they could implement that approach depended on whether they had sufficient strength at home.

The First Seven Years of START in Brief

In 1982, strategic arms negotiations between the United States and USSR that had been on hold since the beginning of the decade reopened with a new name, START (Strategic Arms Reduction Talks). By abandoning the SALT (Strategic Arms Limitation Talks) designation, members of the Reagan administration were signaling that these talks were not simply a continuation of the previous ones and that they sought significant reductions—particularly in the Soviet arsenal—as the result of any treaty.[4]

The superpowers made very little progress on arms control—including START and the Intermediate-range Nuclear Forces (INF) talks—throughout the first half of the 1980s.[5] Both sides seemed more concerned with the INF negotiations at the time. Because NATO proceeded with its deployments in Europe, the USSR postponed the negotiations on long-range systems indefinitely in late 1983. In January 1985, however, the superpowers agreed to resume the dialogue in three separate but linked forums, discussing strategic as well as space and intermediate-range systems.[6]

At a quickly convened summit in Reykjavik in October 1986, the United States and USSR established the basic outline for the START I treaty, agreeing to limit the number of strategic warheads to 6,000 and to restrict the number of nuclear launch vehicles to 1,600. They did not conclude the treaty then, however, because the Soviets maintained that this formula was contingent upon the Americans' accepting restrictions on strategic defense.[7] Despite this disagreement over the linkage of accords on offensive and defensive weapons, the two sides continued to refine their START positions after Reykjavik. Maintaining their commitments to ceilings of 6,000 warheads and 1,600 strategic delivery systems, the negotiators added warhead sublimits of 4,900 on ICBMs and SLBMs, 1,540 on heavy ICBMs, and 3,000 to 3,300 on ICBMs only. Although the United States and USSR even came to agreement on cruise missile counting rules, they were unable to sign an accord during the 1980s.[8] If the United States insisted on pursuing SDI, then the Soviets would not agree to reductions in offensive systems.

While Gorbachev and Reagan could resolve INF, they were unable to surmount their differences regarding offensive and defensive weapons and the extent to which these two sets of systems were interconnected. They had succeeded in achieving a possible framework for a treaty, however. Whether the two sides would actually reach one, without also concluding an agreement constraining the development of SDI, was another question. The answer to this query and the final formula of any agreement would be left for Gorbachev and the new American president, George Bush, to determine.

Executive Autonomy and Bargaining Strategies, 1989–91

The years 1989–91 were certainly eventful in Soviet domestic politics and Soviet–American relations. The turmoil, as we will see, had a mixed impact on arms bargaining. In the USSR, Gorbachev faced new challenges to his autonomy, as the structural changes that he implemented to strengthen his position did not appear to achieve his goal. The Soviet leader's understanding of the bargaining situation had not changed from before; he remained committed to a policy of accommodation. Still, his difficulties at home reminded him that instituting such a policy—especially on the issue of strategic weapons—would take enormous care.

His American counterpart, George Bush, could count on extremely high levels of support with the public and a relatively cooperative Congress. Although both houses were controlled by the opposing party, Bush's veto was overridden only once.[9] So, at the outset of his term, President Bush had a significant amount of autonomy. He was newly elected, very popular, and worked well with Congress. Thus, the president had enormous power over policy, and he was able to make his preferred approach to bargaining the American strategy.

The president's strategy actually evolved over time. Initially, Bush feared that Gorbachev would not succeed in changing the USSR and was concerned about the impressive size and destructive power of the Soviet arsenal. Thus,

Bush conceived of the USSR as a clear menace and stressed the importance of American military power for meeting that threat. In addition, he was not impressed with the idea of working with the Soviets and believed that the United States could pursue policies other than arms control to improve its security. The president, then, preferred a strategy of predomination. Later, however, Bush changed his mind and his approach. After Gorbachev allowed the East Europeans to leave the Communist fold, the president came to recognize that the superpowers were highly interdependent and that there were few alternatives as effective as arms control for promoting security. Bush then became willing to cooperate. This more conciliatory stance made the conclusion of the START agreement possible—particularly after Gorbachev began experiencing many domestic challenges and backtracking in late 1990.

New Thinking, Autonomy, and Bargaining Strategy in the USSR

In each of the other cases, determining preferred strategy was generally a more complicated task than ascertaining autonomy levels. In the last years of the Soviet Union, however, Gorbachev maintained his commitment to new thinking, while the domestic political situation was changing at a rapid pace and in amazing ways.

In chapter 5, we saw that Gorbachev's plan to revamp the assumptions of Soviet foreign policy, new thinking, was central to understanding the USSR's willingness to concede. This policy asserted that military power was not the guarantor of security and that, given the danger of nuclear war, ecological annihilation, and resource constraints, the USSR had few alternatives to arms control. In terms of dealing with the United States, once Reagan demonstrated that he was not simply an ideologue who was only engaging in arms control for political purposes, Gorbachev came to believe that the United States was a worthy partner in this joint endeavor. Thus, the Soviet leader was willing to accommodate the United States—to make greater concessions—to achieve arms control accords that would promote his new understanding of security.[10]

Whether he could implement this approach, however, depended on his domestic political strength. After the 27th Party Congress, Gorbachev possessed moderate autonomy. On that occasion, he was able to eliminate some significant foes of change from their positions and to buy time for reform. Despite the extensive turnover among the elite, however, Gorbachev's support level was mixed. Throughout the apparatus and the leadership there were differences of opinion on how to proceed with reform, and not everyone favored Gorbachev's version. Moreover, Khrushchev's fate loomed large for Gorbachev. He understood that with moderate autonomy he was constrained and sought ways to accrue more power and freedom to maneuver for himself.

At the end of the decade, then, Gorbachev began instituting changes that would transform the Soviet system. The general secretary finally understood that many in the Party were blocking reforms and that he had to reach out to allies in the larger Soviet society. Thus, Gorbachev authorized the creation of a freer press and the Congress of People's Deputies (CPD), a partially elected legislative body, of which he became the leader.[11] He also tolerated the formation of different political organizations and the assembly of groups that were not officially approved.[12] In so doing, the general secretary was broadening his base of support and trying to create a bulwark against potential Party opposition. For the first time, the public became an important constituent of the Soviet leadership. In early 1989, then, massive popular support for Gorbachev as the initiator of the devolution of political power and economic reform served to strengthen his position within the system.[13] After the CPD election, significant support and favorable timing gave Gorbachev a high level of autonomy.

Unfortunately for Gorbachev, this domestic political strength was short-lived. Growing economic problems, societal pressures, and the general secretary's own behavior served to undermine his position over the next year. Despite (or actually because of) Gorbachev's plans for economic revitalization, living standards deteriorated, the shortage of basic goods became severe, and people tired of all the talking that the Soviet leader seemed to sanction.[14] In addition, Gorbachev's calls for democracy brought people into political life who did not share his views of gradual, "socialist," Soviet reform. Encouraged by Gorbachev's acquiescence to the popular revolts against communism throughout Eastern Europe, nationalist movements in the Baltics and the Caucasus began calling for local political control. Other new actors also started to question the legitimacy of the Soviet system. In discussing the atrocities committed under the auspices of building socialism, many activists began to suggest that the system was fundamentally flawed—and not redeemable, as Gorbachev was trying to contend. All these critical groups provoked a backlash. Organizations that glorified communism and Russian nationalism also sprang up.[15] Moreover, Gorbachev himself was not comfortable with the "debate" and "discussion" for which he called. When pushed too far, the Soviet leader could be quite intolerant.[16]

Thus, by early 1990, Gorbachev found himself in a challenging predicament: his approval rating declined from 52 percent in December 1989 to 21 percent in October 1990.[17] He was trying to allow some self-expression and devolution of power, but those who were responding most vigorously wanted to take the country in very different directions. Flanked by ardent anticommunists on one side and a strange coalition of Russian nationalists and Stalinists on the other, Gorbachev was trying to hold onto a rapidly evaporating political center. In 1990, then, with a Party Congress on the horizon and his backing in society and among the Party dropping, Gorbachev's autonomy was also falling.[18]

Although he made it through the Party Congress, changing the composition of the Politburo and receiving tepid support for his policies, Gorbachev was weakened. By the end of 1990, the rifts in Soviet society were starkly apparent, and the Soviet leader's support among his base—now dispersed among Party members and the population—had severely eroded; he could count on the backing of very few. With weakened autonomy, Gorbachev began to reverse himself in foreign and domestic affairs. By December 1990, he was unwilling to defend new thinking and his foreign minister at the Supreme Soviet session. In January 1991, he approved the army's attack against independence activists in Lithuania and Latvia.[19]

Still, the general secretary's backtracking could not stop the momentum for change. Democratic activists pushed for continued liberalization. In 1991, despite the presence of troops in Russian cities throughout the late winter and into the spring, citizens took to the streets in protests against the actions in the Baltics and the attempts to rein in freedoms. A referendum on the state of the union in March and the elections for the Russian presidency three months later also demonstrated the significant support for change. In the union vote, the populations of the six Republics that sought independence refused to participate. In those places where the referendum was held, the result was ambiguous. While support for maintaining the USSR was strong—nearly 77 percent of those voting cast their ballots in the affirmative—majorities also voted for separate motions authorizing republican sovereignty.[20] Moreover, in the election for the presidency of Russia in June, Boris Yeltsin won a resounding victory despite Gorbachev's pleas to voters to support another candidate.[21]

By June, Gorbachev could no longer deny that the future of the USSR was not with the Party but with progressive, societal forces. The Soviet leader—as the one who had ushered in liberalization—felt emboldened to continue with change. While his confidence in his position allowed Gorbachev to renew his innovations in foreign and domestic policy, his self-assurance turned out to be misplaced. His autonomy was very low, and his lack of popular support was matched by opposition to him within the upper reaches of the Party. At a June meeting of the Supreme Soviet, Premier Pavlov tried to arrogate some of the

Soviet president's responsibilities to himself. Moreover, there were growing rumors that some members of Gorbachev's inner circle were preparing for a coup.[22]

Gorbachev, however, ignored these signs, and for once, this politically astute leader[23] was out of touch with the reality of his domestic situation. He was convinced that his position was sufficiently secure to push forward on arms control and took the step to authorize the necessary, final concessions. The result of Gorbachev's decision to try to move the USSR back to new thinking internationally and toward significant domestic political change was a coup against the Soviet leader.[24] But while Gorbachev did not have the autonomy to enact such policies without the support of the party-state machinery, neither did the forces of reaction have the power to dictate politics in USSR. The coup was a defeat for both those opposed to change and Gorbachev, the initiator of reform. In the aftermath of the putsch, the popular and republican forces appeared victorious in the Soviet Union.

In sum, Gorbachev had the domestic political strength to proceed with a policy of accommodation at the negotiating table in 1989. By the autumn of 1990, however, the Soviet leader's autonomy had eroded to such a level that he had to reverse and adapt his approach to the conflictual one favored by the institutional power centers.[25] He was then unable to make concessions and proceed constructively with negotiations until the developments of the spring and early summer of 1991 convinced Gorbachev that the Soviet future was consistent with general political reform. To make the START agreement possible, Gorbachev returned to his accommodative approach and pushed through the last concessions.

Executive Autonomy, Prudence, and Preferred Strategy
in the United States

From 1989 through the end of 1991, George Bush was in an enviable position; the president's performance ratings were consistently good and often astronomical (fig. 6). Moreover, through most of this period, the 1992 election was far in the distance. Consequently, the president did not have to be too concerned with his approval ratings when they dropped to slightly under 60 percent in the fall of 1990 and hovered around that mark through the early winter of 1991. Moreover, the legislature failed on all but its last effort to override his vetoes, and Bush won the important votes of approval in foreign affairs, such as the authorization of the use of force in the Persian Gulf conflict. In short, Bush's position was extremely secure during the last phase of the START I negotiations.

Fig. 6. Bush's approval ratings (percentage who approve). (Data from *Gallup Poll Monthly*, no. 314, Nov. 1991, 24.)

The president was therefore able to bring the national strategy in line with his own values.[26]

When Bush became president in 1989, he promised to ensure that America stayed "strong to protect peace."[27] While an advocate of his predecessor's "peace through strength" approach to the Soviet Union, the new president reportedly had become concerned that in 1988 Reagan had gone "soft" on security. According to Bush, his predecessor had allowed his new relationship with Gorbachev to cloud his judgment. To guarantee that his approach was based on the "facts" and not emotions, Bush ordered a review of American Soviet policy upon coming to office.[28]

What the president learned from that review was that the USSR was still an incredibly dangerous foe and that none of the changes instituted there were, as yet, irreversible. As Bush explained,

> [W]e [must] try to understand the full meaning of the change going on there [the USSR], review our policies, and then proceed with caution.... We will not miss any opportunity to work for peace. The fundamental facts remain that the Soviets retain a very powerful military machine in the service of objectives which are still too often in conflict with ours. So let us take the new openness seriously. But let us also be realistic. And let us always be strong.[29]

James Baker, Bush's close friend and secretary of state designate, echoed his future boss's concern in his confirmation hearings. There, he stated, "We live in a world of powerful adversaries. We cannot take the survival of democracy for granted or assume that if we do not protect our own interests, someone else or some international organization will act on our behalf."[30] While Baker noted that monumental changes were occurring in the USSR, he repeatedly urged caution since there were no guarantees that Gorbachev would succeed in his attempts to reform the Soviet Union.[31]

In effect, Bush and Baker were saying that the nature of the Soviet threat had not changed; the USSR remained a dangerous and hostile enemy. Moreover, the president was particularly impressed with Soviet military power and convinced that such capability was the only guarantee of American security.

In addition, the Bush administration perceived many options for the United States to pursue other than arms control with the Soviets. The United States could maintain its weapons development programs without much trouble, and such independent steps were preferable to working with the USSR or some international organization, particularly at this time when the situation in the Soviet Union was so unstable. Thus, the president preferred to predominate at the bargaining table. American officials argued that there was no reason to compromise on arms control; the Soviets would have to come around to their position if they wanted some kind of an agreement.[32]

In the fall of 1989, however, President Bush's approach to negotiations changed as the events in Eastern Europe unfolded. Soviet acquiescence to the revolutions finally showed Bush that "new thinking" was more than just a slogan. The president came to realize that joint solutions were called for in this new, post–Cold War era, particularly if he hoped for this period to last. Moreover, Bush began to believe that by working with Gorbachev, he could help strengthen the Soviet leader's position and policy. By showing others in the USSR that concession making was worthwhile, Bush hoped to keep the compromises from the Soviets flowing. This change of heart on the part of the president, then, brought about a new approach at the bargaining table at the end of 1990. The president abandoned his search for outright American gains in favor of a strategy of cooperation, where both sides would make compromises to reach an agreement.[33]

Thus, Bush began his term seeking to predominate at the table. By the end of the first year, he changed his strategy to one of cooperation. This change was fortuitous for the arms control process because of the difficulties that Gorbachev then experienced. While the Soviet leader was willing and able to accommodate during much of 1989, that approach became increasingly difficult to enact by the end of 1990 when Gorbachev's autonomy had seriously eroded. American concessions and forbearance during that period were important for keeping the negotiations on track. By the end of 1990, despite significant movement toward a final agreement, the fate of the START accord was in question. The last compromises would come in June, when Gorbachev believed he had the power to authorize them and after Bush provided the aid to entice them.

Finishing START I, 1989–91

While the START negotiations proceeded for almost seven years at a glacial pace, during the last two and a half years of talks, the United States and USSR were able to make progress and conclude an agreement that significantly reduced superpower arsenals. The last phase of START began with both leaders in strong positions domestically. Each therefore was able to pursue his preferred approach at the bargaining table. For Bush, that meant seeking advantages for the U.S. strategic position relative to the Soviet Union. Gorbachev was willing to make one-sided concessions initially, but even he was not amenable to bending as far as the Americans wanted. In less than a year, Bush became less obdurate as he finally became convinced that the security of the two countries was interdependent. With the United States cooperating, the two sides had an easier time resolving their differences at the negotiating table. But the final year of negotiations was not uncomplicated; Soviet domestic politics began to impede the arms control process. Gorbachev was under attack at home, and initially he adjusted to the concerns of traditional forces in an attempt to maintain his autonomy. In the final three months of the negotiations, however, he moved back toward reform, pushing through the last necessary innovations to achieve the START I treaty. These compromises were important and did lead to the signing of an accord, but these steps and others, particularly the plans for a new Union Treaty, ultimately cost Gorbachev his job.

The United States Reverts to Predomination, 1989

In 1989, the START negotiations were stalled. Although the two sides had agreed on an overall ceiling of 6,000 strategic nuclear launch vehicles on each side and some sublimits for the different categories of weapons, the United States and the USSR could not seem to get beyond one big hurdle—the contention that offensive and defensive developments were linked.[34] The Soviets, who had already made a number of concessions to reach this stage, insisted that the START limits were valid only as long as the Americans observed the strict interpretation of the ABM Treaty. They refused to reduce their offensive arsenal if the United States would not keep its promise not to develop and deploy strategic defenses. Thus, for the Soviets no START accord was possible without a commitment to maintain the limits on defense.

When George Bush became president, there was also the possibility that the negotiations could be further complicated. The administration was considering backing away from the already agreed-upon framework, as some members of the new U.S. leadership reportedly contended that Reagan had made too many concessions. They believed that if the United States reversed itself and held firm, the Soviets would cave in to American demands.[35] After careful scrutiny, Bush assented to the ceilings that had been negotiated for warheads and launch vehicles, but he asked for more intrusive verification measures to assure adequate monitoring.[36]

While the American interest in START seemed lukewarm, the USSR advanced some important concessions in the fall of 1989. At a meeting of the two foreign secretaries at Baker's summer home in Wyoming, Shevardnadze provided key concessions to break the START stalemate by revealing that the Soviets would conclude a treaty on offensive arms even if the two sides could not agree on the development of defensive systems. By dropping its demand for linkage between the two issues, the USSR gave up a significant source of leverage over the final formula.[37] Baker and Shevardnadze ironed out other problems at their meeting, too. The ministers signed an "umbrella agreement" promising to implement new types of intrusive verification measures on a test basis. The Bush administration believed that these provisions would make any Senate ratification battle easier since they would provide further proof that the agreement was verifiable. Moreover, from Baker's perspective, this meeting was an important turning point in the relationship.[38]

This change of heart was not simply unique to the secretary of state. With the revolutions in Eastern Europe at the end of 1989, Bush became convinced that Gorbachev's commitment to peace and new thinking was sincere. He agreed to meet the Soviet leader in Malta in December to discuss all the changes that had just occurred and to try to make progress on the arms talks. According to observers, this "nonsummit summit" was significant for the superpower relationship, as the two leaders developed a rapport, and Bush finally concluded "that Gorbachev would prove to be a reliable partner in the new climate."[39] The president had come to believe that American security problems were changing with the new U.S.–USSR relationship. Concerns about Eastern Europe and the future of Germany seemed to displace nuclear weapons on center stage, with thoughts of Latin America and the Middle East not far behind. The United States was necessarily constrained in resolving these issues; the USSR had to be involved in settling these problems, too. Thus, at the end of 1989, Bush estimated that the United States could not promote its security as effectively on its own. The president came to prefer joint solutions for the new and difficult problems facing him in various global hot spots as well as in the familiar arena of nuclear arms. Thus, at Malta, Bush modified the American stance and began to cooperate. There, he gave in to a long-standing Soviet goal for completing the treaty by the next Bush–Gorbachev meeting, to be held some time in June 1990. Previously, the administration had opposed setting such a deadline for fear that the United States would be pressured into making too many concessions in order to finish the treaty by the specified date.[40]

The Final 18 Months: Bush Cooperates, but Gorbachev
Vacillates under Pressure

Although many issues remained to be ironed out in 1990, the prospects for an agreement certainly appeared excellent. With Gorbachev willing to accommodate and Bush ready to compromise, settling the final details should have been relatively easy. While the Soviet and American leaders remained strong, that was certainly true. Throughout early 1990, the negotiators on both sides took a problem-solving approach to the talks and were able to resolve some tricky issues. Later in the year, however, Gorbachev's loss of autonomy impeded and almost derailed the agreement. The U.S. president was understanding of Gorbachev's plight and continued to work constructively (and make some compromises of his own) until the deal was sealed.

The first half of 1990 was a productive one at the table. When negotiators met in February 1990, the two sides agreed that the most problematic ones could be resolved in a second START treaty.[41] This was a signal that both countries were serious about concluding a deal. In addition, the United States and USSR made some more concrete progress on cruise missiles, thanks to Soviet concessions. Regarding air-launched cruise missiles (ALCMs), the two sides agreed to counting rules that would allow the Americans to deploy an extra 1,500 warheads beyond the 6,000-warhead ceiling, while the Soviets could not. The Soviets also accepted the U.S. proposal to refrain from establishing formal counting rules for submarine-launched cruise missiles (SLCMs) and to rely on each side's report of how many it held.[42] This was another significant concession to the United States, since the Soviets had entered the negotiations hoping to limit SLCMs substantially. The Americans, however, adopted the Soviets' preferred position on ALCM range limits.[43] Thus, while important differences remained on the ceilings for ICBM warheads and mobile missiles, the encryption of missile testing data, and verification procedures, Shevardnadze predicted in May that "a treaty on strategic weapons can be finished for signing by the end of this year."[44]

Obstacles seemed to mount at the bargaining table at the end of 1990 and into early 1991, however, as the Soviets repudiated earlier positions. Gorbachev's autonomy had waned significantly, and he began to try to shore up his stance by reversing some concessions. At the bargaining table in late 1990, Gorbachev retracted an earlier concession by changing his mind on the ALCM counting rule agreed to in February 1990. Moreover, by March 1991, "serious strains" were reportedly developing during negotiations. According to one American official, "Soviet and American negotiators in Geneva keep working out technical issues in the strategic arms treaty, only to find them rejected by the Soviet leadership."[45]

The superpowers appeared to make some progress in May 1991 when the United States accepted the Soviet offer on ALCM ranges.[46] But despite this step forward, serious problems remained. Because the USSR was caught trying to circumvent some provisions of the recently signed Conventional Forces in Europe (CFE) treaty, the Americans became very concerned about verification. Bush then decided that he would not try to finish the agreement on strategic weapons until he was satisfied with Soviet compliance of CFE. In early June, the two sides settled their problems relating to the conventional forces treaty, and Bush gave the negotiators the go-ahead on START.[47]

While the numerical limits were basically set, the superpowers could not reach agreement on verification issues. In early July, Bush suggested that the foreign ministers meet to help advance the process and that the United States offer the Soviets some badly needed economic assistance as an incentive to cooperate. According to inside sources, the administration became concerned about losing the START formula. Two months before, Richard Burt, the former head of the American negotiating team, had written, "A delay in finishing the accord would mean that a large portion of the existing treaty would have to be renegotiated under difficult circumstances. The result would surely be an inferior accord." Officials noted that Gorbachev had earlier made "lopsided concessions . . . when he was trying to persuade the West that the Soviets were no longer a threat, and he has been dragging his own military along ever since." The Americans feared that any further delays in finalizing the accord would jeopardize any agreement because Gorbachev potentially could lose "his room for maneuver."[48]

Gorbachev assented to Bush's suggestion, and a week later, Baker and Aleksandr Bessmertnykh, Shevardnadze's replacement as foreign minister, were negotiating the details. To sweeten the deal, the United States also offered the Soviets economic aid.[49] By July 14, they announced that almost all the outstanding issues had been resolved, with both sides making concessions. According to one observer, the United States achieved its goals regarding warhead totals and verification procedures, "while the Soviets got close to what they had been seeking on defining and dealing with new types of missiles."[50] Bush and Gorbachev surmounted the last hurdles just a few days later when Bush agreed to go to Moscow at the end of the month to sign the treaty. After almost a decade, the two presidents concluded the first START agreement, which slashed the number of warheads, cut heavy and other ballistic missiles, and required intrusive verification procedures.[51]

Unilateral Arms Control, 1991

In the aftermath of the START I signing ceremony, the USSR experienced even more turbulence. To prevent the promulgation of a new Union treaty that would have allowed the Baltics and Georgia to secede and would have devolved some powers to the remaining republics, forces opposed to change in the Soviet Union arrested Gorbachev and announced a state of emergency in the USSR.[52] After three tense days, the coup failed and Gorbachev returned to power. In his absence, the political landscape was transformed dramatically. The Baltic republics became independent states, and almost all the other Union republics asserted their sovereignty, although they initially pledged to remain part of the country. In addition, the coup discredited the Party apparatus and legitimized elected officials as the defenders of the law. Anticommunist forces thus won a huge victory.[53]

While the United States cheered the outcome of the coup, administration officials had been concerned about the status of Soviet nuclear weapons throughout those tense days in August. Who had the launch codes while Gorbachev was under house arrest? And now that the Union was disintegrating, who would control the approximately 27,000 tactical, intermediate-range, and strategic-range nuclear weapons that remained?[54]

The putsch itself and its positive resolution (from the perspective of the American administration and anticommunists) caused changes in both the American and Soviet approaches to arms control. The uncertainty about the outcome and the fears about the status of the nuclear weapons led to significant soul-searching among American decision makers. In fact, the United States became increasingly convinced of the importance of strengthening political ties and undertaking steps to improve its relationship with the USSR as a way of reducing the risk of war. In addition, the alternatives to arms reductions—decreasing the amount of destructive capability in general and preventing that power from falling into the wrong hands—seemed few.[55]

Within days of the collapse of the coup, the American president gathered his trusted advisers together to discuss policy options.[56] Then, the administration concluded that the value of an agreement was high (the USSR was a businesslike partner in negotiations and military power was not the essential guarantor of security) and the alternatives to arms control were few. While this pairing could have led Bush to choose either to accommodate or self-adjust, the president understood that time was of the essence. He sought to take advantage of the opportunities presented in the immediate aftermath of the Soviet coup and not to miss his chance. Given the uncertainty about the future of the Soviet state and its ability to safeguard nuclear weapons, the administration decided to take a dramatic step: George Bush chose to self-adjust.[57]

On Friday night, September 27, 1991, President Bush requested television time to announce his plan to decrease drastically the size of the superpower arsenals. The president declared that the United States would unilaterally eliminate all ground- and sea-launched tactical nuclear weapons based in Europe and Asia, take long-range bombers off 24-hour alert, accelerate the reductions mandated by the new START treaty once the Senate ratified it, cancel the development of the mobile MX missile, terminate plans for a short-range attack missile, and simplify some command and control procedures. Bush then challenged the Soviets to follow suit.[58]

Bush's TV offer reflected the changes in his perception of the strategic situation. According to one commentator, "[d]uring the cold war, such an approach to arms control would have been considered beyond the pale. The fear was that the Soviets would pocket any American concessions and never reciprocate."[59] But afterward, the president feared not Soviet intentions, but the collapse of central power in the USSR. The disintegration of the Soviet state revealed the new danger of the unauthorized use of nuclear weapons by renegades, and the only way to mitigate that threat was to enlist the new leadership in the joint project of reducing the amount of firepower available. Thus, the U.S. president recognized the high levels of interdependence between the two sides, the scant alternatives the United States had for acting on its own, and the importance of political measures for resolving these security concerns. Moreover, to address this problem quickly, the best approach was to refrain from lengthy negotiations and hope that the Soviets would reciprocate. The president thus proposed unilateral reductions.[60]

Reflecting the new power realities within the Soviet Union, Gorbachev's initial reaction to the American initiative was positive but noncommittal. Although Gorbachev's preferences had typically been consistent with a similar approach, the Soviet president no longer had the autonomy that would allow him to respond immediately and definitively to such an important proposal. A week later, however, Gorbachev announced that the USSR would match the American plans regarding tactical weapons and would go beyond them by cutting strategic nuclear warheads back more than required by START, instituting a testing moratorium, and reducing troops by another 700,000. In his statement, Gorbachev indicated that his plan reflected the thoughts of the republic leaders and confirmed speculation that his delay in replying occurred in part because he had had to consult them.[61] The Soviets then seized the moment and self-adjusted their position. Gorbachev's vision of the world as a highly interconnected one, in which the United States and USSR were partners and political measures were preferred to military ones for enhancing security, was taken to its logical conclusion.

Arms Control at the End of the Cold War

At the end of the 1980s and at the start of the 1990s, tensions between the United States and the USSR relaxed significantly. This change occurred not simply because of an alteration in the balance of forces, but because the leaders of the two nations recognized that the challenges they faced would be more easily resolved together and that political efforts would be more useful in promoting security in this new era. The two powers arrived at these understandings at different moments. Gorbachev advanced new thinking first, but insufficient autonomy in the system initially stymied his pursuit of innovative security policies. As the decade wore on, he became progressively stronger and bolder. With the democratic opening of Soviet politics in 1989 that provided him with more autonomy, Gorbachev felt empowered to offer concessions that would significantly reduce the USSR's arsenal.

Upon taking office, George Bush was much more impressed with the size and destructive power of the Soviet nuclear arsenal and the USSR's traditionally hostile ideology than with Gorbachev's peaceful promises. The American president could not deny the Soviet leader's sincerity when communism fell in Eastern Europe in 1989, however. Gorbachev's acceptance of the loss of Soviet control there convinced Bush to modify the American stance at the table from one of seeking advantages for his state to one of cooperation. The U.S. leader believed that the complex problems that remained after the dismantling of the Iron Curtain could be addressed only through joint action, and the ability of the United States to solve them alone was limited. Moreover, the defeat of communism in Eastern Europe convinced Bush that he was dealing with a worthy opponent. These realizations allowed the American president to change his approach from one of predomination to cooperation. Bush's understanding of the bargaining situation evolved further after the attempted coup. The putsch and the ensuing concerns about the loss of control of Soviet nuclear weaponry brought about a transformation in Bush's perception of the primacy of political efforts to strengthen security. This modification opened the way for the unilateral reductions that followed on both sides. Bush self-adjusted, and Gorbachev, with the assent of the newly empowered republican leaders, followed suit.

The other frameworks cannot explain these dramatic changes in American and Soviet arms control policies. The START case shows unequivocally that the impetus for agreement did not come from the distribution of military capabilities or from intra-executive branch bargaining. In the last two years of negotiations on strategic weapons, the importance and interplay of both domestic and international level variables were obvious. For George Bush, significant domestic autonomy allowed him to fashion the American approach according to his perception of the international system. Initially he was quite impressed with and concerned about the Soviet arsenal. Gorbachev's behavior as the Soviet empire crumbled in Eastern Europe, however, convinced him that the USSR was an adversary worthy of some cooperation. For Mikhail Gorbachev, the choice was whether to follow his preference of accommodating (in order to reach an agreement) while his autonomy in the system was dwindling. The Soviet leader had long believed that nuclear weapons and accidental war were a more serious threat than U.S. militarism and had been attempting to significantly reduce nuclear arsenals. While the START process wound to its conclusion, however, his domestic position significantly deteriorated. Consequently, the Soviet position at the table became less constructive. But in the last months, with the rising assertiveness of proreform forces in the USSR and the Americans' adopting a constructive approach at the table, Gorbachev took a chance in pushing this process forward. His bravery—or more appropriately, his arrogance—in foreign and domestic politics led to the coup and ultimately the evaporation of his autonomy in the Soviet system.

In the aftermath of START, what had previously been unimaginable—that the superpowers would reduce their nuclear arsenals significantly on their own accord—became a reality. This policy flowed from the change in the American president's understanding of power and the potential for independent action. Then, a very popular George Bush decided to self-adjust. Gorbachev reciprocated, with the support of the newly empowered republican leaders. The formerly powerful institutions—the Party and the military—were severely weakened as a result of their leaders' sponsorship of the coup and could do nothing to prevent these changes in Soviet force structure and operational plans.

CHAPTER 7

Superpower Arms Control and Joint Decision Making in International Relations

Leaders make a difference. In arms control decision making, how executives perceived their bargaining partner, the nature of power in the international system, and their state's alternatives to engaging in joint action affected the strategies they preferred to implement at the table. Whether or not leaders advanced their favorite approach depended on their domestic autonomy. An executive who sought to safeguard his power and have the ability to lead again tomorrow held off on policy innovations when he was weak and moved boldly ahead if he had significant domestic autonomy. While some leaders occasionally miscalculated, they were generally aware of this relationship between domestic and international political imperatives, and students of bargaining should also take both these factors into account when trying to explain the process and result of negotiations.

In the preceding analysis of Soviet and American arms control, while traditional approaches often provided compelling first-cut explanations for outcomes, those accounts were less convincing after closer analysis. Instead, the leadership model, with its integration of both the international and domestic levels, outperformed its challengers across the cases. An executive's perceptions of the value of an agreement and the state's alternatives to arms reduction consistently defined his preferred bargaining strategy, and limited executive autonomy accounted for a nation's deviations from that approach. When a leader had considerable autonomy, he was able to pursue his preferred policy, but when he lacked power, other institutional actors within the domestic political system constrained the executive. In the Soviet system, limited executive autonomy tended to mean intransigence at the bargaining table, since the key organs of the USSR had both ideological and institutional reasons for opposing concessions to the United States. In the United States, insignificant presidential autonomy allowed the Congress or the people to exert more influence over policy. Contrary to its effect on Soviet politics, constituent influence on American politics has shifted over time. Prior to the 1980s, legislators and the public tended to be hostile toward arms control; thus, without considerable executive power, the chance of completing a treaty generally was low. During the Reagan presidency, however, these other groups increasingly supported the conclusion of agreements to limit nuclear weapons. Even then, however, the president could refuse to yield to both the Soviets and domestic pressure if his autonomy were significant.

In addition to accounting for the test ban talks of the 1950s and 1960s, the INF negotiations, and the arms control achievements of 1991, the leadership model can illuminate other instances of joint action in international relations. In fact, it can explain the SALT process and the breakdown of détente in the 1970s. The variables identified in the model—autonomy and bargaining strategy—can also provide insight into the volatility in American–Russian relations in the post–Cold War era. And the relevance of the model is not necessarily limited to the interaction of the former superpowers. Because the approach was derived from theories of adversarial bargaining and interaction, the leadership model may illuminate other long-standing conflicts in the international system. The importance of autonomy and the role of leaders' perceptions of interdependence and the value of agreement suggest that the confrontations in Northern Ireland, the Middle East, and the former Yugoslavia will remain difficult to resolve in the near future.

Recapping the Case Studies

In the four paired cases of arms control—the early test ban talks, the Limited Test Ban Treaty, the Intermediate-range Nuclear Forces talks, and the INF Treaty—as well as the two end-of-the–Cold War minicases—START and the unilateral actions of 1991—the Soviet Union and United States pursued four different types of conflict resolution strategies (table 17). The executive's level of autonomy ultimately determined whether the leader could follow his desired approach or whether he had to modify his stance to conform with the positions of other institutional actors.

Despite their interest in bargaining, executives—whether pursuing their preferred strategies or the default ones—did not always seek to make compromises or reach agreements. Predomination was a highly popular strategy, and even cooperation—seeking approximately equivalent concessions—was pursued cautiously. As the Cold War was ending, however, the Soviets became

TABLE 17. Summary of Bargaining Strategies and Outcomes

Forum	USSR's Strategy	U.S.'s Strategy	Outcome
Test Ban Talks, 1958–60	predomination	cooperation	no agreement
LTBT, 1961–62	predomination	cooperation	no agreement
11/62–8/63	cooperation	cooperation	agreement
INF, 1981–82	predomination	predomination	no agreement
1983	predomination	cooperation	no agreement
INF, 1985–1/86	predomination	predomination	no agreement
2/86–late 1986	cooperation	predomination	no agreement
1987	accommodation	cooperation	agreement
START I, 1989	accommodation	predomination	no agreement
1990–91	accommodation	cooperation	agreement
Fall 1991	self-adjustment	self-adjustment	unilateral reductions

willing to accommodate, and in the fall of 1991, both the United States and the USSR decided to take actions beyond the bargaining framework and self-adjust.

In addition, no single strategy could guarantee the completion of an agreement, as outcomes were necessarily contingent on the behavior of both parties. The United States and the Soviet Union reached a settlement when the strategies or goals from any agreement were complementary and when the specific proposals overlapped. Satisfying both conditions simultaneously did not occur often. The leadership model suggests, however, that the tendency of students of cooperation to focus primarily on the bargaining range to explain success and failure is necessarily flawed. Since bargaining ranges can shift over time as leaders pursue particular outcomes (agreement or no agreement), strategy was often more important in determining whether any accord was even *feasible* in the first place.

Determinants of Preferred Strategy

In most of the cases examined here, both Soviet and American decision makers tended to believe that arms control as a security policy had an insignificant value. This inclination resulted from the very low likelihood that any leader during the Cold War would simultaneously judge the opponent to be "businesslike" and identify something other than military force to be the key component of security. The strategies varied because of differences in a leader's evaluation of the alternatives to arms control. While Khrushchev (prior to the Cuban Missile Crisis), Reagan, and Bush (at the outset of his term) contended that their nation was highly independent, Eisenhower, Khrushchev (after the crisis), Kennedy, Bush (after a year in office), and Gorbachev recognized the links between the two countries and therefore that the alternatives to arms control were few. Each man identified different constraints on national behavior. For Eisenhower, the prevailing belief around the world that the United States was not interested in peace and was declining relative to the USSR made him realize that America had to take action in concert with the Soviet Union to dispel notions of its bellicosity and impotence. After the brush with nuclear confrontation, Khrushchev recognized the close linkage of the superpowers' fates, especially in an era of budget constraints, new reconnaissance techniques, and the growing Sino-Soviet conflict. Kennedy believed that the American ability to maintain its power was restricted because on its own, it could not slow down the rate of development of the arsenals of either the USSR or third parties. Only joint action could achieve such a goal. Almost 30 years later, Bush came to a similar conclusion on the interdependence of the two states. Because U.S. and Soviet security were linked, Bush recognized that he could best provide for U.S. safety by working with, not against, Gorbachev.

Most radically, Gorbachev contended that the enormous stockpiles, the potential for the breakdown in command and control, and the possibility of ecological devastation were far more serious threats than the danger that the United States might one day order a massive thermonuclear strike. Thus, to rein in the arsenals and reduce the likelihood of accidental war or unintended escalation, Gorbachev understood that he had to enlist the United States in his project. Security could only be mutual, and in contemporary conditions, it was best pursued through political and not military means. When, in the aftermath of Reykjavik, Gorbachev also determined that his opponent was one "with whom he could do business," the last Soviet general secretary adopted an almost revolutionary approach to the arms bargaining table. Gorbachev became willing to make more concessions than he expected in return from his bargaining partner.

Initially, the United States misunderstood Gorbachev's approach. Several observers thought that he was only biding time for the development of a new, revitalized, and more aggressive Soviet Union. Interestingly, however, after the domestic political upheaval in the USSR, George Bush's understanding of the character of the American–Soviet relationship and the nature of security changed, too. This American president then went beyond the bargaining process and self-adjusted the U.S. position. The Soviets reciprocated, and as a result, the United States and USSR achieved arms control breakthroughs in the fall of 1991 that went beyond START.

Just as perceiving arms control as valuable was unusual, so too was an executive's conceiving that the state's alternatives were limited. Typically, leaders did not want to be dependent on their opponent and preferred to use state resources to develop their nation's power. In many ways, the Cold War culture as well as key domestic institutions were predicated on the notion that joint action with the adversary was both foolhardy and dangerous. Thus, to hold the view that there were multiple alternatives to arms control and that the two states were independent was consistent with the ideas and the interests of constituents and principal institutions. Pursuing such a policy allowed an executive to maintain commitments to powerful individuals and bureaucracies, preserving their budgets, prestige, and importance. Moreover, such an approach did not require a change in the general rhetoric or understanding of the superpower relationship. In essence, then, to assert that there were several alternatives to arms control allowed executives such as Khrushchev (until November 1962), Reagan, and Bush (through most of his first year) to pursue transactional strategies in which they engaged in an exchange of valued goods with their constituents.

Even executives who perceived interdependence continued to employ a transactional approach to leadership if they had a low estimation of the value of arms control. In some ways, they justified cooperation as the appropriate choice on a particularly limited issue, but they never saw a need for fundamentally reconceiving the relationship. They reached this conclusion because they generally believed in the centrality of military power or the treachery of their adversary. So Eisenhower, Khrushchev (after the crisis), Kennedy, and Bush (through the second and third years of the START negotiations) also practiced transactional leadership. These leaders made their cooperation understandable to the electorate and the major institutional actors as the best possible bargain, one that would not preclude further weapons development and would not challenge the missions of key organizations.

Only Gorbachev (after 1987) and Bush (after the attempted Soviet coup) recognized both the intertwining of the fates of the two states and the significant utility of arms control. They each then argued that the relationship had to be changed dramatically, and both had to justify engaging in a joint project with the adversary. The defense of this policy was much harder for Gorbachev in 1987 than for Bush in the euphoria that followed the defeat of the putsch in 1991. Throughout the late 1980s and into the 1990s, however, Gorbachev struggled in transformative efforts, and ultimately his attempt to see the world differently—for example, to allow those people who had been under Soviet or Russian domination to leave the fold if they desired—brought about his downfall. But where Gorbachev failed personally, he paved the way for the new republican leaders to carry on. For them, the struggle to undermine the Cold War culture, particularly among the older generation of Russians, continues. But this transformation was interrupted somewhat, as Yeltsin was weakened by both the institutional tug-of-war of 1992–93 and the precipitous decline in his popularity that followed the onset of economic reform.

In the United States, Bush's effort also had mixed success. While the nation happily greeted political change in Russia and the former Soviet Union, the tendency was to oversell what had happened there. In the "new world order," democracy and liberalism would reign. When instead authoritarianism seemed likely and chaos flourished, Americans—leaders and public alike—did not understand. The response was to return to old thinking, expanding NATO and containing the possible Russian threat. The Clinton administration, in fact, appears at times to have left the transformative project behind and returned to the practice of transactional leadership in security policy. The enemy still exists, and the roles of defense contractors and the foreign policy establishment are to supply our friends with the hardware and advice to prevent Russian aggression.[1]

Impact of Autonomy

Some leaders, of course, would not have been able to transform the relationship even if they had believed that a major change was in order. As we have already seen, executives did not always have the luxury of acting as they preferred; domestic political concerns often compelled them to adopt another course. When leaders lacked autonomy—there was an upcoming election or selection and their support levels were low or mixed—they could not pursue an unpopular policy. They would then adjust their approach to one that was consistent with the strategy of the other power centers in the system. For most of the period, this meant that weak leaders generally sought to predominate, but interestingly, in the 1980s in the United States, because of congressional and public concern about the risk of nuclear war, the impact of domestic pressure was to force cooperation.

These case studies also indicate that autonomy problems could be brought on by a leader's foreign policy failures. For instance, the overflight of the U-2 and the lack of progress at the INF bargaining table in the early 1980s both had effects on the autonomy of American leaders. The U-2 incident initiated the lame-duck phase for Eisenhower, and the widespread public perception of Reagan's willingness to risk nuclear war fed the freeze movement, helped elect a more pro–arms control House of Representatives in 1982, and made the president appear vulnerable in his reelection campaign. In the USSR, Gorbachev's concessions to the West—at the arms control bargaining table (for INF and

START) as well as his acquiescence to the East European revolts against Soviet rule (which many of his constituents in the Party considered failures)—also undermined his political position and forced him to back away from his policy of accommodation in the last year of the START negotiations.

Interstate Feedback

Domestic developments in one country at times had an impact on the bargaining approach of the other's leadership. For instance, Reagan's potential weakness in 1984 encouraged Soviet leaders to respond with disinterest in American attempts to return to the INF negotiating table. Another example of this phenomenon was Bush's reply to Gorbachev. For a time, the U.S. president feared that the fragility of Gorbachev's position meant that the utility of bargaining with the opponent was limited. Others might unseat Gorbachev, and the USSR would be the same menace it had been prior to this reformist general secretary's coming to power. Later, Bush understood that Gorbachev needed to show that his approach to the United States was fruitful in order to strengthen his domestic position.

In these cases, there was also perhaps a less surprising form of feedback, a spillover between foreign policy developments in one country and external behavior of the other. While the U-2 incident undermined Eisenhower's position, it also served to force a change in Khrushchev's behavior, since the first secretary's American policy had been predicated on the notion that Eisenhower was a "reasonable man." To maintain his credibility at home, then, Khrushchev had to amend his approach as a result of Eisenhower's taking responsibility for that ill-fated mission. In addition, Kennedy's failure to follow through with the invasion of Cuba at the Bay of Pigs affected Khrushchev's assessment of the new president and then influenced the Soviet leader's approach to the bargaining table. And Gorbachev's promulgation of the "Sinatra Doctrine" for Eastern Europe—letting each country "do it their way"—had an enormous impact on George Bush.

Purely domestic political concerns also exerted influence on the negotiations. Throughout the 1980s, the long-lasting Brezhnev succession affected Soviet bargaining behavior. While no general secretary was particularly strong, each had to play to the powerful interests in Soviet society and engage in transactional approaches at the table. Only until after the 27th Party Congress, when Gorbachev's position became relatively secure, did he embark on his accommodative strategy. In the United States, Ronald Reagan bent to domestic political demands in 1983 and 1987, becoming more willing to compromise with the Soviets as the public and the majority of the Congress advocated. Moreover, in late 1990 and early 1991, when Gorbachev was increasingly under attack from both the Right and the Left, the USSR's bargaining behavior shifted as the Soviet leader attempted to hold on to his position.

In effect, then, the cases demonstrate that there was an interesting type of feedback between the developments in the two systems. Since strategy depended on an assessment of the opponent, domestic political events had an effect not only on a leader's autonomy but also on his opponent's perception of the nature of that state. In addition, problems in foreign policy, which could help undermine a leader's autonomy at home, also affected that assessment of the nature of the adversary abroad.

The Leadership Model and SALT

While it provides an excellent account for the cases examined here, the leadership model can also illuminate and explain other instances of superpower arms control. From 1968 through 1979, the USSR and the United States were involved in the Strategic Arms Limitation Talks (SALT).[2] The first set of negotiations, SALT I, ended in 1972 and resulted in the Anti-Ballistic Missile (ABM) Treaty—restricting the development and deployment of ABMs—as well as the Interim Agreement—limiting the numbers of ICBMs and SLBMs that each side could possess. In SALT II, signed in 1979 but never ratified, the two countries agreed to place a ceiling on strategic launchers and rein in the qualitative arms race.

The leaders, their perceptions of the value of and alternatives to arms control, and their domestic political positions appear to have also played an important role in these cases. In 1969, Nixon pursued a cooperative strategy at the table, trading American concessions on strategic ballistic missile systems for Soviet ones on ABMs precisely because the U.S. president believed that the value of arms control was limited (parity, the U.S. opening to China, and the encouragement of U.S.–USSR economic ties had made the Soviets a businesslike opponent, although military power was still the essential element of security), and resource constraints meant that alternatives to arms control were few. Nixon thus sought to cooperate with the Soviets, exchanging approximately equivalent concessions with the other power. Brezhnev adopted the same approach as he perceived that parity had forced his opponent to be sober and that destructive capability was key. While Brezhnev wanted to fund the continued buildup of Soviet forces, he hoped to fix the target (by placing a ceiling on the growth of U.S. forces) at which he had to aim. Thus, he perceived that his options other than arms control for achieving that goal were limited.

In the SALT I talks, the two sides played complementary strategies and were able to come to a settlement. They restricted their development of antiballistic missiles, thereby constraining the complexity of successfully delivering weapons to their target. In addition, regarding offensive strategic systems, the agreement froze the number of ballistic missile launchers at their existing levels. Although this ceiling allowed the USSR to have more land- and submarine-based systems, the United States was confident that it was still a good deal. Neither American forward based systems nor strategic bombers, which were far more numerous and capable than their Soviet counterparts, were counted in the totals. In addition, the Interim Agreement did not put any limit on the number of warheads that either side could place on a missile. The United States was about to begin MIRVing its ICBMs and SLBMs, so it knew that it was going to maintain numerical superiority in deliverable bombs. (The Soviets were behind in MIRV technology.) Moreover, the accuracy of American delivery systems was still far better than that of the Soviet systems, meaning that U.S. MIRVs would pack an impressive punch.

The Soviets, too, thought that this was a good bargain. They had been trying to catch up to American strategic power for more than two decades, and SALT and the Moscow summit were both a sign and a symbol of having accomplished that feat.[3] Moreover, the Soviets understood that future breakthroughs in MIRV and navigation technology would also allow them to add warheads to and improve the accuracy of their existing launchers.

To justify this bargain and to bolster his domestic political position, President Nixon engaged in an oversell of what SALT represented. The exaggeration regarding the achievement of SALT and the meaning of détente turned out to be a serious mistake for the arms control process as well as the American–Soviet relationship. In arguing that SALT I was good for the United States, Nixon failed to explain adequately that the agreements were not simply a victory for the United States; rather, the United States had had to make concessions, too. Thus, when some people—particularly in Congress, but also citizens throughout the country—looked at the treaty outline and saw that the numbers appeared to favor the Soviets, the deal began to look flawed.

A second mistake that the U.S. president made was to maintain that détente entailed a fundamental transformation of the superpower relationship. Really, what had been achieved in 1972 was an approximately even exchange between two parties. The basic nature of the competition had not changed, and when the Soviets continued to confront Western interests—by supporting insurgents in the lesser-developed world, continuing to modernize their strategic arsenal, deploying intermediate-range nuclear missiles, which were not limited in the SALT agreements—many in the United States felt betrayed. But in SALT, the Soviets had not promised that they would reform; the two sides simply made equivalent concessions to reach a treaty.[4]

The motivations of the leaders and the bargain struck seven years later in SALT II were similar.[5] This time the two sides promised not only to limit the total number of strategic launchers (including bombers) but also to restrict the numbers of warheads and the extent of modernization that either side could undertake. But Carter's insensitivity to the need to manage swiftly the ratification process in the summer of 1979 (as Kennedy had done 16 years before) and then the precipitous weakening of the president made the ratification of SALT II impossible.[6] Thus, the feedback between international events like the seizing of American hostages in Iran in November 1979 and the Soviet invasion of Afghanistan a month later helped heighten Carter's autonomy problems. SALT II became another foreign policy failure—an unratified agreement with a bellicose adversary. To respond to his perceptions of a changed international and domestic context as well as to bend to the wishes of the electorate, President Carter moved away from constructive interaction with the USSR in 1980. This modification was too late to salvage the election for Carter, and it spelled rejection of not only SALT II but a strategy of cooperation with the Soviets.[7]

A lesson from the superpower arms control experience is that transformative leadership cannot be entered into lightly. A leader must have the domestic political strength to carry it through (which Gorbachev did not in July 1991). Moreover, the executive's analysis that a transformation of the relationship had occurred could not be wrong or politically motivated. The consequences of the Nixon oversell of détente, as Jimmy Carter learned, were the undoing of his presidency. And in bringing Ronald Reagan to the White House, it produced a new deep freeze in the Cold War.

Implications of This Study

The End of the Cold War and the American–Russian Relationship

While this study has been primarily concerned with arms control negotiations between the former superpowers, the findings provide insight into the end of the Cold War, contemporary American–Russian relations, other types of arms control, and the general problem of bargaining between adversaries. Contrary to the opinions of some observers, this book seriously undermines the argument that the United States "won" the Cold War and that the Soviets "lost."[8] Most adherents of this view point to Soviet concessions in arms control and retrenchment in the Third World to make their case. But the analysis here of INF and START does not reveal that "peace through strength" compelled the USSR to agree to U.S. arms control positions. In fact, this study demonstrates how contingent Soviet concessions were on Gorbachev and his "new thinking." He developed this approach not out of a fear of the United States and its enormous strength, but rather out of concern for the enormous destructive power that both superpowers possessed and the horror that it could someday be used.

Moreover, that this policy was dependent on Gorbachev and not "peace through strength" is clear from statements that former Soviet leaders have made about the primacy of the general secretary, as well as the attempts to undermine Gorbachev's position and then reverse his policies. Opponents to new thinking attempted to remove Gorbachev from power with the August 1991 putsch. While the Union Treaty was their impetus, the State Committee for the State of Emergency contended that Soviet foreign policy as a whole had been badly misguided. According to the explanation that they provided at the outset of the putsch, the coup plotters stated "only yesterday, a Soviet person . . . abroad felt himself a worthy citizen of an influential and respected state, now he is often a second-rate foreigner, the attitude to whom is marked by either contempt or sympathy." Indeed, they argued that "the pride and honor of the Soviet people must be restored in full," and in their view, the only way to accomplish that goal was to oust the man who caused all the problems.[9] Thus, Gorbachev led the CPSU in a foreign policy direction that many of its members opposed. Had the Central Committee not selected Gorbachev in March 1985—and there was a choice—it is highly unlikely that the USSR would have made concessions at the bargaining table, instituted extensive domestic political reforms, abrogated the Brezhnev Doctrine, and ended its confrontation with the West at the end of the 1980s.

In solidifying the end of the Cold War, both Bush and Gorbachev took actions, motivated not by "strength" but by concern for nuclear safety, that helped secure the end of the superpower confrontation. Both leaders were willing to enact changes in their force structures without the benefit of a formal agreement in order to stabilize the situation while the USSR disintegrated. And this momentum to reduce nuclear arsenals continued even after the initial glow over the collapse of communism had faded. Since the end of 1991, there have been remarkable arms control achievements, including but not limited to the completion of START II, which reduced the number of warheads to about a third of the levels allowed under START I; the signing of the Convention on the Prohibition of the Development, Production, Stockpiling and Use of Chemical Weapons and Their Destruction; and the expansion of existing accords that limit conventional weapons in Europe and enhance confidence-building measures in the region.[10]

Given these impressive results, some analysts began to argue that "[t]he future U.S.–Russian arms control agenda seems ... to be moving towards discussions on how to facilitate greater levels of cooperation in order to attain common goals" and "there is no longer a military threat from the East."[11] But that view was far too optimistic. The Russian Duma has refused to ratify this second treaty, and plans for START III are on hold.[12] In fact, Russian politicians have learned that nationalism and anti-Westernism attract voters. In the parliamentary elections in 1993 and 1995, the most successful parties—the Liberal Democratic Party of Russia and the Communist Party of the Russian Federation, respectively—were those that appealed to national pride and promised to act decisively to assert Russian interests. By the time of the 1996 presidential elections, Yeltsin learned this lesson, too. To assure his victory, he shuffled his Cabinet, firing the last of the "liberals"; decided to annihilate recalcitrant Chechen fighters, their captives, and those unlucky enough to be in the army's way; and found a place in his administration for the outspoken nationalist and second runner-up in the first round of the presidential contest, Aleksandr Lebed.[13]

Although Yeltsin won that election, he did so at great expense to his health and, some would argue, Russian democracy.[14] The president had a heart attack shortly after the first round of voting and withdrew from public life for nearly six months to regain strength, undergo a quintuple bypass operation, and recuperate. While Yeltsin's recovery seemed miraculous in early 1997, by the end of the year he again appeared to be very ill. As long as his physical condition, and therefore his hold on power, is questionable, Yeltsin's ability to follow his preferred strategy (which seems to recognize the constraints on independent Russian action and the benefits of working with the United States) will be limited. Besides his health problems, Yeltsin faces a legislature (the Duma) that is controlled by forces antagonistic to the West. The majority of the population is sympathetic to the Duma's position and would like to see Russia strongly reassert itself in world affairs. Thus, Yeltsin's physical condition and support problems provide him with limited autonomy. The best hope for Russian-American relations at the end of the century is that they will be erratic, with the president mixing his preferred, constructive approach with a more hostile one favored by his many opponents.[15]

Precisely what can be achieved in the relationship, of course, is also dependent on the American political scene. Since 1993, foreign policy and particularly Russian–American relations have not been a primary consideration for the average U.S. voter or for the American administration. The election of 1996, with Clinton winning a second term handily and the Republicans maintaining control of both houses of Congress meant that Clinton's autonomy in foreign affairs would be moderate: the president's timing appeared good, but his support was mixed (an opposition-dominated Congress and a supportive public). Given the security of his position as a second-term president and his popularity, however, the president could decide to lead.[16]

For the Clinton administration, the more interesting question is *would* the president seek to put his own stamp on arms control and Russian policy. In the post–Cold War era, when there are no longer two superpowers and the Russian–American security relationship does not have the same urgency, an American president has the luxury *not* to lead. However, just as the oversell of the change in Soviet-American détente fueled a renewal of the Cold War in the 1980s, American confidence in the compatibility of Russian and U.S. policy in this new era could have a dangerous feedback of its own. In early 1998, the disagreements between Russia and the United States over the handling of arms inspections in Iraq generally took the U.S. administration by surprise and were met with indignation in the Congress. Containing the fallout from that interchange and understanding the sources of Russian conduct are essential for maintaining a partnership between these two former superpowers and enemies.[17]

Arms Control in Other Contexts

While the United States and the Soviet Union or Russia have had the most experience with arms control, they are certainly not the only states that could be engaged in this endeavor. In fact, countries in the Middle East and South Asia, among other places, either have tried or are trying to develop nuclear capability and other weapons of mass destruction. If nations begin to deploy these armaments, some experts predict a "proliferation ripple effect" to follow. Moreover, the conventional arms trade and stockpiles continue to grow.[18] Thus, the potential for arms control remains real, and the superpower experience suggests that in pursuing arms control, state leaders will play an important role. Autonomy from militaristic forces in society provides executives with opportunities to make progress on limiting arms, whereas dependency on these groups suggests that such actions will be very difficult. Moreover, this book highlights the complexity in reaching agreements. The participants have to be playing complementary strategies. For instance, no matter how compromising one party is, if the other side refuses to settle, there can be no agreement. And, if the number of countries that are participating as equals in the negotiations increases, so too does the complexity of the process, as the leaders of several countries have to synchronize their approaches in order to reach a negotiated settlement. Such an outcome will not simply occur with time. Contrary to what some argue, states do not automatically become more reasonable as the talks proceed.[19] Seemingly intractable problems can be solved only when a significant change in leaders' perceptions of the international situation occurs or if domestic political pressures for moderation develop.

Outside actors can try to influence the process, however, by changing a leader's perception of his nation's capacity for independent action. Here, the threat of force, embargoes on weapons or products used to make them, trade sanctions, international condemnation, or the reduction of economic aid might serve to change a leader's assessment of alternatives and could convince an executive to pursue negotiations seriously. The recent show of force and diplomatic efforts to convince Saddam Hussein to reopen his country to weapons inspection is an interesting case in point.

Leadership and Conflict Resolution

Finally, insights from this study of superpower arms control behavior might enhance our understanding of other cases of international negotiation. Throughout the Cold War, nuclear weapons were perceived by decision makers on both sides as essential to their safety. Yet, the Soviets and the Americans were willing to negotiate about limiting the source of their power and security. Today, other antagonists face analogous situations as they negotiate about the fates of their nations. Specifically, the conflicts in Northern Ireland, the former Yugoslavia, and the Middle East appear to be similar cases of long-term conflict between adversaries regarding central security issues.

In contemplating the potential for a resolution of these confrontations, the leadership model provides some ideas. What is clear from this study of arms control is that leaders in both democracies and authoritarian or totalitarian states have to be concerned with their domestic political positions. Leaders always have constituents (although exactly who comprises this group will vary across regime types) and must maintain the support of their electorate or selectorate. Thus, executives operate under constraints, particularly in policy areas of such importance as national security. Domestic political expediency does not always drive policy, however. Leaders make decisions about when to pursue their preferred aims and when to respond to the wishes of others in the system. Sometimes, of course, executives' and constituents' preferences correspond. But there are cases in which leaders might seek a shift in the policy approach.

An executive's conclusion that a new strategy is required comes from a transformation of his understanding of the value of an agreement and the extent of his nation's dependence on this rival.

Thus, to understand the potential for a negotiated resolution of the conflicts in Northern Ireland, the former Yugoslavia, and the Middle East, analysts should start by recognizing that the default position for any politician would be to demonize the other side. Within each society, many groups would support the position of predomination. Few families have been untouched by the violence, and everywhere military or paramilitary groups have been formed to "fight for justice." Thus, the typical approach at the bargaining table would be predomination; a party would typically resist all agreements with its historical adversary unless that accord were clearly in its favor. As we have seen in our study of arms control (and as is logically obvious), it is impossible for two opponents to reach an agreement if both predominate, if both seek relative gains from the agreement (unless one side is fooled about the actual content of the agreement). Thus, as long as leaders are weak and actors pursue the default strategy, there is no hope for negotiated solutions.

This examination of superpower bargaining behavior shows, however, that parties do not *have* to pursue a default strategy. They may try another approach at the table if a leader believes that it is warranted, based on his perception of the bargaining situation, and has the autonomy to convince constituents to follow his lead.[20] Thus, the potential for negotiated solutions expands as leaders have the domestic political strength to consider challenging the traditional wisdom. Moreover, if leaders can extend their understanding of security to constitute more than just safety from the hated other's incursions and to encompass the interconnection of the fates of the various ethnic and religious groups, including the challenges of economic development, environmental protection, and the reduction of daily violence, then they can find more reasons to work effectively with an opponent. Problems like poverty, pollution, and the insecurity caused by violence and the spillover from them generally affect all parties to the conflict and require mutual solutions. If leaders can reframe the problems they face to envision the resolution of such common difficulties (rather than the more typical conceptualization of a struggle over the control of territory or a battle for historical justice), then they may be able to rethink the kinds of strategies that are appropriate, perhaps even adopting cooperation, accommodation, or self-adjustment.

In the three conflict-prone regions mentioned here, there have been a few steps toward resolution recently, but the progress is tenuous. While Protestants and Catholics in Northern Ireland, along with the British and the Irish governments, achieved the beginnings of a peace settlement in 1994, the Irish Republican Army (IRA) broke its promised cease-fire in February 1996. Frustration on the part of some of the fighters with the pace of the progress and with British reversals led them to take this action. They blamed British prime minister John Major for not pursuing the peace fairly. At the time, the Conservative leader was just barely holding on to majority in Commons with the help of the Protestant Unionist parties, his popularity ratings were extremely low, and he had to call an election in a little more than a year. Given his particular vulnerability to the Unionists and the coming election, Major was in no position to advance innovative proposals and make concessions.[21]

With the resounding victory of Tony Blair in 1997, the momentum for a peaceful resolution initially shifted. Blair made peace and the negotiations a priority, and he did not have the links that his predecessor had to the Unionist factions. The new prime minister and his government were even willing to talk to Sinn Fein, the political wing of the IRA, about the conditions it would have to satisfy to return to the table. Given the popular distress with the renewed fighting as well as the realization of Blair's sincerity on this issue, the chance for progress in the peace talks appeared improved. But success at the table remains contingent upon obedience to the cease-fire, and the peace has not held. Despite the war-weariness of the majority of the population and the commitment of the British and Irish governments to peaceful resolution, the negotiators representing the Northern Irish parties have not been able (or perhaps willing) to stop the violence. As long as the attacks and the killings continue, the task of reaching an agreement at the table in which both sides cooperate remains enormously complex; players that are not party to or in favor of the negotiations can seek to derail accords with continued violence. The bloodshed makes it hard for Protestants and Catholics to view each other as reasonable bargaining partners and encourages each group to seek independent solutions (or retaliatory responses). Assuming the sincerity of the people at the negotiating table, the lack of autonomy of the faction leaders over the paramilitaries associated with their causes or over splinter groups opposing settlement means that the peace will be difficult to consolidate.[22]

In the Middle East, the breakdown of the peace process has followed as Yasir Arafat has lost control over various Palestinian groups. Thus, other nationalist organizations such as Hamas have sought to undermine the settlement by attacking Israeli civilians. These actions have fueled a response on the Israeli side that included the murder of the Prime Minister Rabin; tough action by Shimon Peres, Rabin's successor, who was trying to revise his reputation as a dove to position himself for the 1996 presidential elections; and the victory in that contest of a true hawk, Binyamin Netanyahu.

Netanyahu's preferred approach to the situation has been one akin to "peace through strength." Moreover, his position has been relatively shaky since his election. Not only was his margin of victory extremely narrow, but his administration has been plagued by scandals more recently. Neither his domestic position—his support problems and his dependence on parties that favor no concessions to the Palestinians and the expansion of settlements—nor his personal opinions seem to bode well for the peace process.[23]

Finally, although there is a kind of peace in Bosnia, the concern is that once the NATO troops are removed from the Balkans, the calm will evaporate and the region will again be enveloped in war. Unfortunately, there is not much reason to hope otherwise. The leaders of the region who brought the war are still quite powerful—some, like Milosevic and Tudjman, are officially still in place, while others, like Karadzic, exert control from behind the scenes—and their most important constituents still seem to be military and paramilitary forces. Thus, neither the inclinations of leaders nor those of their chief constituencies appear to be toward peace. Unless these states can be demilitarized and become more democratic and leaders can reconceptualize security can anyone expect the problems in this region to be resolved.[24]

Thus, security problems are not simply created or settled by great structural forces in the international system, nor does bureaucratic bargaining between officials at the highest levels of government determine states' responses. Instead, these challenges and their solutions depend much more on leaders, their perceptions of the international system, their relationship with their constituents, and the election or selection cycle. National leaders face constraints, both domestic and international, but they also have the opportunity to effect change—for better or worse. Those that have been willing to take the risks to reconceive national security—like Mikhail Gorbachev or Yitzhak Rabin—will be remembered as transformational leaders who made a better future possible for both the citizens of their countries and the people of the world.

Notes

Preface

1. "1994 Convention Update: *The New Agenda of World Politics*," *International Studies Newsletter* 20, nos. 2 & 3 (1993): 1–2; Dunbar Lockwood, "Nuclear Arms Control," in *SIPRI Yearbook 1993: World Armaments and Disarmament,* ed. SIPRI (New York: Oxford University Press, 1993), 549; and Adam Daniel Rotfeld, "Introduction: Parameters of Change," in *SIPRI Yearbook 1993: World Armaments and Disarmament,* ed. SIPRI (New York: Oxford University Press, 1993), 1–2.

2. Samuel B. Bacharach and Edward J. Lawler, *Bargaining: Power, Tactics, and Outcomes* (Washington, DC: Jossey-Bass, 1981), 61–62.

3. Important constructivist works include Nicholas Greenwood Onuf, *World of Our Making: Rules and Rule in Social Theory and International Relations* (Columbia: University of South Carolina Press, 1989); David Campbell, *Writing Security: United States Foreign Policy and the Politics of Identity* (Minneapolis: University of Minnesota Press, 1992); three articles by Alexander E. Wendt, "The Agent-Structure Problem in International Relations Theory," *International Organization* 41 (1987): 341–70; "Anarchy Is What States Make of It: The Social Construction of Power Politics," *International Organization* 46 (1992): 391–425; and "Constructing International Politics," *International Security* 20 (1995): 71–81; Audie Klotz, *Norms in International Relations: The Struggle against Apartheid* (Ithaca, NY: Cornell University Press, 1995); and Peter J. Katzenstein, ed., *The Culture of National Security: Norms and Identity in World Politics* (New York: Columbia University Press, 1996).

4. On the interplay of domestic and international politics, see Robert D. Putnam, "Diplomacy and Domestic Politics: The Logic of Two Level Games," *International Organization* 42 (1988): 427–60. Regarding strategy and interaction, see especially Robert Axelrod, *The Evolution of Cooperation* (New York: Basic Books, 1984); Robert O. Keohane, *After Hegemony: Cooperation and Discord in the World Political Economy* (Princeton, NJ: Princeton University Press, 1984); the articles collected in Kenneth Oye, ed., *Cooperation under Anarchy* (Princeton, NJ: Princeton University Press, 1986); and Arthur Stein, *Why Nations Cooperate: Circumstance and Choice in International Relations* (Ithaca: Cornell University Press, 1990).

5. These insights come from the work of Theodore J. Lowi, *The Personal President:*

Power Invested, Promise Unfulfilled (Ithaca, NY: Cornell University Press, 1985); Bruce Russett, *Controlling the Sword: The Democratic Governance of National Security* (Cambridge: Harvard University Press, 1990); and Thomas Risse-Kappen, "Public Opinion, Domestic Structure, and Foreign Policy in Liberal Democracies," *World Politics* 43 (1991): 479–512 on the American system and from Myron Rush, *The Rise of Khrushchev* (Washington, DC: Public Affairs Press, 1958), *Political Succession in the USSR* (New York: Columbia University Press, 1968), and *How Communist States Change Their Rulers* (Ithaca, NY: Cornell University Press, 1974); George Breslauer, *Khrushchev and Brezhnev as Leaders: Building Authority in Soviet Politics* (Boston: George Allen & Unwin, 1982); Bruce Parrott, "Soviet National Security under Gorbachev," *Problems of Communism* 37, no. 6 (1988): 1–36; and Philip Roeder, "Do New Soviet Leaders Really Make a Difference? Rethinking the 'Succession Connection' Hypothesis," *American Political Science Review* 79 (1984): 958–76, and *Red Sunset: The Failure of Soviet Politics* (Princeton: Princeton University Press, 1993) on the Soviet one.

6. Throughout this book I will use masculine pronouns and nouns to refer to American and Soviet leaders because in the postwar period, all such policymakers were men.

7. For more on the types of leadership, see James MacGregor Burns, *Leadership* (New York: Harper & Row, 1978), 19–20.

8. The leadership model predicts the strategies that the two countries will choose, the nature of the interaction, and the general likelihood, given these bargaining approaches, that the states will reach agreement. For instance, if one state seeks to predominate and another aspires to cooperate, the first country should offer proposals that will provide for the unequivocal improvement of its position, and the second should suggest deals that require the two countries to make mutual, equivalent compromises. Ultimately, these two goals (unequivocal victory and mutual compromise) cannot be achieved simultaneously, so the leadership model predicts that when a state that is playing a strategy of predomination is bargaining with another that is pursuing cooperation, an accord is impossible.

9. A notable exception is Steve Weber, *Cooperation and Discord in U.S.–Soviet Arms Control* (Princeton, NJ: Princeton University Press, 1991). Two more recent works, volumes edited by George, Farley, and Dallin and by Evans, Jacobson, and Putnam are very consciously theoretical (and had an important impact on this investigation) but are interested in security "cooperation" and broader issues of international bargaining. In general, analysis of arms control has mirrored the theoretical and empirical development in international relations. Many early works followed from a rational actor, economistic model. In the 1970s and early 1980s, analysts tended to view the subject from a bureaucratic or organizational politics perspective. By the mid-1980s, the study and practice of arms control fell on some hard times, with many authors (and policymakers) trying to defend (as well as explain) the phenomenon. For examples, see Hedley Bull, *The Control of the Arms Race* (New York: Praeger, 1965); Thomas Schelling and Morton Halperin, *Strategy and Arms Control* (New York: Twentieth Century Fund, 1961); Franklin Long and George Rathjens, eds., *Arms Defense Policy and Arms Control* (New York: W. W. Norton, 1976); Christer Jonsson, *Soviet Bargaining Behavior: The Nuclear Test Ban Case* (New York: Columbia University Press, 1979); Strobe Talbott, *Endgame: The Inside Story of SALT II* (New York: Harper & Row, 1979);

Gerard Smith, *Doubletalk: The Story of the First Strategic Arms Limitation Talks* (Garden City, NY: Doubleday, 1980); Albert Carnesale and Richard N. Haass, eds., *Superpower Arms Control: Setting the Record Straight* (Cambridge, MA: Ballinger, 1987); Alexander George, Philip J. Farley, and Alexander Dallin, eds., *U.S.–Soviet Security Cooperation: Achievements, Failures, and Lessons* (New York: Oxford University Press, 1988); Peter B. Evans, Harold K. Jacobson, and Robert D. Putnam, eds., *Double-Edged Diplomacy: International Bargaining and Domestic Politics* (Berkeley and Los Angeles: University of California Press, 1993).

10. Lewis Dunn, "New Nuclear Threats to U.S. Security," in *New Nuclear Nations: Consequences for U.S. Policy,* ed. Robert D. Blackwill and Albert Carnesale (New York: Council on Foreign Relations, 1993), 20–50; Michael Klare "Adding Fuel to Fires: The Conventional Arms Trade in the 1990s," in *World Security: Challenges for a New Century,* 2d ed., ed. Michael Klare and Dan Thomas (New York: St. Martin's Press, 1994), 134–54; and Michael Klare, "Deadly Convergence: The Arms Trade, Nuclear/Chemical/Missile Proliferation, and Regional Conflict in the 1990s," in *World Security: Trends and Challenges at Century's End,* ed. Michael Klare and Dan Thomas (New York: St. Martin's Press, 1991), 170–96.

11. Francis Fukuyama, *The End of History and the Last Man* (New York: Free Press, 1992). Many scholars argue that post–Cold War conflict is different; it involves intrastate confrontation, not interstate strife. See Michael Klare, "Redefining Security: The New Global Schisms," *Current History* 95 (1996): 353–58. Even in such situations, a group typically asserts the independence of a segment of the existing state and seeks to be treated as the leadership of a new country. Thus, negotiations between the two parties would involve two statelike entities that perceive each other to be adversaries.

12. Don Oberdorfer, *The Turn: From the Cold War to a New Era* (New York: Touchstone, 1992) 49–77.

Chapter 1

1. For the core of the realist position, see Hans Morgenthau, *Politics among Nations: The Struggle for Power and Peace,* 5th ed. (New York: Knopf, 1973); Kenneth Waltz, *Theory of International Politics* (Reading, MA: Addison-Wesley, 1979); and Joseph Grieco, "Anarchy and the Limits of Cooperation: A Realist Critique of the Newest Liberal Institutionalism," *International Organization* 42 (1988): 485–508. For the domestic politics approach, see the articles in Long and Rathjens, *Arms Defense Policy;* Marshall Shulman, "SALT and the Soviet Union," in *SALT: The Moscow Agreements and Beyond,* ed. Mason Willrich and John B. Rhinelander (New York: Free Press, 1974), 101–24; and several works by Strobe Talbott, including *Endgame* and *Deadly Gambits: The Reagan Administration and the Stalemate in Nuclear Arms Control* (New York: Vintage Books, 1985).

2. Bernard Bechhoefer, *Postwar Negotiations for Arms Control* (Washington, DC: Brookings Institution, 1961); Coit D. Blacker and Gloria Duffy, *International Arms Control: Issues and Agreements,* 2d ed. (Stanford, CA: Stanford University Press, 1984), 102–3.

3. Talbott, *Deadly Gambits;* Jonathan Haslam, *The Soviet Union and the Politics of Nuclear Weapons in Europe, 1969–1987* (Ithaca, NY: Cornell University Press, 1990).

4. Robert S. Norris et al., "Nuclear Weapons," *SIPRI Yearbook 1991: World Armaments and Disarmament,* ed. Stockholm International Peace Research Institute (New York: Oxford University Press, 1991), 25.

5. See especially Graham T. Allison and Frederic A. Morris, "Armaments and Arms Control: Exploring the Determinants of Military Weapons," in *Arms, Defense Policy, and Arms Control,* ed. Franklin A. Long and George W. Rathjens (New York: W. W. Norton, 1976), 99–130; John Steinbruner and Barry Carter, "Organizational and Political Dimensions of Strategic Posture: The Problems of Reform," in *Arms, Defense Policy, and Arms Control,* ed. Franklin A. Long and George W. Rathjens (New York: W. W. Norton, 1976), 131–54; Shulman, "SALT and Soviet Union"; Talbott, *Deadly Gambits;* Talbott, *Endgame;* and Glenn Seaborg, *Kennedy, Khrushchev, and the Test Ban.* (Berkeley and Los Angeles: University of California Press, 1981).

6. SALT II, however, was not ratified. While some contend that critics stopped this treaty from becoming law, others note that had President Carter managed the process better and moved the agreement toward ratification immediately after signing it, then the Senate would likely have approved the treaty. See Dan Caldwell, *The Dynamics of Domestic Politics and Arms Control: The SALT II Treaty Ratification Debate* (Columbia: University of South Carolina Press, 1991). Another interesting point about SALT II is that despite the opposition of many in the Reagan administration to the agreement, the president observed the provisions of the treaty until late 1986. Thus, despite their criticisms, many officials perceived the benefits of the accord.

7. One of the first to levy such criticism was Stephen Krasner, "Are Bureaucracies Important? (or Allison Wonderland)," *Foreign Policy,* no. 7 (1972): 165–79.

8. Important works in the bargaining literature include Thomas Schelling, *Arms and Influence* (New Haven: Yale University Press, 1966) and *The Strategy of Conflict* (Cambridge: Harvard University Press, 1960); Glenn Snyder and Paul Diesing, *Conflict among Nations: Bargaining and Decision-Making in International Crises* (Princeton, NJ: Princeton University Press, 1977); Howard Raiffa, *The Art and Science of Negotiation* (Cambridge, MA: Belknap Press of Harvard University Press, 1982); Bacharach and Lawler, *Bargaining;* Dean Pruitt, "Strategy in Negotiation," in *International Negotiation: Analysis, Approaches, Issues,* ed. Victor Kremenyuk (San Francisco: Jossey-Bass, 1991), 78–89; I. William Zartman, "The Structure of Negotiation," in *International Negotiation: Analysis, Approaches, Issues,* ed. Victor Kremenyuk (San Francisco: Jossey-Bass, 1991), 65–77; and Leonard Greenhalgh and Deborah I. Chapman. "Joint Decision Making: The Inseparability of Relationships and Negotiation," in *Negotiation as a Social Process,* ed. Roderick M. Kramer and David M. Messick (Thousand Oaks, CA: Sage Publications, 1995), 166–85.

9. Greenhalgh and Chapman, "Joint Decision Making," 167.

10. Grieco, "Anarchy and Limits"; Kenneth A. Oye, "Explaining Cooperation under Anarchy" in *Cooperation under Anarchy,* ed. Kenneth A. Oye (Princeton, NJ: Princeton University Press, 1986): 1–25; Robert Axelrod and Robert O. Keohane, "Achieving Cooperation under Anarchy: Strategies and Institutions," in *Cooperation under Anarchy,* ed. Kenneth A. Oye (Princeton, NJ: Princeton University Press, 1986): 226–54.

11. Keohane, *After Hegemony,* 51–54, esp. 51.

12. Ibid. Other important works on cooperation include Axelrod, *Evolution of Cooperation;* Matthew Evangelista, "Cooperation Theory and Disarmament Negotiations in the 1950s," *World Politics* 42 (1990): 502–28; Joanne Gowa, "Anarchy, Ego-

ism, and Third Images: *The Evolution of Cooperation* and International Relations," *International Organization* 40 (1986): 167–86; Grieco, "Anarchy and Limits"; Helen Milner, "International Theories of Cooperation among Nations: Strengths and Weaknesses," *World Politics* 44 (1992), 466–96; Deborah Welch Larson, "Crisis Prevention and the Austrian State Treaty," *International Organization* 41 (1987): 27–60; A. Stein, *Why Nations Cooperate;* and Janice Gross Stein, ed., *Getting to the Table: The Processes of International Prenegotiation* (Baltimore: Johns Hopkins University Press, 1989). In addition, Grieco's critique of this literature was particularly insightful and influential.

13. A state engages in dictate when it uses its own resources or threatens to resort to force to achieve a desired outcome. On the use of threats, see Schelling, *Arms and Influence,* 2, 7, 100, 103.

14. Bacharach and Lawler, *Bargaining,* 61–62.

15. Note that early bargaining theories from economics typically assumed that both parties were rational maximizers with similar interests. See Fred Charles Ikle, *How Nations Negotiate* (New York: Harper & Row, 1964); and Schelling, *Strategy of Conflict* and *Arms and Influence.* Greenhalgh and Chapman ("Joint Decision Making") provide an important critique. For the role that power can play in a relationship when interdependence is asymmetrical, see Robert O. Keohane and Joseph S. Nye, *Power and Interdependence: World Politics in Transition* (Boston: Little, Brown, 1977).

16. In his analysis of U.S.–Soviet security cooperation, Alexander George identified the "perception of mutual dependence" as an explanatory variable of state behavior. Throughout this text, I use the perception of alternatives and interdependence interchangeably, with the perception of many alternatives being consistent with the assessment of low levels of interdependence. Alexander George, "Incentives for U.S.–Soviet Security Cooperation and Mutual Adjustment," in *U.S.–Soviet Security Cooperation: Achievements, Failures, and Lessons,* ed. Alexander George, Philip J. Farley, and Alexander Dallin (New York: Oxford University Press, 1988), 641–54.

17. For the classic formulation of the goals of arms control, see Schelling and Halperin, *Strategy and Arms Control,* 1–6, 9–24.

18. See the focus on "capability" (power) and "credibility" (will) throughout Schelling, *Strategy of Conflict* and *Arms and Influence.*

19. Others who identify nonmilitary aspects of security include Joseph J. Romm, *Defining National Security: The Nonmilitary Aspects* (New York: Council on Foreign Relations Press, 1993) and the authors in the collections by Sean Lynn-Jones and Steven E. Miller, eds., *Global Dangers: Changing Dimensions of International Security* (Cambridge: MIT Press, 1995); and Michael Klare and Daniel Thomas, eds., *World Security: Challenges for a New Century,* 2d ed. (New York: St. Martin's Press, 1994).

20. While other concerns might seem to pale in comparison to a threat of superpower nuclear war, a larger meaning of security that recognizes that the United States and USSR faced other types of challenges and might seek to respond in different ways besides building up their military arsenals should not be logically excluded. A broader understanding of power and security is especially important if, for instance, we accept the notion that during the Cold War a taboo against using nuclear weapons developed. Joseph S. Nye, Jr., "Nuclear Learning and U.S.–Soviet Security Regimes", *International Organization* 41 (1987): 371–402.

21. The balance of power, ideological and domestic political differences, psycho-

logical pathologies, and the interaction between these variables overdetermined superpower conflict. But once the U.S.-USSR relationship existed as an adversarial one, a shared understanding among decision makers and publics within both societies about the nature of the opponent, the wealth and destructive forces produced specifically to deter or defeat the other party, and the practices of matching the other's ability to develop weapons, gain allies, recruit clients, and record scientific or social achievements sustained the hostility in the interaction. Wendt, "Constructing International Politics," 73.

22. Few students of bargaining note the importance of the perception of the opponent. One of the reasons for this omission is the tendency to rely on simple, game-theoretic representations of the bargaining problem. Students of social psychology and the political scientists who have incorporated insights from that field, however, have recognized the impact of the relationship and perceptions of it in the bargaining process. See Greenhalgh and Chapman, "Joint Decision Making," 166–85; and critics of the deterrence model—Robert Jervis, *Perception and Misperception in World Politics* (Princeton, NJ: Princeton University Press, 1976); Richard Ned Lebow, *Between Peace and War: The Nature of International Crisis* (Baltimore: Johns Hopkins University Press, 1981); Richard Ned Lebow and Janice Gross Stein, *We All Lost the Cold War* (Baltimore: Johns Hopkins University Press, 1994). Others who explore the role of images of the adversary in designing security policy include Franklyn Griffiths, "The Sources of American Conduct: Soviet Perspectives and their Policy Implications," *International Security* 9 (1984): 3–50; Richard K. Herrmann, *Perceptions and Behavior in Soviet Foreign Policy* (Pittsburgh: University of Pittsburgh Press, 1985); and Deborah Welch Larson, *Origins of Containment: A Psychological Explanation* (Princeton, NJ: Princeton University Press, 1985).

23. Robert D. Putnam, "Diplomacy and Domestic Politics," 427–60. Others who had previously noted this interplay include Blacker and Duffy, *International Arms Control;* and Shulman, "SALT and Soviet Union."

24. Putnam, "Diplomacy and Domestic Politics." Putnam's work inspired a collection of articles published in Evans, Jacobson, and Putnam, *Double-Edged Diplomacy;* and Jeffrey W. Knopf, "Beyond Two-Level Games: Domestic-International Interaction in the Intermediate Range Nuclear Forces Negotiations," *International Organization* 47 (1993): 599–628. While highly critical of two-level game adherents' inattention to what he calls "transboundary" connections (transgovernmental, transnational, and cross-level—between leaders and publics across countries), Knopf simply accepts the "COG" terminology. Still, Knopf identifies an important omission, and transboundary connections are taken into account here in the causal variables, "autonomy," "alternatives to," and "values of" agreements.

25. Putnam, "Diplomacy and Domestic Politics"; and Andrew Moravcsik, "Introduction: Integrating International and Domestic Theories of International Bargaining," in *Double-Edged Diplomacy: International Bargaining and Domestic Politics,* ed. Peter B. Evans, Harold K. Jacobson, and Robert D. Putnam (Berkeley and Los Angeles: University of California Press, 1993), 3–42.

26. Two contributors to the Evans, Jacobson, and Putnam, *Double-Edged Diplomacy* volume who are extremely mindful of the executive-constituent link are Jack Snyder, "East-West Bargaining Over Germany: The Search for Synergy in a Two-Level Game,"

104–27; and Janice Gross Stein, "The Political Economy of Security Agreements: The Linked Costs of Failure at Camp David," 77–103.

27. Thanks here to Steve McGovern for his help conceptualizing the American system.

28. Lowi has developed this argument throughout his career. See Theodore J. Lowi, "The Public Philosophy: Interest-Group Liberalism," *American Political Science Review* 61 (1967): 5–21; *The End of Liberalism: The Second Republic of the United States,* 2d ed. (New York: W. W. Norton, 1979); *Personal President.*

29. Richard Neustadt, *Presidential Power: The Politics of Leadership from FDR to Reagan* (New York: Free Press, 1990), 10.

30. Lowi, *Personal President;* Russett, *Controlling the Sword;* Risse-Kappen, "Public Opinion," 479–512.

31. The following discussion benefits from the works of Lowi, *End of Liberalism* and *Personal President;* William B. Quandt, "The Electoral Cycle and the Conduct of American Foreign Policy," in *American Foreign Policy,* 3d ed., ed. C. W. Kegley, Jr. and E. R. Wittkopf (New York: St. Martin's Press, 1987), 91–93; Russett, *Controlling the Sword;* and Miroslav Nincic, "U.S. Soviet Policy and the Electoral Connection," *World Politics* 42 (1990): 370–96.

32. Russett, *Controlling the Sword,* 13; Lowi, *Personal President,* 12.

33. The following works have had a critical impact on my understanding of the Soviet system: Rush, *Rise of Khrushchev, Political Succession,* and *Communist States;* Breslauer, *Khrushchev and Brezhnev;* Parrott, "Soviet National Security"; Roeder, "New Soviet Leaders" and *Red Sunset;* Jack Snyder, "The Gorbachev Revolution: A Waning of Soviet Expansionism?" *International Security* 12, no. 3 (1987–88): 93–131. While there are certainly distinctions among these works, all analyze the Soviet system as a "normal" one in which politicians must gain the support of key institutional actors to gain and remain in power.

34. See esp. Roeder, *Red Sunset,* 24–27, 76–77.

35. Jack Snyder, *The Myths of Empire: Domestic Politics and International Ambition* (Ithaca, NY: Cornell University Press, 1991) and "Gorbachev Revolution"; Roeder, *Red Sunset* and "New Soviet Leaders"; Stephen M. Meyer, "The Sources and Prospects of Gorbachev's New Political Thinking on Security," *International Security* 13 (1988): 124–63; Griffiths, "Sources of Conduct."

36. Roeder, *Red Sunset,* 210–45; George Breslauer, "Evaluating Gorbachev as Leader," *Soviet Economy* 5, no. 4 (1989): 299–340; Jerry F. Hough, "Gorbachev's Endgame," in *The Soviet System in Crisis,* ed. A. Dallin and G. Lapidus (Boulder, CO: Westview Press, 1991), 224–50; Hedrick Smith, *The New Russians* (New York: Avon Books, 1991), 419–29; David Remnick, *Lenin's Tomb: The Last Days of the Soviet Empire* (New York: Vintage Books, 1994), 219–25.

37. Others put more emphasis on the primacy of domestic politics. See, for instance, James M. Goldgeier, *Leadership Style and Soviet Foreign Policy: Stalin, Khrushchev, Brezhnev, and Gorbachev* (Baltimore: Johns Hopkins University Press, 1994).

38. The most influential leadership scholars include James MacGregor Burns, *Leadership*; and Bernard M. Bass, *Bass & Stogdill's Handbook of Leadership: Theory, Research, and Managerial Applications* (New York: Free Press, 1990). Others who have built on these works and have had an impact on this study include Valerie Bunce,

Do New Leaders Make a Difference? Executive Succession and Public Policy under Capitalism and Socialism (Princeton, NJ: Princeton University Press, 1981); Noel M. Tichy and Mary Anne Devanna, *The Transformational Leader* (New York: Wiley, 1990); Jameson W. Doig and Erwin C. Hargrove, Introduction to *Leadership and Innovation: A Biographical Perspective on Entrepreneurs in Government,* ed. Jameson W. Doig and Erwin C. Hargrove (Baltimore: Johns Hopkins University Press, 1987) 1–23; John W. Gardner, *On Leadership* (New York: Free Press, 1990); Neustadt, *Presidential Power;* Stephen Skowronek, *The Politics Presidents Make: Leadership from John Adams to George Bush* (Cambridge: Belknap Press of Harvard University Press, 1993); Oran R. Young, "Political Leadership and Regime Formation: On the Development of Institutions in International Society," *International Organization* 45, no. 3 (1991): 281–308.

39. Besides the "two-level game" analysts, others who have stressed this interaction and been influential here include Peter Gourevitch, "The Second Image Reversed: The International Sources of Domestic Politics," *International Organization* 32 (1978): 881–911; and Daniel Deudney and G. John Ikenberry, "International Sources of Soviet Change," *International Security* 16 (1991–92): 74–118.

Chapter 2

1. SIPRI, Appendix 18A, "Nuclear Explosions, 1945–1994," *SIPRI Yearbook 1995: Armaments, Disarmament, and International Security* (New York: Oxford University Press, 1995), Table 18A.2, 722.

2. Killian, *Sputnik, Scientists, and Eisenhower: A Memoir of the First Special Assistant to the President for Science and Technology* (Cambridge: MIT Press, 1977), 151; Seaborg, *Kennedy, Khrushchev,* 11; Divine, *Blowing on the Wind: The Nuclear Test Ban Debate, 1954–1960* (New York: Oxford University Press, 1978), 174–75.

3. The British were also participants in the negotiations, but they participated as junior partners.

4. At the 19th Party Congress in 1952, Stalin replaced the Politburo with a new, larger body called the Presidium. Rush, *Political Succession,* 50.

5. After Stalin died, Khrushchev became the first secretary of the Central Committee. This new title was in place until 1966, when the CPSU leader was again called the general secretary. Ibid., 64.

6. Rush, *Rise of Khrushchev,* 62–64; Linden, *Khrushchev and Soviet Leadership, 1957–1964* (Baltimore: Johns Hopkins University Press, 1966), 27–37. Also see Mikhail Heller and Aleksandr M. Nekrich, *Utopia in Power: The History of the Soviet Union From 1917 to the Present* (New York: Summit Books, 1986), 555.

7. For excessive praise of Khrushchev, see speeches at the 21st Party Congress collected in Leo Gruliow, ed., *Current Soviet Policies III: The Documentary Record of the Extraordinary 21st Congress of the CPSU* (New York: Columbia University Press, 1960), by Podgorny, 74; Furtseva, 90, 91; Gromyko, 95; Suslov, 99, 100; Mukhitdinov, 104, 105; Pospelov, 125; Mikoyan, 128; Ignatov, 137; and Kuusinen, 160. Also see Rush, *Political Succession,* 108–13 on the limits of Khrushchev's power.

8. On the differences in Soviet leadership politics after Stalin, see especially Rush,

Political Succession. On the importance of policy as a component of a leader's authority, see Breslauer, *Khrushchev and Brezhnev*, and James G. Richter, *Khrushchev's Double Bind: International Pressures and Domestic Coalition Politics* (Baltimore: Johns Hopkins University Press, 1994). Richter, in particular, provides an excellent account of the interaction between domestic and international policies as part of Khrushchev's formula for rule. Ultimately, his penchant for innovation, or what became known as "harebrained schemes" in the Soviet lexicon, resulted in his downfall because he was not paying attention to the voices of other strong players in the Soviet system. See William J. Tompson, "The Fall of Nikita Khrushchev," *Soviet Studies* 43 (1991): 1101–21.

9. Vladislav Zubok and Constantine Pleshakov, *Inside the Kremlin's Cold War: From Stalin to Khrushchev* (Cambridge: Harvard University Press, 1996), 182–87; William Curti Wohlforth, *The Elusive Balance: Power and Perceptions During the Cold War* (Ithaca, NY: Cornell University Press, 1993), 140–41.

10. "Press Conference with N. S. Khrushchev, Chairman of the Council of Ministers," *Current Digest of the Soviet Press* [*CDSP*] 12, no. 23 (1960): 6; "Concluding Remarks by Comrade N. S. Khrushchev at a Meeting of the USSR Supreme Soviet," *CDSP* 12, no. 19 (1960): 4; Linden, *Khrushchev and Soviet Leadership*, 94; Michel Tatu, *Power in the Kremlin: From Khrushchev to Kosygin*, trans. Helen Katel (New York: Viking Press, 1970), 41; N. S. Khrushchev, *Khrushchev Remembers: The Last Testament*, vol. 2, trans. Strobe Talbott (Boston: Little, Brown & Co., 1974), 362, 374; Anatoly Dobrynin, *In Confidence: Moscow's Ambassador to America's Six Cold War Presidents* (New York: Times Books, 1995), 41–42; Michael R. Beschloss, *May Day: Eisenhower, Khrushchev, and the U-2 Affair* (New York: Harper & Row, 1986), 273–304; Dwight D. Eisenhower, *Waging Peace, 1956–1961: The White House Years* (Garden City, NY: Doubleday, 1965), 442–46.

11. Stephen Ambrose, *Eisenhower*, vol. 2: *The President* (New York: Simon & Schuster, 1984), 343, 370, 388–91, 580.

12. "Control Figures for Development of the USSR National Economy, 1959–1965," *Current Soviet Policies III*, 25. Also Zubok and Pleshakov, *Inside Kremlin's Cold War,* 185–86; Wohlforth, *Elusive Balance,* 139–41; Dobrynin, *In Confidence,* 36.

13. N. S. Khrushchev, "Report to the XX Party Congress, February 14, 1956," in *The International Situation and Soviet Foreign Policy: Reports of Soviet Leaders,* ed. Myron Rush (Columbus, OH: Charles E. Merrill, 1970), 182; "Declaration of the Conference of Representatives of Communist and Workers' Parties of Socialist Countries, Held in Moscow, November 14–16, 1957," *CDSP* 9, no. 47 (1957) 3–4; "Report to the XXI (Extraordinary) Party Congress," *Current Soviet Policies III,* 58; and "Control Figures," 25. Also Arnold Horelick and Myron Rush, *Strategic Power and Soviet Foreign Policy* (Chicago: University of Chicago Press, 1966).

14. Khrushchev quoted in "Report," 58, emphasis added; quotation from Seven Year Plan in "Control Figures," *Current Soviet Policies III,* 25. On the policy of deception, see Horelick and Rush, *Strategic Power,* esp. 29; and Wohlforth, *Elusive Balance,* 159. For the socialist states' formulation, see "Declaration," 3–4; on Malinovsky's lie, "Speech by R. Ya. Malinovsky, Chelyabinsk Election District, Russian Republic, January 15, 1960," *CDSP* 12, no. 3 (1960): 13–14; and Desmond Ball, *Politics and Force Levels: The Strategic Missile Program of the Kennedy Administration* (Berkeley and Los

Angeles: University of California Press, 1980), 50–51, 55; who contended that the USSR had only two ICBMs on its test sites during 1960 and no other operational intercontinental missiles.

15. Khrushchev, "Report to XX Congress," 182. See also "Declaration"; "Report to the XXI (Extraordinary Party) Congress." Khrushchev revealed that some communists were uncomfortable with the strategy of negotiations in "Disarmament Is the Path toward Strengthening Peace," *CDSP* 12, no. 2 (1960): 3–16, 23. Zubok and Pleshakov make a similar argument in *Inside Kremlin's Cold War,* 182–88.

16. "Concluding Remarks by Comrade N. S. Khrushchev at 21st Party Congress February 5, 1959," *Current Soviet Policies III,* 203. Also see Mikoyan's speech in the same volume, 128–32.

17. One of the more prominent skeptics was Defense Minister Malinovsky. Compare his speech to the Congress in Gruliow, *Current Soviet Policies III,* 151–53, with those of Khrushchev in the same volume. Other evidence that there was high-level opposition within the USSR to Khrushchev's policy of negotiating with the West can be found in G. Ratiani, "Who is Frightened by Forthcoming Meetings?" *CDSP* 11, no. 34 (1959): 11–12.

18. Linden, *Khrushchev and Soviet Leadership,* 90–97; Tatu, *Power in Kremlin,* 41; Herbert Dinerstein, Leon Goure, and Thomas Wolfe, "U.S. Editors' Analytical Introduction," in *Soviet Military Strategy,* ed. V. D. Sokolovskii (Englewood Cliffs, NJ: Prentice Hall, 1963), 14; Zubov and Pleshakov, *Inside Kremlin's Cold War,* 203–4; Richter, *Khrushchev's Double Bind,* 132–33.

19. Richard A. Melanson, "The Foundations of Eisenhower's Foreign Policy: Continuity, Community, and Consensus," in *Reevaluating Eisenhower: American Foreign Policy in the 1950s,* ed. Richard A. Melanson and David Mayers (Urbana: University of Illinois Press, 1987), esp. 38–43; Ambrose, *Eisenhower,* 130–33, 404, 525.

20. Matthew Evangelista argues that Eisenhower and Dulles were opposed to agreement from 1955 to August 1957 in "Cooperation Theory," 502–28. See also Ambrose, *Eisenhower,* 131–32, 256–57.

21. Evangelista, "Cooperation Theory," 519; Blacker and Duffy, *International Arms Control,* 97; Bechhoefer, *Postwar Negotiations,* 405–6. While Ambrose's account provides ample evidence to indicate that the president was seeking relative gains from any agreement, he also maintains that the president "remained committed to disarmament" in his first term. Ambrose, *Eisenhower,* 343.

22. Zubok and Pleshakov, *Inside Kremlin's Cold War,* 192. The result of a study of Third World and Western public opinion is provided in "The Impact of Sputnik on the Stand of the U.S. versus the USSR," Report 52, December 31, 1957, Office of Research and Intelligence [INR], USIA, WHOF, OSA NSA, NSCS, Briefing Notes Subseries, File name: United States Information Agency (1) [1954–1960] Box 18, DDEL, ii. The Allied reaction can also be found in "Western European Opinion Trends on U.S. and Soviet Strength," National Security Files [NSF]—Subjects: Opinion Polls, Box 302, John F. Kennedy Library, Dorchester, MA [JFKL], 1–2.

23. Bechhoefer, *Postwar Negotiations,* 431–32, 445; Zubok and Pleshakov, *Inside Kremlin's Cold War,* 193.

24. Divine, *Blowing on the Wind,* 174–75; Ambrose, *Eisenhower,* 447; Killian, *Sputnik, Scientists, and Eisenhower,* 152. Tables 7 and 8 also show that the Soviet public re-

lations strategy was more successful in some places than others. While citizens of the United States and Western Europe were impressed with Soviet nuclear prowess, they were not convinced that its superiority would hold. Moreover, Westerners tended to be more skeptical of the Soviet commitment to peace.

25. Memorandum from Eisenhower to John Foster Dulles, March 21, 1958, ACWF, DDES, Box 31, File name: DDE Dictation, 3/58, Dwight D. Eisenhower Library [DDEL], 1–2. Ambrose stresses that after the Suez Crisis in 1956, the president became particularly concerned with the Third World's impression of the United States. Ambrose, *Eisenhower,* 376–80.

26. "MCP, March 24, 1958," ACWF, DDES, Box 31, File name: Staff Notes, 3/58 (1), DDEL, 1.

27. Ibid., 1–2. After Sputnik, the American public was out of step with the rest of the world. U.S. citizens were opposed to the cessation of testing while everyone else opposed the continuation of the tests. See George W. Gallup, *The Gallup Poll: Public Opinion 1935–1971,* vol. 2 (New York: Random House, 1972), 1487–88, 1541, 1552.

28. "MCP, March 24, 1958," ACWF, DDES, Box 31, File name: Staff Notes, 3/58 (1), DDEL, 3, emphasis added.

29. The quotations here are Eisenhower's. Ibid., 3–4, emphasis added. This proposal was for troop and weapons reductions.

30. Telegram, Dulles to Macmillan, Re Nuclear Matters, 8/21/58, ACWF, Dulles-Herter Series [DHS], Box 8, File name: Dulles, August, 1958, DDEL, 1–2. Macmillan was initially an opponent to the test ban talks. Prior to his reelection campaign in 1959, the British prime minister became an advocate of the cessation of nuclear explosions, just like the majority of Britons.

31. Bechhoefer, *Postwar Negotiations,* 492.

32. "MCP, March 24, 1958," ACWF, DDES, Box 31, 5. The British and the French had expressed their disinterest in any kind of test ban while they lagged behind in the understanding of nuclear phenomena. Ike knew that to get their cooperation to pursue the cessation of tests, he would have to be able to share American secrets with them. At the time, however, U.S. law prohibited that action.

33. "Report of the NSC Ad Hoc Working Group on the Technical Feasibility of a Cessation of Nuclear Testing," March 27, 1958, WHOF, OSA NSA, NSCS, Box 2, File name: [Atomic Testing] Killian Report—Technical Feasibility of Cessation of Nuclear Testing [1958], DDEL, ii, iii.

34. Secretary Quarles expressed this opinion in "MCP, March 24, 1958," ACWF, DDES, Box 31, File name: Staff Notes, March 1958 (1), DDEL, 6. Similarly, AEC Chairman Strauss mentioned the negative attitudes in "MCP, June 9, 1958," ACWF, DDES, Box 33, File name: June 1958: Staff Notes (3), DDEL, 2.

35. Gallup, *Gallup Poll,* vol. 2, 1487–88, 1541, 1552. Opponents of the test ban within the administration continued to inform the president of public opposition. See, for example, "MCP, June 9, 1958," ACWF, DDES, Box 33, File name: June 1958—Staff Notes (3), 2.

36. "Memorandum for the Chairman, Ad Hoc Panel of Nuclear Test Cessation [Killian] from Donald A. Quarles, Secretary of Defense, Subject: the Effects of a total Suspension or Cessation of Nuclear Testing, 3/12/58," WHOF, OSA NSA, NSCS, Briefing Notes Subseries, Box 2, File name: "[Atomic Testing] Killian Report—Technical

Feasibility of Cessation of Nuclear Testing [1958]," DDEL, 1–2; "Memorandum on the Discussion at the 361st Meeting of the National Security Council, 4/3/58," prepared by S. Everett Gleason, ACWF, NSCS, Box 10, File name: 361st Meeting of the NSC, 4/3/58, 4; "Summary of Meeting Held in the State Department from 4:00 to 6:20 pm on August 13," WHOF, OSA NSA, NSCS, Briefing Notes Subseries, Box 2, File name: [Atomic Testing] Suspension of Nuclear Testing and Surprise Attack (2) [1958– 60], DDEL, 1–2; and "MCP, May 19, 1959," ACWF, DDES, Box 41, File name: Staff Notes—May 1959 (2), 3.

37. Bechhoefer, *Postwar Negotiations,* 453–57; Seaborg, *Kennedy, Khrushchev,* 11–15. The USSR denied that verifying a ban was a problem. See "Soviet Government Memorandum to the U.S. Government," *CDSP* 10, no. 26 (1958): 15; and "Soviet Government Memorandum of July 7, 1958 to the U.S. Government," *CDSP* 10, no. 28 (1958): 11.

38. Bechhoefer, *Postwar Negotiations,* 491–92.

39. Ibid., 492; Adam Ulam, *Expansion and Coexistence: The History of Soviet Foreign Policy, 1917–1967* (New York: Praeger, 1968), 619; Horelick and Rush, *Strategic Power,* 50–57.

40. U.S. Disarmament Administration, "U.S. Working Paper on New Seismic Data, January 5, 1959", *Geneva Conference on the Discontinuance of Nuclear Weapons Tests: History and Analysis of Negotiations* (Washington, DC: Department of State Publication 7258, 1961), 331; Bechhoefer, *Postwar Negotiations,* 494–95.

41. "MCP, January 5, 1959," ACWF, DDES, Box 38, File name: Staff Notes—1/59 (2), 1.

42. On electoral concerns, see "MCP, March 24, 1960," ACWF, DDES, Box 48, File name: Staff Notes—March 1960 (1), 2. Ambrose, *Eisenhower,* 523–25, 541. Dying of cancer, Dulles had resigned his post, and Eisenhower appointed Herter on April 18, 1959. Dulles passed away a little more than a month later.

43. "Report," *CSP,* 60; "Speech by Mikoyan," *CDSP,* 58–59; "A. I. Mikoyan's Press Conference," *CDSP* 11, no. 4 (1959): 28. For Khrushchev's rhetoric and his portrayals of American leaders, see, for example, "Press Conference of Comrade N. S. Khrushchev, Chair of USSR Council of Ministers," *CDSP* 11, no. 12 (1959): 12–14; "Our Friendship Will Endure Forever—Cordial Meetings of USSR Party and Government Delegates with the Working People," *CDSP* 11, no. 21 (1959): 13.

44. See Bechhoefer, *Postwar Negotiations,* 495; Seaborg, *Kennedy, Khrushchev,* 19–20; "Report of the Technical Working Group on the Detection and Identification of High Altitude Nuclear Explosions, July 10, 1959," *Geneva Conference,* 367–74.

45. Seaborg, *Kennedy, Khrushchev,* 21; U.S. Disarmament Administration, "Report, July 10, 1959," *Geneva Conference,* 390–95. See Bechhoefer, *Postwar Negotiations,* 495; Seaborg, *Kennedy, Khrushchev,* 19–21; U.S. Disarmament Administration, "Report, July 10, 1959," *Geneva Conference,* 367–74; and U.S. Disarmament Administration, "Report of Technical Working Group II on Seismic Problems, December 18, 1959," *Geneva Conference.*

46. "Mission of Peace," *CDSP* 11, no. 39 (1959): 4; "A Visit That Will Go Down in History," *CDSP* 11, no. 39 (1959): 13; "Long Live Reason, May Darkness Vanish," *CDSP* 11, no. 40 (1959): 12; "On the International Situation," *CDSP* 11, no. 44 (1959): 3–11; "The Soviet Press Should Be the Strongest and Most Militant! Speech by N. S.

Khrushchev at the Kremlin Reception for Soviet Journalists on November 14, 1959," *CDSP* 11, no. 46 (1959): 4; Ambrose, *Eisenhower,* 542.

47. "MCP, December 29, 1959," ACWF, DDES, Box 46, File name: Staff Notes—12/59, 1–3.

48. U.S. Disarmament Administration, *Geneva Conference,* 100; U.S. Disarmament Administration, *Documents on Disarmament, 1960,* 90–91; Bechhoefer, *Postwar Negotiations,* 500.

49. "MCP, March 24, 1960," ACWF, DDES, Box 48, File name: Staff Notes—March 1960 (1), 1–2.

50. Khrushchev, "Disarmament Is Path," 3–16, 23; Linden, *Khrushchev and Soviet Leadership,* 93; Wohlforth, *Elusive Balance,* 145–48.

51. Wohlforth, *Elusive Balance,* 145–48; Eisenhower, *Waging Peace,* 442–46; Beschloss, *May Day,* 243–72; Ambrose, *Eisenhower,* 570.

52. See "Mighty Demonstration of Unity and Friendship," *CDSP* 12, no. 21 (1960): 3–4; Beschloss, *May Day,* 273–304; and Khrushchev, *Khrushchev Remembers,* vol. 2, 362, 374.

53. Kistiakowsky quoted in Ambrose, *Eisenhower,* 580. On page 570, Ambrose wrote, "His [Eisenhower's] own desire to make a breakthrough in the arms race, as his final act as a world leader, was greater than ever [in early 1960]."

54. For the documentary evidence of these negotiations, see U.S. Disarmament Administration, *Geneva Conference,* 100–122. Regarding Khrushchev, domestic political considerations were on his mind, too, since the U-2 had demonstrated that he had been wrong. See Richter, *Khrushchev's Double Bind,* 132; Zubok and Pleshakov, *Inside Kremlin's Cold War,* 203–9.

55. Zubok and Pleshakov, *Inside Kremlin's Cold War,* 208.

Chapter 3

1. Again, the British were also a party to the negotiations, but the focus here is on bargaining between the alliance leader, the United States, and the USSR.

2. As quoted in Richter, *Khrushchev's Double Bind,* 132.

3. For the details of Khrushchev ascendance, see Rush, *Rise of Khrushchev;* Linden, *Khrushchev and Soviet Leadership,* 27–37; and Breslauer, *Khrushchev and Brezhnev,* 50–80. For evidence of the cult, see the text of the speeches by Marshall V. I. Chuikov and Major General Saburov provided in "Immortal Feat of Soviet People: Meeting of Representatives of the Moscow Public to Mark the Twentieth Anniversary of the Beginning of the Great Patriotic War," *CDSP* 13, no. 25 (1961): 5–6; Marshal Yeremenko, "Twentieth Anniversary of the Battle on the Volga: In the Days of the Heroic Epic," *CDSP* 15, no. 4 (1963): 5–6; "Motion Pictures: The Great Battle on the Volga," *CDSP* 15, no. 4 (1963): 7; and "Colonel Starinov's Secret: An Unknown Page in a Heroic Struggle," *CDSP* 15, no. 6 (1963): 21–23.

4. For Khrushchev's attacks against the Albanians, see "Twenty-Second Congress of the CPSU: Report of the Central Committee of the CPSU to the Twenty-Second Party Congress—Report by Comrade N. S. Khrushchev, First Secretary of the Central Committee, October 17, 1961," Part 4, *CDSP* 13, no. 43 (1961): esp. 5; and "Concluding Remarks by Comrade N. S. Khrushchev, First Secretary of the Party Central Committee at

the Twenty-Second Party Congress, October 27, 1961," *CDSP* 13, no. 46 (1961): esp. 26. For the removal of Stalin's body, see "Announcement," *CDSP* 13, no. 45 (1961): 20. Former Soviet policymakers and scholars have corroborated this argument about Khrushchev's position. See especially Gromyko's, Burlatsky's, and Shaknazarov's comments in James G. Blight and David Welch, eds., *On the Brink: Americans and Soviets Reexamine the Cuban Missile Crisis* (New York: Hill & Wang, 1989), 90, 80, 235, 237.

5. Zubok and Pleshakov, *Inside Kremlin's Cold War,* 268–69; "The Present International Situation and the Foreign Policy of the Soviet Union: Report by Comrade N. S. Khrushchev at the Session of the USSR Supreme Soviet," *CDSP* 14, no. 51 (1962): 3–8; "From Positions of Reason," *CDSP* 14, no. 43 (1962): 12; "Reason Triumphs," *CDSP* 14, no. 43 (1962): 13; William E. Griffith, *The Sino-Soviet Rift* (Cambridge: MIT Press, 1964).

6. Neustadt, *Presidential Power.*

7. "Memorandum for the President from Theodore C. Sorensen, Subject: Atomic Testing and the Political Atmosphere, January 25, 1962," NSF, Nuclear Weapons Series, Box 299, JFKL, File name: Nuclear Weapons Testing, 1/23/62–1/26/62, JFKL, 1. Also see Theodore C. Sorensen, *Kennedy* (New York: Harper & Row, 1965), 308–9 and 339–42.

8. Zubok and Pleshakov found this document and provide the excerpt in, *Inside the Kremlin's Cold War,* 239.

9. Dobrynin, *In Confidence,* 45. See also Zubok and Pleshakov, *Inside Kremlin's Cold War,* 236, 243; William Taubman, "The Correspondence: Khrushchev's Motives and his Views of Kennedy," *Problems of Communism* 41 (special edition, 1992): 15. According to Beschloss, Kennedy's willingness to accede to Soviet claims of parity in Vienna 1961 reinforced Khrushchev's assessment of his realism and Kennedy's willingness to compromise. Michael R. Beschloss, *The Crisis Years: Kennedy and Khrushchev, 1960–1963* (New York: HarperCollins, 1991), 202. See also Wohlforth, *Elusive Balance,* 177.

10. See "Answers by Comrade N. S. Khrushchev to questions of Hans Thirring, Austrian Professor," *CDSP* 13, no. 1 (1961): 13; "Concluding Remarks," 24. Other examples of Soviet bluster include N. S. Khrushchev, "Great Fraternity of Free Peoples: Bulgaria Ceremoniously Greets Soviet Guests," *CDSP* 14, no. 20 (1962): 6; "Speech by Malinovsky," 19–22; "Voters Meet Candidate for Deputy to the USSR Supreme Soviet," *CDSP* 14, no. 13 (1962): 5–6; "General and Complete Disarmament Is the Guarantee of Peace and Security for All Peoples," *CDSP* 14, no. 27 (1962): 3; and "Marxism-Leninism Is Our Banner," *CDSP* 15, no. 24 (1963): 7.

11. Dobrynin, *In Confidence,* 36; Wohlforth, *Elusive Balance,* 139–41. For the general importance of strategic deception in Khrushchev's policy, see Horelick and Rush, *Strategic Power.*

12. Zubok and Pleshakov stress, however, that Khrushchev was worried about the Chinese attempts to argue that their system was more appropriate for many newly independent states. See their discussion of the Sino-Soviet relationship (*Inside Kremlin's Cold War,* 210–35).

13. According to Richter (*Khrushchev's Double Bind,* 157), Khrushchev's "arguments for a change in policy direction depended less on the claim . . . that the West had forsaken the politics of strength, and more on the dangers of nuclear war that confronted

both sides." Regardless of the audience, thereafter the first secretary "consistently argued that war could bring no victory."

14. The Chinese and their mouthpiece, the Albanians, had asserted that the Soviets should have gone to war over Cuba because the United States was a "paper tiger" and "the balance of forces on the world scene on the whole is on the side of socialism and revolutionary peoples, not of imperialism and its lackeys." "To the CC of the CPSU," *CDSP* 15, no. 11 (1963): 4. For Soviet justifications of their actions in Cuba, see "Tenth Congress of the Italian Communist Party: Speech by Comrade Frol Kozlov, head of CPSU Delegation," *CDSP* 14, no. 49 (1962): 7; "Present International Situation," 3; and "Speech by Comrade N. S. Khrushchev at the Sixth Congress of Socialist Unity Party of Germany," part 2, *CDSP* 15, no. 4 (1963): 13.

15. For Kennedy's ideas, see State of the Union, as well as his Inaugural Address and Special Message on the Defense Budget, March 28. Also see McGeorge Bundy, "The Presidency and the Peace," *Foreign Affairs* 42, no. 3 (1964): 355, 357; and Memorandum to the President from William Foster, March 3, 1962, Presidential Office Files [POF], Subject Series, Disarmament—Nuclear Test Ban Negotiations, Box 100, JFKL, File name: ENDC: U.S. Position, March 3, 1962, 2.

16. See John F. Kennedy, *Strategy of Peace,* ed. Allan Nevins (New York: Harper & Brothers, 1960); M. B. Schnapper, ed., *New Frontiers of the Kennedy Administration: The Texts of the Task Force Reports Prepared for the President* (Washington, DC: Public Affairs Press, 1961); and Rockefeller Brothers Fund, *Prospect for America: The Rockefeller Panel Reports* (Garden City, NY: Doubleday, 1961). Several future members of the Kennedy administration helped write *New Frontiers* and the *Prospect for America,* including Jerome Wiesner, Chester Bowles, and Dean Rusk.

17. "Special Message on the Defense Budget, March 28, 1961" *Congressional Quarterly Almanac* [*CQ Almanac*]*, 1961* (Washington, DC: Congressional Quarterly Press, 1961), 902–6. For evidence that the administration hoped that the United States and the USSR could work together, see "Notes on the Discussion of the Thinking of the Soviet Leadership, Cabinet Room, February 11, 1961," National Security Files [NSF], Countries Subseries—USSR, Box 176, File name: General, 2/2/61–2/14/61, John F. Kennedy Library, Dorchester, MA [JFKL], 2; Arthur M. Schlesinger, *A Thousand Days: John F. Kennedy in the White House* (Boston: Houghton Mifflin, 1965), 369–72; and Sorensen, *Kennedy,* 543–49.

18. See "Special Message on the Defense Budget," *CQ Almanac, 1961,* 902.

19. "State of the Union Message, 1961" *CQ Almanac, 1961,* 858–59. Seaborg also provides notes from a meeting of the president with members of Congress in which Kennedy identified his concern with proliferation. Seaborg, *Kennedy, Khrushchev,* 48. After the Cuban Missile Crisis, Kennedy's worries about proliferation appear to have deepened. "Remarks of President Kennedy to the NSC Meeting of January 22, 1963," NSF, Meetings and Memoranda, NSC Meetings, 1963, File name: No. 508, January 22, 1963, JFKL, 5 and "Instructions for the Honorable W. Averell Harriman," NSF, Meetings and Memoranda, NSC Meetings, 1963, File name: No. 515, July 9, 1963, JFKL, 1.

20. "The Only Sane Course Is Peaceful Coexistence: On U.S. President Kennedy's State of the Union Message," *CDSP* 13, no. 5 (1961): 30. American Ambassador Llewelyn Thompson also noted that the Soviet press "takes a cautiously hopeful view

of future U.S.-Soviet relations." See Incoming Telegram to the Secretary of State from Thompson, #1814, February 1, 1961, NSF, Countries—USSR Series, Box 176, File name: General 1/1/61–1/21/61, JFKL, 1.

21. There was room for compromise on the issues of how to allow the Soviets to inspect American nuclear devices under the auspices of the seismic research program, how to preserve the ability to conduct peaceful nuclear explosions under a test ban regime, how to determine the number of necessary on-site inspections, and how many inspections to require per year for verification of compliance. See Seaborg, *Kennedy, Khrushchev,* 36–43, for his accounts and notes of meetings.

22. United States Arms Control and Disarmament Agency [U.S. ACDA], "Statement by the Soviet Representative (Tsarapkin) at the Geneva Conference on the Discontinuance of Nuclear Weapons Tests, March 21, 1961," *Documents on Disarmament [DD], 1961* (Washington, DC: U.S. Government Printing Office, 1962), 42–55.

23. As in the previous negotiations, the Soviets were asking for a four- to five-year moratorium, a high-altitude test ban, and fewer control posts on Soviet territory. See chapter 2.

24. "Statement by the United States Representative (Dean) at the Geneva Conference on the Discontinuance of Nuclear Weapons tests, March 21, 1961," *DD, 1961.,* 55–65; U.S. Disarmament Administration, *Geneva Conference,* 126–27. See "Anglo-American Draft Treaty on the Discontinuance of Nuclear Weapons Tests, April 18, 1961," *DD, 1961,* 82–126, for text of the document; "Statement by the Soviet Representative (Tsarapkin) at the Geneva Conference, April 28, 1961," *DD, 1961,* 134–41, for the Soviet reaction; and Seaborg, *Kennedy, Khrushchev,* 57–58 for discussion.

25. For evidence of the American interest in mutual concession making, see "Notes on the Discussion of the Thinking of the Soviet Leadership, Cabinet Room, February 11, 1961," NSF, Countries Subseries—USSR, Box 176, File name: General, 2/2/61–2/14/61, JFKL, 2. Also see "Soviet *Aide-Memoire* to the United States Regarding the Nuclear Test Ban Negotiations, 6/4/61," *DD, 1961,* 162–66; Schlesinger, *Thousand Days,* 369–72; Sorensen, *Kennedy,* 543–49; Seaborg, *Kennedy, Khrushchev,* 67; and Beschloss, *Crisis Years,* 213–36.

26. On the Soviet performance in Geneva in early 1961, see "Clouds over Geneva," *CDSP* 13, no. 14, 28; "What is Happening at the Geneva Conference," *CDSP* 13, no. 15, 26; Zubok and Pleshakov, *Inside Kremlin's Cold War,* 241–48; and Dobrynin, *In Confidence,* 43–46. On American reactions to that behavior and subsequent actions, see Schlesinger, *Thousand Days,* 369–72; Sorensen, *Kennedy,* 543–49; "Radio and TV Address," POF, Countries—USSR, General, 3/61–7/61, Box 125a, JFKL, 1–8; Seaborg, *Kennedy, Khrushchev,* 76–78; and Beschloss, *Crisis Years,* 236.

27. Letter from Harold Brown, Director of Defense Research and Engineering, to Jerome Wiesner, August 3, 1961, NSF, Nuclear Weapons Subseries, File name: Nuclear Weapons Testing, July 16, 1961–August 9, 1961, Box 299, JFKL, 1–2; Memorandum for the President from McGeorge Bundy, August 8, 1961, Subject: The NSC Meeting on Nuclear Tests, NSF, Nuclear Weapons Subseries, File name: Nuclear Weapons Testing, July 16, 1961–August 9, 1961, Box 299, JFKL, 2–3. See also Seaborg, *Kennedy, Khrushchev,* 74–75.

28. The United States had increased its forces in Europe in response to the Soviet actions in Berlin. On the building of the Berlin Wall, see Beschloss, *Crisis Years,* 266–73;

Zubok and Pleshakov, *Inside Kremlin's Cold War,* 250–53; and Richter, *Khrushchev's Double Bind,* 142–43. See also "Statement by the Government on the Resumption of Nuclear Weapons Tests, August 30, 1961," *DD, 1961,* 337.

29. Seaborg, *Kennedy, Khrushchev,* 82–84, 87. Neither the United States nor the USSR had the capability of testing such enormous devices underground.

30. Ibid., 114, 117.

31. See the text of the speech, "Address by Deputy Secretary of Defense Gilpatric to the Business Council, 10/21/61," *DD, 1961,* 544–50. Hilsman contends that the administration decided that Gilpatric, a deputy assistant secretary of defense, should make the announcement since he was senior enough to be taken seriously but not so important a personage to be considered threatening. Roger Hilsman, *To Move a Nation: The Politics of Foreign Policy in the Administration of John F. Kennedy* (Garden City, NY: Doubleday, 1967), 163.

32. "Soviet Draft Agreement, November 28, 1961," *DD, 1961,* 664–68; "Statement by the Soviet Representative (Tsarapkin) at the Geneva Conference, November 28, 1961" and "Statement by the Soviet Representative (Tsarapkin) at the Geneva Conference, December 5, 1961," *DD, 1961,* 674–77, 703–6; "Soviet Draft Agreement on the Discontinuance of Nuclear and Thermonuclear Weapons Tests, November 28, 1961," *DD, 1961,* 664–68; "Statement by United States Representative (Stevenson) to First Committee of the General Assembly: Establishing the Eighteen Nation Disarmament Committee, December 13, 1961," *DD, 1961,* 722–25.

33. "Bermuda Communique, December 22, 1961," *DD, 1961,* 742–44; "White House Statement: Anglo-American Agreement for Tests on Christmas Island," *DD, 1962,* 31–32.

34. Notes from the February 27, 1962, meeting in Seaborg, *Kennedy, Khrushchev,* 136–38. "Memorandum of a Conversation at the Department of State, Subject: A Program to Explain the U.S. Position on Testing in the Atmosphere, January 4, 1962," NSF, Box 300, File name: Nuclear Weapons Testing, 1/27–2/10–62, JFKL, 1–2; Memorandum of the NSC Meeting, February 27, 1962, NSF, Meetings and Memoranda Series, Box 313, File name: No. 497, February 2, 1962, JFKL, 1; "Radio and TV Address by Kennedy on Nuclear Testing and Disarmament, March 2, 1962" *DD, 1962,* 66–73. The Eighteen Nation Disarmament Committee (ENDC) opened on March 15.

35. For Soviet reaction, see "Statement by Foreign Minister Gromyko to the ENDC, March 15, 1962," *DD, 1962,* 95; Editorial, "Real Way to Lasting Peace," *CDSP* 14, no. 8 (1962): 25; "On Eve of Negotiations in Geneva," *CDSP* 14, no. 10 (1962): 23; "Voters Meet Candidate," 6–7; "Message from Khrushchev to Macmillan, April 12, 1962," *DD, 1962,* 325; and "Tsarapkin Statement to the Test Ban Subcommittee at the ENDC, March 21, 1962," *DD, 1962,* 164. See also Seaborg, *Kennedy, Khrushchev,* 126–31, 134, 162–63.

36. Seaborg, *Kennedy, Khrushchev,* 141–43.

37. "Eight Nation Joint Memorandum, April 16, 1962," *DD, 1962,* 334–36. For reaction to the Eight Nation Memorandum, see "United States Paper Submitted to the ENDC, 4/17/62," "Statement by the Soviet Representative (Zorin) to the Test Ban Subcommittee of the ENDC, April 19, 1962," and "Statement by United States Representative (Dean) to ENDC, April 20, 1962," *DD, 1962,* esp. 336–38, 416–19, and 421, respectively. On the resumption of testing, see "Statement by United States Representative

(Dean), April 26, 1962" and "Statement by Soviet Representative (Zorin), April 26, 1962," *DD, 1962,* 456–57 and 458–61, respectively.

38. William Foster, Memorandum for the President, Subject: U.S. Progress Regarding a Treaty to Ban Nuclear Weapons Tests and Other Disarmament Proposals, July 30, 1962, POF, Subjects Series, Disarmament Subseries, Box 100A, File name: Disarmament—Nuclear Test Ban Negotiations—July 30, 1962 Meeting, JFKL, 2. See also Seaborg's accounts of a series of July meetings, *Kennedy, Khrushchev,* esp. 164.

39. Memorandum from Robert McNamara to JFK, "The U.S.-USSR Balance with and without a Test Ban," POF, Subjects Series, Disarmament—Nuclear Test Ban Negotiations, Box 100, JFKL, File name: July 30, 1962 Meeting, 3–4.

40. "Report by the Department of Defense on Project Vela, July 7, 1962," *DD, 1962,* 633–35; Seaborg, *Kennedy, Khrushchev,* 164–68.

41. "Anglo-American Proposal Submitted to ENDC: Draft Treaty Banning Nuclear Weapons Tests in all Environments, 8/27/62," "Anglo-American Proposal Submitted to ENDC: Draft Treaty Banning Nuclear Weapons Tests in the Atmosphere, Outer Space, and Underwater, 8/27/62," and "Dean Statement to ENDC: New Anglo-American Test Ban Proposals, August 27, 1962," *DD, 1962,* 792–804, 804–7, and 807–19, respectively. "National technical means" (NTM) was a euphemism that referred to surveillance and reconnaissance methods that each side possessed. Verification by NTM meant that neither side would depend on the other to furnish any information.

42. "Kuznetsov statement to ENDC: Anglo-American Test Ban Proposals, August 29, 1962," *DD, 1962,* 820–29.

43. Khrushchev, *Khrushchev Remembers,* vol. 2, 509–14; Schlesinger, *Thousand Days,* 794–819; Graham Allison, *Essence of Decision: Explaining the Cuban Missile Crisis* (Boston: Little, Brown, 1971); Ronald Pope, *Soviet Views on the Cuban Missile Crisis: Myth and Reality in Foreign Policy Analysis* (Washington, DC: University Press of America, 1982); Raymond Garthoff, *Reflections on the Cuban Missile Crisis* (Washington, DC: Brookings Institution, 1987); Blight and Welch, *On the Brink;* Bruce Allyn, James G. Blight, and David A. Welch, "Proceedings from the Moscow Conference on the Cuban Missile Crisis, January 27–28, 1989" (Center for Science and International Affairs, Harvard University, December 1989); "Kennedy-Khrushchev Correspondence," *Problems of Communism* 41 (special edition, 1992): 30–120.

44. "Present International Situation," esp. 4, 6. More immediate statements include "From Positions of Reason," 12; and "Reason Triumphs," 13. For the Chinese attacks, see Griffith, *Sino-Soviet Rift,* 64–103. The Soviet defense is mounted in K. Voroshilov, "The Cause of Great October Lives and Triumphs," *CDSP* 14, no. 44 (1962): 17; "Forty-Fifth Anniversary of the Great October Socialist Revolution: Report by Comrade A. N. Kosygin at the Formal Meeting in the Kremlin Palace of Congresses," *CDSP* 14, no. 45 (1962): 3–8, esp. 6–7; and "Tenth Congress," 7. Some Eastern European leaders wholeheartedly supported Khrushchev, including Gomulka, Zhivkov, and Novotny, as in *CDSP* 14, nos. 44 and 45 (1962).

45. Dobrynin, *In Confidence,* 86–88; Taubman, "Correspondence," 15–17, n. 8; "Kennedy-Khrushchev Correspondence," *Problems of Communism* 41 (special edition, 1992): 60–62.

46. Zubok and Pleshakov, *Inside Kremlin's Cold War,* 268–70; Dobrynin, *In Confidence,* 93; Arthur Schlesinger Jr., "Onward and Upward from the Missile Crisis," *Prob-*

lems of Communism 41 (special edition, 1992): 7; Fedor Burlatskiy, "The Lessons of Personal Diplomacy," *Problems of Communism* 41 (special edition, 1992): 12–13.

47. The misunderstanding over OSI demonstrates the fear that both sides had of being exploited, as superpower cooperation was new and tenuous. Luckily, the leaders came to understand that each was simply looking for a good bargain, and this episode did not preclude the final settlement. "Letter From Premier Khrushchev to President Kennedy, December 19, 1962," *DD, 1962,* 1239–41; U.S. ACDA, "Letter from President Kennedy to Premier Khrushchev, December 28, 1962," *DD, 1962,* vol. 2, 1277–78; U.S. ACDA, "Letter from Premier Khrushchev to President Kennedy, January 7, 1963," *DD, 1963,* 3; Beschloss, *Crisis Years,* 572; Tatu, *Power in Kremlin,* 311; Dobrynin, *In Confidence,* 100–102.

48. "Letter from Adrian Fisher to Senator Dodd, March 14, 1963," WAH Papers, Special Files, Public Service, 1915–81 Series, Trips and Missions Subseries, Box 560, File name: Test Ban Treaty Background II, 2; Sorensen, *Kennedy,* 730–31.

49. Positive signs included a continuing rapprochement with Yugoslavia, worsening relations with China, and interest in April in (and ultimately the conclusion in June of) the Hot Line Agreement. The latter accord established a direct teletype connection between the two capitals. The difficulty in sending messages quickly and reliably during the Cuban missile crisis was the impetus for this deal. Blacker and Duffy, *International Arms Control,* 117–18; "Useful Agreement," *CDSP* 15, no. 25 (1963): 21; "Emendation," *CDSP* 15, no. 13 (1963): 5; "Letter from the CPSU Central Committee to the Central Committee of the CCP," *CDSP* 15, no. 14 (1963): 3–9.

50. This decision came as Soviet-Chinese relations worsened. Chinese diplomats had recently distributed a critique of Khrushchev's foreign policy to residents of major Soviet cities. Enraged at the audacity of this measure, the USSR expelled Chinese diplomats and attacked the PRC at the next Central Committee meeting. Then, the Soviets also revealed that the Western arms control delegation would arrive to discuss the test ban at the same time that a high-level Chinese Communist Party delegation would be visiting Moscow. By scheduling an overlap in the two meetings, the Soviets were downgrading the importance of their negotiations with the Chinese and signaling their increased interest in concluding a test ban. Griffith, *Sino-Soviet Rift,* 143–61; "Speech by Comrade N. S. Khrushchev at the Sixth Congress of the Socialist Unity Party of Germany," part 2, *CDSP* 15, no. 4 (1963): esp. 13–15; "Exchange of Letters Between the CPSU Central Committee and the CCP Central Committee," *CDSP* 15, no. 11 (1963): 3–6; "Emendation," 5, "Letter from CPSU to CCP," 3–9; "Statement of the CPSU Central Committee" and "Marxism-Leninism Is Banner," *CDSP* 15, no. 24 (1963): 3–6.

51. Seaborg, *Kennedy, Khrushchev,* 180; "Kennedy News Conference Remarks on Test Ban Negotiations, {Extract}, April 24, 1963," *DD, 1963,* 181–82. Regarding public opinion, back in December 1962, 63 percent of Americans polled believed peace with the USSR was possible. By early July 1963, however, only 49 percent held that view. George W. Gallup, *The Gallup Poll: Public Opinion 1935–1971,* vol. 3 (New York: Random House, 1972), 1799, 1826.

52. "Interview of Premier Khrushchev with the Editor of *Il Giorno* {Extract}, April 20, 1963," *DD, 1963,* 174–75.

53. "Speech by Comrade N. S. Khrushchev at Berlin Rally on July 2, 1963," *CDSP* 15, no. 27 (1963): esp. 9.

54. "Hungarian-Soviet Friendship Rally: Speech by Comrade N.S. Khrushchev," *CDSP* 15, no. 29 (1963): 7.

55. "Embassy Telegram #167 to Rusk from Harriman, July 7, 1963," WAH Papers, Special Files, Public Service, 1915–81 Series, Trips and Missions Subseries, Box 561, File name: Test Ban Treaty, 1; Carl Kaysen, "Instructions for the Honorable W. Averell Harriman," Draft, July 8, 1963, WAH Papers, Special Files, Public Service, 1915–81 Series, Trips and Missions Subseries, Box 560, File name: Test Ban Treaty Background 3, Library of Congress, 2. An examination of the cable traffic indicates that the last week was devoted to bickering over the language of the withdrawal clause and warding off Soviet (and British) attempts to conclude simultaneously a nonaggression pact between NATO and the Warsaw Treaty Organization. The telegrams are located in two files, Test Ban Treaty Briefing Book Incoming and Test Ban Treaty Briefing Book Outgoing, in Box 560, WAH Papers, Special Files, Public Service, 1915–81 Series, Trips and Missions Subseries. See also Seaborg, *Kennedy, Khrushchev,* 256.

56. "Handling of Ban Series Communications," WAH Papers, Box 561, File name: Test Ban Treaty Briefing Book, Instructions, Communiques, Miscellaneous, 1–2.

57. While a majority of the attentive public said they approved the ban, many others did not know about it. The public could potentially be manipulated by opponents if those opposed were to rally the uninformed to their cause. The Gallup poll reported that of those asked during the period August 15–20, 1963, 60 percent had heard of the LTBT. When those who were familiar with the treaty were asked whether the Senate should approve it, 63 percent said yes, 17 percent said no, and 20 percent had no opinion. Gallup, *Gallup Poll,* vol. 3, 1826.

58. U.S. ACDA, "Message from President Kennedy to the Senate: Transmittal of Test Ban Treaty: August 8, 1963," *DD, 1963,* 299–302; U.S. ACDA, "Radio-TV Address by President J. Kennedy, July 26, 1963," 250–56. Regarding the signing ceremony, see Bromley Smith, "Memorandum of Conference with the President, July 22, 1963," NSF, Meetings with the President Series, Box 317, JFKL, File name: Harriman Mission to Moscow July 1963, 1.

59. Telephone conversation between Secretary Rusk and the president, July 24, 1963, Item 23B6, "Winning Senate Support for the Nuclear Test Ban Treaty, 1963," JFKL, 2. Also see the conversation between the national security adviser and JFK on July 25, 1963, Item 23D3, in which Bundy advises that "the shortest possible gap between signature and your, your [sic] striking the key note is . . . essential."

60. Telephone conversation between the president and Senator Mike Mansfield, August 12, 1963, Item 25B2, "Winning Senate Support," JFKL, 1, 2–3.

61. "Statement by the Chairman of the Joint Chiefs of Staff," August 15, 1963, *Geneva Conference,* vol. 3, 347–51. See also Seaborg, *Kennedy, Khrushchev,* 281.

Chapter 4

1. Another popular explanation is consistent with the realist school. Since I wanted to assess the explanatory power of both realist and domestic politics explanations for one of the INF cases, I decided to develop the realist one when examing the successful completion and the domestic politics account for the failure of the accord. (In that manner, I would be reversing the juxtaposition of the approach and outcome that I had in the

test ban cases. I used realism for the failure and domestic politics for the success.) Moreover, I believed that I was choosing the stronger contender for each instance.

Still, because of the prevalence of the realist explanation for the breakdown of the talks in 1983, let me provide a brief outline of why I discounted it here. Realists contend that military power was imbalanced during that time period. The United States had lost significant ground to the USSR over the course of the 1970s in both its strategic and theater capability. Thus, the United States had no incentive to limit its arsenal. Similarly, the USSR, as the superior power, was not interested in taking any action that would hurt its stance. The talks failed precisely because both sides were carefully guarding their power positions and rightly suspicious of joint endeavors with the enemy.

While there is some truth in that argument, there are also serious deficiencies in the realist position. First, the contention that the USSR was superior to the United States in strategic capability is extremely difficult to sustain (see table 12). In addition, the Soviet preponderance of ground-based nuclear missiles in the European theater could be matched by American ballistic missiles, submarines, and bombers deployed outside of it. Moreover, if the supposed "imbalance" in Europe were so relevant, why did the United States not plan to deploy more INF to match the USSR's holdings? Second, why were the two negotiators able to come up with a compromise solution—and these were two men not known for their dovelike tendencies—in the Walk-in-the-Woods formula? While realists would expect the rebuff of their superiors, the deal should be surprising nonetheless. Finally, the United States did not "hang tough" throughout the negotiations, but rather offered an "Interim Agreement" in early 1983. The realists cannot explain why the United States advanced this proposal at that time.

2. For elements of this argument, see Talbott, *Deadly Gambits;* and Oberdorfer, *Turn,* 41–42, 97–102.

3. David Schwartz, *NATO's Nuclear Dilemmas* (Washington, DC: Brookings Institution, 1983); Thomas Risse-Kappen, *The Zero Option: INF, West Germany, and Arms Control* (Boulder, CO: Westview Press, 1988), 7–19; Haslam, *Politics of Nuclear Weapons,* 58–88; Raymond Garthoff, "The Soviet SS-20 Decision," *Survival* 25, no. 3 (1983): 110–19; and Stephen M. Meyer, "Soviet Theater Nuclear Forces," *Adelphi Papers,* nos. 187 and 188 (London: International Institute for Strategic Studies, 1983 and 1984).

4. Helmut Schmidt, "The 1977 Alastair Buchan Memorial Lecture," *Survival* 20, no. 1 (1978): 2–10; Risse-Kappen, *Zero Option,* 20–47; Haslam, *Politics of Nuclear Weapons,* 89–100; Talbott, *Deadly Gambits,* 34–37.

5. Risse-Kappen, *Zero Option,* 48–59; Haslam, *Politics of Nuclear Weapons,* 101–5.

6. Talbott, *Deadly Gambits,* 41.

7. See, for instance, interesting firsthand accounts by Yegor Ligachev, *Inside Gorbachev's Kremlin: The Memoirs of Yegor Ligachev,* trans. Catherine A. Fitzpatrick, Michele A. Berdy, and Dobrochna Dyrcz-Freeman (New York: Pantheon, 1993); Mikhail Gorbachev, *Memoirs* (New York: Doubleday, 1995), 136–57; and Georgi Arbatov, *The System: An Insider's Life in Soviet Politics* (New York: Times Books, 1993), 211–27.

8. See the articles in Fred I. Greenstein, ed. *The Reagan Presidency: An Early Assessment* (Baltimore: Johns Hopkins University Press, 1983); Theodore J. Lowi,

"Ronald Reagan—Revolutionary?" in *The Reagan Presidency and the Governing of America,* ed. Lester M. Salamon and Michael S. Lund (Washington, DC: Urban Institute, 1984), 29–56; and James W. Caesar, "The Theory of Governance of the Reagan Administration," also in *The Reagan Presidency and the Governing of America,* 57–87.

9. Myron Rush, "Succeeding Brezhnev," *Problems of Communism* 32, no. 1 (January–February 1983), 2–7; Myron Rush, "Guns over Growth in Soviet Policy," *International Security* 7 (1982–83): 167–79; Roeder, *Red Sunset,* esp. 68, 71, 155–56; Gorbachev, *Memoirs,* 126–39.

10. Jokes provide evidence of the widespread knowledge of the health problems of Soviet leaders. Rush, "Succeeding Brezhnev," 4; Gorbachev, *Memoirs,* 136–39; Ligachev, *Inside Gorbachev's Kremlin,* 36–39; Remnick, *Lenin's Tomb,* 146; Oberdorfer, *Turn,* 78–79.

11. Remnick, *Lenin's Tomb,* 180–97; Dobrynin, *In Confidence,* 477–521. For an academic discussion, see Seweryn Bialer, *Stalin's Successors: Leadership, Stability and Change in the Soviet Union* (New York: Cambridge University Press, 1980), esp. 72–74, 91–95.

12. Harry Gelman, *The Brezhnev Politburo and the Decline of Detente* (Ithaca, NY: Cornell University Press, 1984); Raymond Garthoff, *Detente and Confrontation: American-Soviet Relations from Nixon to Reagan* (Washington, DC: Brookings Institution, 1985).

13. Soviet opponents of détente equated the United States of the 1980s to Nazi Germany and warned that the lessons about aggressors gleaned from the World War II experience were still relevant. Such proponents of this view included Defense Secretary Ustinov, Leningrad Party leader and Politburo member Romanov, and Marshal Nikolai Ogarkov. On the general secretaries and their positions, see "Conference of Military Leader in the Kremlin," *CDSP* 34, no. 43 (1982): 1–3; Rush, "Guns over Growth"; and Jerry Hough, "Andropov's First Year," *Problems of Communism* 32, no. 6 (1983): 49–64.

14. Fred I. Greenstein, "The Need for an Early Appraisal of the Reagan Presidency," in *The Reagan Presidency: An Early Assessment,* ed. Fred I. Greenstein (Baltimore: Johns Hopkins University Press, 1983), 15–16. Also Lester M. Salamon and Michael S. Lund, "Governance in the Reagan Era: An Overview," in *The Reagan Presidency and the Governing of America,* ed. Lester M. Salamon and Michael S. Lund (Washington, DC: Urban Institute Press, 1984), 10–12, 17–18.

15. In 1982, the freeze narrowly lost in a 204–202 House vote, with the president making last-minute phone calls to bring about its defeat. In the 1982 general election, however, "Voters in eight states and several major cities, which together include about one-fourth of the country's population, called for a worldwide nuclear freeze . . . despite warnings from the Reagan Administration that such a policy would damage the security of the United States." John Herbers, "Widespread Vote Urges Nuclear Freeze," *New York Times* [*NYT*], 4 November 1982, A22. With an accompanying victory of several freeze supporters in House races and losses of its opponents, the House passed the measure in 1983, although the Senate never did. Pressure by the pro-freeze and antinuclear movement was "intense" during 1983 especially. See also David Shribman, "Pushing for a Nuclear Freeze," *NYT,* 6 September 1983, B10; Margot Hornblower, "Nuclear Freeze Resolution Passes House Test Votes," *Washington Post* [*WP*], 17 March 1983, A1;

Margot Hornblower, "5000 Freeze Supporters Pour In as Hill Action Nears," *WP,* 8 March 1983, A2; and table 14.

16. Typically, the party in power loses some ground in these elections. The extent to which one views the results of 1982 as negative for the president depends, in a sense, on one's benchmark. Some have compared it to the 1934 election, because Roosevelt was also engaged in a "revolution," and found 1982 to be a defeat. See Lowi, "Ronald Reagan—Revolutionary?" Others have looked at the progressive acceptance of the public of Reagan's views—particularly on domestic politics—and see 1982 as an important year in which no ground was lost and significant numbers of people were won over. Everett Carll Ladd, "The Reagan Phenomenon and Public Attitudes toward Government," in *The Reagan Presidency and the Governing of America,* ed. Lester M. Salamon and Michael S. Lund (Washington, DC: Urban Institute, 1984), 221–49. On arms control issues, however, those opposed to Reagan's policies both in the House and in the American polity were to become much louder and more active after the 1982 election. Regarding these particular problems, see Hedrick Smith, "New House Seems Less in Tune with Reagan," *NYT,* 4 November 1982, A1; and Adam Clymer, "Contradictory Lessons of '82 Election," *NYT,* 4 November 1982, A1.

17. Throughout Reagan's first term, people identified the Democratic party as "more likely to keep the United States out of World War III" and as the party best able to handle the country's most important problem. See *Gallup Reports,* no. 223, April 1983, and no. 226, July 1984. Furthermore, people's concern about the threat of war and nuclear weapons jumped during 1983 from 25 percent (threat) and 20 percent (weapons) in March to 45 percent and 37 percent, respectively, in October. See Eymert Den Oudsten, "Public Opinion on Peace and War," *SIPRI Yearbook 1986: World Armaments and Disarmament* (New York: Oxford University Press, 1986), 18.

18. See, for example, Ronald Reagan, "Inaugural Address," January 20, 1981, *CQ Almanac,* 97th Cong., 1st sess. (1981), vol. 37, 11E–13E; Alexander Haig, "A New Direction in U.S. Foreign Policy," *United States Department of State Bulletin [DSB],* vol. 81, no. 2051, 64; and Lawrence S. Eagleburger, "U.S. Policy toward the USSR, Eastern Europe, and Yugoslavia, Testimony before the Subcommittee on Europe and the Middle East, House Foreign Affairs Committee, June 10, 1981," *DSB,* vol. 81, no. 2053, 73.

19. Eugene V. Rostow, "America's Blueprint for Controlling Nuclear Weapons: Testimony before the Senate Foreign Relations Committee, June 22, 1981," *DSB,* vol. 81, no. 2053, 59; "Secretary Haig Visits Europe: Address before Berlin Press Association, September 13, 1981," *DSB,* vol. 81, no. 2056, 45–47; George Bush, "Remarks before the Dominican Republic Congress, October 12, 1981," *DSB,* vol. 82, no. 2058, 13; L. S. Eagleburger, "Preserving Western Independence and Security: Address before the North Atlantic Assembly, October 15, 1981," *DSB,* vol. 82, no. 2058, esp. 40; Alexander Haig, "Secretary's Remarks: NATO Council Meeting, January 12, 1982," *DSB,* vol. 82, no. 2059, esp. 22; Eugene V. Rostow, "The Unnecessary War," *DSB,* vol. 82, no. 2059, esp. 32; Ronald Reagan, "Arms Control and the Future of East-West Relations: Eureka College Commencement Address, May 9, 1982," *DSB,* vol. 82, no. 2063, esp. 34; and Ronald Reagan, "Building Peace through Strength: American Legion, Seattle, WA, August 23, 1983," *DSB,* vol. 83, no. 2079, esp. 28.

20. See, for example, Ronald Reagan, "Interview with Walter Cronkite," *DSB,* vol. 81, no. 2049, 9; "Secretary Haig Interviewed for French Television," *DSB,* vol. 81, no. 2049;

13–16; Ronald Reagan, "Visit of British Prime Minister Thatcher," *DSB,* vol. 81, no. 2049, 26; Alexander Haig, "A New Direction in U.S. Foreign Policy," *DSB,* vol. 81, no. 2051, 5; Caspar Weinberger, "Requirements of our Defense Policy: Address before UPI Luncheon, May 5, 1981," *DSB,* vol. 81, no. 2052, 46–48; Rostow, "America's Blueprint," 59–64; and George Shultz, "Secretary-Designate Shultz Appears before Senate Committee," *DSB,* vol. 82, no. 2065, esp. 50. The United States and USSR concluded SALT I in 1972 and SALT II in 1979. Although the U.S. Senate never ratified the second treaty, the Reagan administration observed its provisions until December 1986.

21. Reagan, "Inaugural Address," 12E.

22. Lawrence J. Korb, "The 1991 Defense Budget," in *Setting National Priorities: Policy for the Nineties,* ed. Henry J. Aaron (Washington, DC: Brookings Institution, 1990), 120.

23. *CQ Almanac,* 96th Cong., 2d sess. (1988), 79B–80B. Also see Strobe Talbott's analysis of the administration's conduct of the INF and START negotiations in *Deadly Gambits.*

24. The following account benefits from Schwartz, *NATO's Nuclear Dilemmas;* Talbott, *Deadly Gambits;* Risse-Kappen, *Zero Option;* and Haslam, *Politics of Nuclear Weapons.*

25. Blacker and Duffy, *International Arms Control,* 264.

26. See Garthoff, *Detente and Confrontation,* 883–94; and Talbott, *Endgame,* 58–78, for accounts of the Comprehensive Proposal debacle.

27. Talbott, *Deadly Gambits,* 157–60, and Risse-Kappen, *Zero Option,* 67.

28. Perhaps as more archival materials from the 1980s are released, we will learn that at least one of the parties was playing a strategy of obfuscation instead of predomination. With the sources available, I have concluded that each would have liked an agreement, as long it was advantageous. As we will see in chapter 5, there are reasons to suspect that some members of the U.S. administration perhaps favored obfuscation, although the president did not.

29. In polls conducted during the period January 28–31, 1983, 35 percent of those asked approved of the way the president was handling his job, while 56 percent disapproved. "Reagan Popularity," *Gallup Report,* nos. 244–45 (January–February 1986): 23. In addition, in 1983 and 1984, 70 percent or more of those asked indicated that they would favor a verifiable agreement that froze Soviet and American nuclear arsenals. See *Gallup Report,* no. 212 (May 1983): 26, and *Gallup Report,* no. 229 (October 1984): 6.

30. Oberdorfer, *Turn,* 79–96.

31. Not only were Americans learning about the potentially devastating environmental impact of nuclear war, but their Catholic bishops questioned the moral implications of nuclear deterrence. It was hard to escape the concern with war, as even a made-for-TV movie about life in Lawrence, Kansas, following a nuclear strike, *The Day After,* aired just days prior to the Bundestag vote on whether to accept the American deployments. See Jonathan Schell, *The Fate of the Earth* (New York: Knopf, 1982); R. P. Turco et al. "Nuclear Winter: Global Consequences of Nuclear Explosions," *Science* 222:1283–92; Carl Sagan, "Nuclear War and Climatic Catastrophe: Some Policy Implications," *Foreign Affairs* 62 (1983–84): 257–92; and National Conference of Catholic Bishops, *A Pastoral Letter on War and Peace* (Washington, DC: United States Catholic Conference, 1983). Opinion polls also showed that in October 1983, of those

asked about their "greatest concerns," 45 percent mentioned the "threat of war" and 37 percent mentioned "fear of nuclear weapons." (In this poll, individuals could name more than one concern.) See Den Oudsten, "Public Opinion," 18.

32. Scholars generally believe that leadership opposition to arms control, particularly on the American side, fed the peace and freeze movements.

33. Garthoff, *Detente and Confrontation,* 870–71.

34. To characterize Paul Nitze—the author of NSC-68 and a founding member of the Committee on the Present Danger, a group that lobbied extensively against the SALT II Treaty—as a "liberal" is very strange, to say the least. For accounts of the infighting, see Oberdorfer, *Turn;* and Talbott, *Deadly Gambits.* For more on Nitze, see Strobe Talbott, *The Master of the Game: Paul Nitze and the Nuclear Peace* (New York: Alfred A. Knopf, 1988).

Chapter 5

1. For examples of this type of logic, see George Shultz, "The INF Treaty: Strengthening U.S. Security," *Department of State Bulletin (DSB),* vol. 88, no. 2132, esp. 31, 39; Caspar W. Weinberger, "Arms Reductions and Deterrence," *Foreign Affairs* 66 (1988): 700–19; Lynn E. Davis, "Lessons of the INF Treaty," *Foreign Affairs* 66 (1988): 720–34; John Lewis Gaddis, "Hanging Tough Paid Off," *Bulletin of the Atomic Scientists* 45, no. 1 (January–February 1989): 11–14; David T. Jones, "How to Negotiate with Gorbachev's Team," *Orbis* 33 (1989): 357–73; and Haslam, *Politics of Nuclear Weapons.*

2. In 1983, when the USSR walked out of the talks, the United States had no INF deployed in the theater. By the end of 1984 (just prior to the two parties' agreement to return to the table), the United States had 102 intermediate-range nuclear launchers and warheads, while the USSR had 499 launchers and 1,273 warheads. In 1987, the United States possessed 316 of each, and the Soviets had 470 launchers and 1,280 warheads. The planned U.S. deployment of 572 warheads was still far short of the Soviet totals. The missiles counted in the total are the Pershing II and Tomahawk GLCM for the United States and the SS-20, SS-4, and SS-5 for the Soviet Union. Sources for the number of American INF are the Stockholm International Peace Research Institute's *SIPRI Yearbook* for 1979–1987. Soviet data come from Cochran et al., *Nuclear Weapons Databook,* vol. 4 (New York: Harper & Row, 1989), 191. Note that the Soviet figures *include* SS-20s based in Asia.

3. Daniel Deudney and G. John Ikenberry, "Who Won the Cold War?" *Foreign Policy,* no. 87 (1992): 123–38.

4. Oberdorfer, *Turn,* 51–68.

5. More than 70 percent of those asked in late 1984 said they favored a verifiable freeze of Soviet and American arsenals. *Gallup Report,* no. 229 (October 1986): 6.

6. Ronald Reagan, "The U.S.-Soviet Relationship," *DSB,* vol. 84, no. 2083, 1–4. Although the INF deployments had started, by the end of 1983, the United States had only 25 warheads in place, as opposed to 1,247 for the USSR. It appears that something other than these few warheads was responsible for Reagan's new rhetoric.

7. "Evil Empire . . . Come in Evil Empire," *NYT,* 17 January 1984, A24; Jonathan Moore, "The Reelection Value of an Arms Control Initiative," *NYT,* 22 February 1984, A23. Also on electoral motives, see "The Race for Arms," *NYT,* 25 September 1984,

A26; and Hedrick Smith, "Like it or Not, Two Sides Share a Need for Talks," *NYT,* 30 September 1984, sec. 4, 1.

8. Leslie Gelb, "House Puts a Hold," *NYT,* 18 June 1984, sec. 2, 8, and 21 June 1984, sec. 2, 10.

9. Hedrick Smith, "Arms Control: Election-Year Pressure on Reagan," *NYT,* 13 June 1984, A4. See also Bernard Gwertzman, "Reagan Asserts Ties with Soviets are Paramount," *NYT,* 1 June 1984, A1, A6; Wayne Biddle, "House Military Bill Sets Stage for a Struggle with Senate on Arms Control," *NYT,* 2 June 1984, 29; Biddle, "Arms Spending Debate to Continue in Senate," *NYT,* 11 June 1984, A10; Biddle, "Congress Moves to Get Hands on Arms Control," *NYT,* 17 June 1984, sec. 4, 2; Gelb, "House Puts a Hold."

10. The Soviets wanted the "space weapons" to be on the table, while the Americans hoped to discuss offensive and defensive systems. Francis X. Clines, "Reagan, Still Optimistic over Arms Talks, Warms against Protests," *NYT,* 23 June 1984, 2; Bernard Gwertzman, "U.S. Tells Soviet It Would Talk about All Arms," *NYT,* 30 June 1984, 1, 4; Gwertzman, "U.S. Says It Weighs Kremlin's Motives in New Arms Offer," *NYT,* 1 July 1984, 1, 7; Seth Mydans, "Soviet Condemns U.S. Reply to Bid on Space Weapons," *NYT,* 2 July 1984, A1, A9; Gwertzman, "Shultz Again Says U.S. Wants to Discuss Space Arms," *NYT,* 8 July 1984, 3; Leslie Gelb, "Reagan is Willing to Delay a Parley on Space Weapons," *NYT,* 15 July 1984, 1, 15.

11. Ronald Reagan, "Reducing World Tensions: Address at the Opening of the 39th United Nations General Assembly," *DSB,* vol. 84, no. 2092, 1–7; Bernard Gwertzman, "Reagan Reported Ready to Press Gromyko for Cabinet-Level Talks," *NYT,* 22 September 1984, 1, 5; Steven R. Weisman, "Reagan, at UN, Asks Soviets for Long-Term 'Framework' to Press for Arms Control," *NYT,* 25 September 1984, A1, A12; and Leslie Gelb, "Reagan Initiative on Arms is Hinted," *NYT,* 3 November 1984, 9.

12. Oberdorfer, *Turn,* 87–96.

13. Ibid., 102–5.

14. Reagan had first mentioned SDI in a television address on March 23, 1983. Ibid., 27.

15. Reagan used the "evil empire" designation for the first time in a speech on March 8, 1983, in Orlando, Florida. Ibid., 23.

16. Gorbachev, *Memoirs,* 154–68; Ligachev, *Inside Gorbachev's Kremlin,* 54–72; Oberdorfer, *Turn,* 79–81.

17. See *Pravda,* 12 March 1985, 1–2, for the news of Gorbachev's selection and Chernenko's death. See also H. Smith, *New Russians,* 77; and Dusko Doder and Louise Branson, *Shadows and Whispers* (New York: Random House, 1986), 267.

18. In the speech, Gromyko said he could "personally" confirm that Gorbachev was a man of principles, and he listed the candidate's qualifications for the job: Gorbachev was experienced, had worked brilliantly, thought analytically, and always found solutions that corresponded to the Party line. "Rech' Tovarishcha A. A. Gromyko," [Speech of Comrade A. A. Gromyko] *Kommunist,* no. 5 (March 1985): 6–7.

19. "Speech by Comrade Ye. K. Ligachev," *Current Soviet Policies X: The Documentary Record of the 19th Party Conference of the Communist Party of the Soviet Union* (Columbus, OH: Current Digest of the Soviet Press, 1988), 79–81, esp. 80.

20. Ligachev, *Inside Gorbachev's Kremlin.* For Grishin's ambitions, see 57–62; on the succession, 72–78. See also Doder and Branson, *Shadows and Whispers,* 100.

21. Georgi Arbatov, "America Also Needs Perestroika," in *Voices of Glasnost: Interviews with Gorbachev's Reformers,* ed. Stephen F. Cohen and Katrina vanden Heuvel (New York: W. W. Norton, 1989), 312. Neither Ligachev nor Arbatov named Gorbachev's rival while the USSR was still in existence.

22. Gorbachev, *Memoirs,* 166. Gorbachev also explained that he and Gromyko had a private meeting 20 minutes prior to the full Politburo gathering in which the foreign minister pledged his support. Moreover, in other sections of his memoirs, Gorbachev suggested that prior to his selection, Tikhonov, the Soviet chief of state, was a consistent thorn in his side and that others in the leadership made their jealousy of him clear. These remarks seem to reinforce the contention that there was opposition to Gorbachev at the highest levels. See *Memoirs,* 154, 156, 163–67.

23. Remnick contended that interviews with several Politburo members confirmed that the vote was unanimous, which again does not undermine the account here (*Lenin's Tomb,* 519). According to Gorbachev, "my ill-wishers must have known the mood among the people, and the feeling of the regional first secretaries, who were increasingly determined not to let the Politburo juggle another old, sick or weak person into the top position again. [In fact, s]everal groups of oblast Party first secretaries came to see me. They appealed to me to take a firm stand and assume the tasks of the General Secretary" (*Memoirs,* 165). Ligachev provides a consistent version of events. Ligachev, *Inside Gorbachev's Kremlin,* 54–78. Aleksandr Yakovlev also discusses the division in the Party in "A New Step is Needed," *CDSP* 43, no. 26 (1991): 3.

24. Ligachev, *Inside Gorbachev's Kremlin,* 72–78. Ligachev was Gorbachev's "second secretary" and was often portrayed as a leader of the hard-line faction in the late 1980s; Gromyko was considered a member of the old guard, as Stalin's ambassador to the United States and as Soviet foreign minister under Khrushchev, Brezhnev, Andropov, and Chernenko; and Yakovlev was considered the intellectual godfather of perestroika and one of the most radical of the reformists in the Party.

25. Eduard Shevardnadze, *The Future Belongs to Freedom,* trans. Catherine Fitzpatrick (New York: Free Press, 1991), xviii–xix. Others have made similar arguments; see Breslauer, "Evaluating Gorbachev," 299–340; and Tatyana Zaslavaskaya, "Socialism with a Human Face," in *Voices of Glasnost: Interviews with Gorbachev's Reformers,* ed. Stephen F. Cohen and Katrina vanden Heuvel (New York: W. W. Norton, 1989), 134. As we will see in chapter 6, Gorbachev would need to be even more watchful after 1989, when the ambiguity of his goals was reduced.

26. *Pravda,* 13 March and 24 April 1985. In making this statement, I am not arguing that Gorbachev had his *whole* agenda planned out. Gorbachev himself, who is not usually known for modesty, admitted that in his memoirs. Some earlier speeches and writings indicate that he did want to pursue broad-based reforms of the system, including a confidential memorandum to the Central Committee written in May 1978 and cited in Georgi Smirnov, "Restructuring the 'Citadel of Dogmatism,'" in *Voices of Glasnost: Interviews with Gorbachev's Reformers,* ed. Stephen F. Cohen and Katrina vanden Heuvel (New York: W. W. Norton, 1989), 85. Throughout 1985, however, his watchword was *uskoreniye* (acceleration). Many observers of Soviet politics thus concluded that he was simply a technocrat.

27. In that first year, Ligachev, Chebrikov (KGB), Ryzhkov, and Shevardnadze were all made full members, while Romanov, Tikhonov, and Grishin were kicked out. Yeltsin

and Sokolov (defense minister) also became Candidate Members. *CDSP* 37, no. 52 (1985): 6.

28. *CDSP* 37, no. 52 (1985): 10, 15–17; *Pravda,* 28 September 1985, 1. See also *Pravda,* 15 October 1985, 1; and *Pravda,* 3 June 1985. See Thane Gustafson and Dawn Mann, "Gorbachev's First Year: Building Power and Authority," *Problems of Communism* 35, no. 3 (1986): 1–19; Thane Gustafson and Dawn Mann, "Gorbachev's Next Gamble," *Problems of Communism* 36, no. 4 (1987): 18; and Jerry Hough, "Gorbachev Consolidating Power," *Problems of Communism* 36, no. 4 (1987): 30. That year, there were shake-ups in several Party committees, including the ones in Moldavia, Kurgan, Issyk-Kul (Kirgizia), Blagoveshchensk, Vologda, Uzbekistan, the Kiev province, the Khakass province, Tadzhikistan, the Moscow province, and Kirgizia. In addition, several ministers and members of Gosplan were fired. See reports in *CDSP* 37, nos. 26, 27, 29, and 31 (1985). On the change at the top of the Foreign Ministry and its significance as well as other personnel changes, see Gorbachev, *Memoirs,* 179–82.

29. Jerry Hough, *Opening up the Soviet Economy* (Washington, DC: Brookings Institution, 1987), 28.

30. Gorbachev, *Memoirs,* 194–99. "Friends and foes of change" is an allusion to the title of chapter 5 of Stephen F. Cohen's *Rethinking the Soviet Experience: Politics and History Since 1917* (New York: Oxford University Press, 1985).

31. Some observers have noted that new thinking reflected intellectual currents in the West that had long criticized a realpolitik approach to international relations. See, for instance, Robert G. Herman, "Identity, Norms, and National Security: The Soviet Foreign Policy Revolution and the End of the Cold War," in *The Culture of National Security: Norms and Identity in World Politics,* ed. Peter J. Katzenstein (New York: Columbia University Press, 1996), 271–313. For other Western assessments of new thinking, see Robert Legvold, "The Revolution in Soviet Foreign Policy," in *The Soviet System in Crisis,* ed. A. Dallin and G. Lapidus (Boulder, CO: Westview Press, 1991), 487–97; Meyer, "Sources and Prospects," 124–63; Parrott, "Soviet National Security," 1–36; and J. Snyder, "Gorbachev Revolution," 93–131.

32. Mikhail Gorbachev, *Perestroika: New Thinking for Our Country and the World* (New York: Harper & Row, 1987), 139–43; Anatoly Dobrynin, "Za Bez'yadernyi Mir, Na Vstrechu XXI Veka [Toward a Nonnuclear World, On the Brink of the Twenty-first Century]," *Kommunist,* no. 9 (1986): 18–31; Aleksandr Bovin, "Novoe Myshlenie: Trebovanie Yadernogo Veka [New Thinking: Requirement of the Nuclear Age]," *Kommunist,* no. 10 (1986): 113–24; "The Strategy of Acceleration Is Leninism in Action: Report by Comrade E. A. Shevardnadze at the Ceremonial Meeting Dedicated to the 116th Anniversary of V. I. Lenin's Birth," *CDSP* 38, no. 16 (1986): 10; and Shevardnadze, *Future Belongs to Freedom,* xvii. A highly influential discussion of the security dilemma in Western literature is Robert Jervis, "Cooperation under the Security Dilemma," *World Politics* 30, no. 2 (1978): 167–214.

33. See accounts in Oberdorfer, *Turn,* 186–87; and Gorbachev, *Memoirs,* 415.

34. Shevardnadze, *Future Belongs to Freedom,* 54. In particular, many perceived the deployment of the SS-20s as a significant mistake. See David Holloway, "State, Society, and the Military," in *The Soviet System in Crisis,* ed. A. Dallin and G. Lapidus (Boulder, CO: Westview Press, 1991), 616–32; Gorbachev, *Memoirs,* 443; and Arbatov, *System,* 197–201.

35. The impact of developments in Western thought in conjunction with the foreign

and domestic political challenges that the USSR faced was relevant to Soviet international relations specialists. See Herman, "Identity, Norms."

36. Gorbachev, *Memoirs,* 416–18; Oberdorfer, *Turn,* 208–9, 216. Gorbachev himself is rather imprecise in dating his change of view of Reagan. He mentions that the first summit in Geneva in November 1985 was important for showing him that he could "do business" with Reagan, but he also goes on to say that at that meeting, "Reagan appeared to me not simply a conservative, but a political 'dinosaur.'" Moreover, in the preparations for the Reykjavik meeting, Gorbachev says he was prepared for the Americans to try to take advantage of him. Only after the Reykjavik meeting does Gorbachev use the term *a breakthrough* in the relationship. In addition, Gorbachev's early public reaction to the antinuclearism Reagan revealed in Geneva was less than positive. Oberdorfer, *Turn,* 144. For these reasons, I believe the change occurred in the aftermath of Reykjavik. Moreover, it is only in late 1986 that Gorbachev knows that other domestic forces in the United States are going to be exerting pressure on Reagan to be more reasonable. Deudney and Ikenberry, on the other hand, identify the first Reagan-Gorbachev summit in Geneva in November 1985 as the point at which the transformation occurred. See their "Who Won the Cold War?" 127.

37. "On Perestroika and the Party's Personnel Policy: Report by M. S. Gorbachev, General Secretary of the CC at the Plenary Session of the CPSU CC," *CDSP* 39, no. 4 (1987): 5–6.

38. Gorbachev, *Memoirs,* 195–99. See also Roeder, *Red Sunset,* 211–45; Breslauer, "Evaluating Gorbachev," 299–340; and Archie Brown, "Political Change," in *The Soviet System: From Crisis to Collapse,* rev. ed., ed. Alexander Dallin and Gail W. Lapidus (Boulder, CO: Westview Press, 1995), 111–24.

39. *Pravda,* 30 May 1987, 6; *Pravda,* 31 May 1987, 1; Parrott, "Soviet National Security," 19. Defense Minister Sokolov and Commander-in-Chief of the Air Defense Forces Koldunov were fired immediately. In replacing Sokolov, Gorbachev turned to General Dmitri Yazov, a relatively junior official, whom the general secretary believed was a supporter of perestroika. A few weeks later, several high-ranking officials, including the commander, of the Moscow Air District were also dismissed. See also Randall E. Newnham, "Gorbachev and the Soviet Military: A Chronology," *Gorbachev and His Generals: The Reform of Soviet Military Doctrine,* ed. William C. Green and Theodore Karasik (Boulder, CO: Westview Press, 1989), 220–21; and Dale Herspring, "On Perestroyka: Gorbachev, Yazov, and the Military," *Problems of Communism* 36, no. 4 (1987): 104. (Gorbachev ultimately misjudged Yazov, who later provided only a halfhearted defense for the INF treaty to internal skeptics, openly criticized Shevardnadze in late 1990 over the events in Eastern Europe, and was one of the August 1991 coup plotters.)

40. Bernard Weinraub, "Reagan's Last Years: How Effective Can They Be?" *NYT,* 19 November 1986, A10.

41. Gerald M. Boyd, "The Mood of White House Officials: Despair as Damage Builds," *NYT,* 1 December 1986, A10; Weinraub, "Reagan's Last Years,"; Gerald M. Boyd, "Reagan Friends Said to Ask for Changes," *NYT,* 24 November 1986, A14; R. W. Apple Jr., "The Iran Affair: A Presidency Damaged," *NYT,* 26 November 1986, A1, A12.

42. David E. Rosenbaum, "The 100th Congress is Full of Partisan Risk," *NYT,* 11 January 1987, sec. 4, 1; Michael R. Gordon, "Reagan is Warned by Senator Nunn Over

ABM Treaty," *NYT,* 7 February 1987, 1, 4; and "Correction," *NYT,* 16 February 1987, A3.

43. In addition to *Gallup Report,* no. 264, see Weinraub, "Reagan's Last Years"; Apple, "Iran Affair"; and E. J. Dionne Jr., "Public Skeptical on State of Union," *NYT,* 27 January 1987, A1, A12.

44. "President Reagan's Second Inaugural Address, January 21, 1985," *DSB,* vol. 85, no. 2096, esp. 3; "State of the Union, February 6, 1985," *DSB,* vol. 85, no. 2097, 9; George Shultz, "The Future of American Foreign Policy: New Realities and New Ways of Thinking, January 31, 1985," *DSB,* vol. 85, no. 2096, esp. 14.

45. 1984 Republican Party Platform, *CQ Almanac,* 98th Cong., 2d sess. (1984), vol. 40, 41B–62B, at 60B.

46. Ronald Reagan, "President's Address before a Joint Session of Congress, November 21, 1985," *DSB,* vol. 86, no. 2106, 13–16, esp. 13; Reagan, "U.S.–Soviet Relations: Radio Address, November 23, 1985," *DSB* vol. 86, no. 2107, 23; K. L. Adelman, "Geneva Arms Control Talks," *DSB* vol. 86, no. 2108, 28–32, esp. 30. For other examples of this logic, see these speeches printed in *DSB:* Shultz, "Arms Control: Objectives and Prospects" vol. 85, no. 2098, 24–28; Nitze, "The Objectives of Arms Control," vol. 85, no. 2098, 27–63; Shultz, "The Meaning of Vietnam," vol. 85, no. 2099, 13–16; Reagan, "MX Missile and U.S.-USSR Negotiations on Nuclear and Space Arms," vol. 85, no. 2099, 60; Shultz, "Arms Control, Strategic Stability, and Global Security," vol. 85, no. 2104, 20–25, esp. 24; Reagan, "An Essay on Peace: Graduation Speech, Glassboro, NJ, June 19, 1986," vol. 86, no. 2114, 21–23; Adelman, "Arms Control: Turning the Corner: ABA, August 12, 1986," vol. 86, no. 2115, 7–10; Reagan, "Prospects for World Peace: Speech to the UN General Assembly, September 22, 1986," vol. 86, no. 2116, 1–7; Reagan, "The Current State of Soviet–American Relations," vol. 87, no. 2123, 10–11; Rowny, "Effective Arms Control Demands a Broad Approach," vol. 87, no. 2124, 22–24; Reagan, "U.S.–Soviet Relations," vol. 87, no. 2129, 7; and Shultz, "The INF Treaty: Strengthening U.S. Security," vol. 88, no. 2132, 31–40.

47. *Pravda,* 8 April 1985, 1; *Pravda,* 30 July 1985, 1.

48. Occasionally, the United States would indicate that it would accept some restrictions on SDI; however, the administration still viewed the issues of INF, strategic-range weapons, and space weapons separately. The Soviets returned to the table with the understanding that they were linked. Gorbachev periodically unlinked them to give the negotiations a boost. See Leslie Gelb, "Gap in Arms Talks: Is it Narrowing?", *NYT,* 18 October 1985, A14; Gelb, "U.S. Officials Reveal Disunity on Arms Goals," *NYT,* 25 October 1985, A1, A15; R. W. Apple Jr., "No Breakthroughs," *NYT,* 22 November 1985, A1, A12; Gelb, "Winners and Losers," *NYT,* 22 November 1985, A12; Gordon, "U.S. Unveils 3-Year Plan on Missile Cuts," *NYT,* 25 February 1986, A3; Gelb, "U.S. Aides Report Compromise Offer by Soviet on Arms," *NYT,* 29 June 1986, 1, 10. See also Talbott, *Master of the Game,* 265, 304, 315, 325.

49. "For a Peaceful, Free and Prosperous Future," *CDSP* 37, no. 40 (1985): 7–10; Richard Bernstein, "Gorbachev Urges Arms Agreement with Europeans," *NYT,* 4 October 1985, A1, A12; Bernard Weinraub, "Reagan Sees Shift by Soviet," *NYT,* 4 October 1985, A1, A13.

50. *Pravda,* 16 January 1986, 1–2; Serge Schmemann, "Gorbachev Offers to Scrap A-Arms within 15 Years," *NYT,* 16 January 1986, A1, A10; Michael R. Gordon,

"Reagan, Welcoming Gorbachev's Plan, Says He'll Study It Carefully," *NYT,* 16 January 1986, A10; Bernard Weinraub, "Reagan 'Grateful' for Soviet Plan on Nuclear Arms," *NYT,* 17 January 1986, A1, A8; Leslie Gelb, "Weighing the Soviet Plan," *NYT,* 17 January 1986, A1, A8.

51. "Speech by Comrade M. S. Gorbachev," *CDSP* 38, no. 30 (1986): 1–3; Leslie H. Gelb, "U.S. Reply on A-Arms is Said Not to Link Defense Cuts," *NYT,* 21 July 1986, A1, A3.

52. Oberdorfer, *Turn,* 174–83; Gorbachev, Memoirs 414–15; Deudney and Ikenberry, "Who Won Cold War?" 127–28.

53. Oberdorfer, *Turn,* 191.

54. Ibid., 191–200.

55. "On Arms, Democrats Feel Shell-Shocked," *NYT,* 17 October 1986, A22; Bernard Weinraub, "Reagan Triumphs from Failure in Iceland," *NYT,* 17 October 1986, A22; Oberdorfer, *Turn,* 205.

56. Oberdorfer, *Turn,* 208–9; Gorbachev, *Memoirs,* 416–18.

57. Weinraub, "Reagan's Last Years"; Apple, "Iran Affair"; Boyd, "Mood of White House Officials"; Rosenbaum, "100th Congress"; Gordon, "57 Senators in Letter Ask Reagan to Observe '79 Arms Pact," *NYT,* 16 December 1986, A12; Gordon, "Reagan Warned by Senator Nunn over AMB Treaty," *NYT* 7 February 1987, 1.

58. Weinraub, "Regan's Exit Was Inevitable; Baker's Entrance a Surprise," *NYT,* 1 March 1987, 1, 12; Weinraub, "Nancy Reagan's Power is Considered at Peak," *NYT,* 3 March 1987, A1, A11.

59. Gerald M. Boyd, "Panel Said to Find Reagan was Told of Iran Dealings," *NYT,* 25 February 1987, A1, A12; "Excerpts from the Tower Commission News Conference," *NYT,* 27 February 1987, A8; Stephen Engelberg, "A Web of Maneuvers," *NYT,* 27 February 1987, A1, A10; Fox Butterfield, "The Missing Notes," *NYT,* 27 February 1987, A1, A11; Steven V. Roberts, "Inquiry Finds Reagan and Chief Advisers Responsible for 'Chaos' in Arms Deal," *NYT,* 27 February 1987, A1, A9; "The Findings: In Muskie's Words," *NYT,* 27 February 1987, A1.

60. Bill Keller, "Moscow, In Reversal, Urges Agreement 'Without Delay' to Limit Missiles in Europe," *NYT,* 1 March 1987, 1, 7; Michael Gordon, "U.S. Expresses Hope for Action on Accord Soon," *NYT,* 1 March 1987, 1, 6; James M. Markham, "Soviet, In Geneva, Said to Back Idea of Site Inspection," *NYT,* 5 March 1987, A1; E. J. Dionne Jr., "Poll Shows Reagan Approval Rating at 4-Year Low," *NYT,* 3 March 1987, A1, A11; Thomas W. Netter, "U.S. and Russians Agree to Extend Talks on Missiles," *NYT,* 3 March 1987, A1, A6.

61. Michael R. Gordon, "U.S. Says Soviet Arms Bid Offers Much but Has Gaps," *NYT,* 3 March 1987, A6; James M. Markham, "A Europe of Two Minds," *NYT,* 3 March 1984, A1, A6; David K. Shipler, "Gorbachev Offers to Render Europe Clean of Missiles," *NYT,* 15 April 1987, A1, A6; Risse-Kappen, *Zero Option,* 123.

62. See chapter 4.

63. David Shipler, "New Task for Shultz," *NYT,* 17 April 1987, A8; Talbott, *Deadly Gambits,* 58–60; James M. Markham, "Joint Stand Eludes Allies on Eliminating Missiles," *NYT,* 29 April 1987, A10; Markham, "Bonn Coalition Openly Split on Short Range Arms," *NYT,* 8 May 1987, A9; Markham, "Soviet Missile Proposals Put Kohl in a Tough Spot," *NYT,* 19 May 1987, A3; Serge Schmemann, "Bonn's Coalition Agrees

to Endorse Missiles' Removal: Weeks of Dispute Ended," *NYT,* 2 June 1987, A1, A8; Schmemann, "West German Parliament Backs Plan on Medium Range Missiles," *NYT,* 5 June 1987, A2; Risse-Kappen, *Zero Option,* 131–42.

64. Gorbachev, *Memoirs,* 443; Shevardnadze, *Future Belongs to Freedom,* 97; Primakov, "A New Philosophy of Foreign Policy," *CDSP* 39, no. 28 (1987): 1–4, esp. 4; "On the Path to Nuclear Disarmament: S. Akhromeyev Answers Questions from *Pravda* Correspondent A. Gorokhov," *CDSP* 39, no. 51 (1987): 13–14; "October and Perestroika: The Revolution Continues: Report by M. S. Gorbachev, General Secretary of the CPSU CC, at the Joint Ceremonial Meeting of the CPSU CC, the USSR Supreme Soviet, and the Russian Republic Supreme Soviet Devoted to the 70th Anniversary of the Great October Socialist Revolution," *CDSP* 39, no. 44 (1987). The INF decision was a sensitive one, and the debate continued after December 1987. For more insight into the arguments surrounding the Soviet compromises and confirmation that there was a debate on the policy of new thinking, see especially the essays in *SShA: Ekonomika, Politika, i Ideologiya,* no. 12 (December 1988): 23–41.

65. Oberdorfer, *Turn,* 245–57.

66. There was no significant battle over ratification in the United States, as the agreement's few opponents could be found on the extreme right of the Republican party. The final vote in favor in May 1988 was 93–5, far in excess of the needed 67 yea votes. See "Senate Votes 93–5 to Approve Ratification of the INF Treaty," *CQ Weekly Report* 42, no. 22 (1988): 1431–35.

67. Throughout the spring, Weinberger had the habit of following Secretary Shultz around and contradicting him. Reports leaked that the two were battling over policy and that Reagan was siding with Shultz. The infighting continued through the summer. See Talbott, *Master of the Game,* 248–67, 346–50; Craig R. Whitney, "U.S. and Arms Control: Internal Discord," *NYT,* 9 April 1987, A10; David K. Shipler, "U.S. Said to Widen Goals for Banning Mid-Range Missiles," *NYT,* 13 April 1987, A1, A8; Steven V. Roberts, "Adviser [Rowny] Rebuked by White House For Arms Remarks," *NYT,* 29 April 1987, A1, A10; Michael R. Gordon, "On Rowny's Dissent," *NYT,* 1 May 1987, A16; Gordon, "NATO [Defense] Ministers Urge New Stance by U.S. on Mid-Range Arms Pact," *NYT,* 16 May 1987, 1, 4; Gordon, "Weinberger Comment on Missiles Said to Upset White House Aides," *NYT,* 17 May 1987, 1, 19; Neil Lewis, "Shultz Responds Tartly to NATO Chief's Criticism," *NYT,* 21 June, 1987, 17; and Gordon, "Washington Talk: Arms and the Administration," *NYT,* 7 August 1987, A16.

68. Michael R. Gordon, "Perle is Bowing Out, His Goals and Acerbity Intact," *NYT,* 13 March 1987, A16; Judith Miller, "'Sometimes I Say Things Differently,'" *NYT,* 13 March 1987, A16; Gordon, "Adelman Quits as Head of Arms Control Group," *NYT,* 31 July 1987, A3; John H. Cushman, Jr., "Top Arms Control Official Quits: Criticizes Haste in Seeking Treaty," *NYT,* 21 November 1987, 1, 6. Talbott suggested that the whole administration was obfuscating in *Deadly Gambits.*

69. According to Jonathan Dean, "the unprecedented verification provisions of the INF treaty will allow for the monitoring of mutual compliance with considerable confidence." INF was the first of the U.S.–Soviet arms control treaties that required on-site inspections at production plants, bases, and support areas. See "The INF Treaty Negotiations," in *SIPRI Yearbook 1998: World Armaments and Disarmament,* ed. Stockholm International Peace Research Institute (New York: Oxford University Press, 1988), 387.

70. William C. Wohlforth argues that the Soviets were concerned about the impending deterioration of their power position, and this concern encouraged conciliatory behavior in "Realism and the End of the Cold War," *International Security* 19, no. 3 (1994–95): 91–129. Deudney and Ikenberry raise the point that SDI would be easy to thwart and continued commitment to the system was questionable. See their "Who Won Cold War?"

71. Gorbachev, *Memoirs,* 177.

72. Ibid., 443–45.

Chapter 6

Chapter 6 is a revised version of "Finishing START and Achieving Unilateral Reductions," *Journal of Peace Research* 34, no. 2 (1997). Reprinted by permission of Sage Publications Ltd.

1. Regina Cowen Karp, "The START Treaty and the Future of Strategic Nuclear Arms Control," in *SIPRI Yearbook 1992: World Armaments and Disarmament,* ed. SIPRI (New York: Oxford University Press, 1992), 20–22; Fred Chernoff, "Ending the Cold War: The Soviet Retreat and the U.S. Military Build-up," *International Affairs* (London) 67, no. 1 (1991): 111–26; Rush, "Guns over Growth"; Dmitri Steinberg, "The Soviet Defence Burden: Estimating Hidden Defence Costs," *Soviet Studies* 44 (1992): 237–63.

2. Rush, "Guns over Growth"; Holloway, "State, Society"; Gorbachev, *Memoirs,* 215–36.

3. James A. Baker III with Thomas M. De Frank, *The Politics of Diplomacy: Revolution, War, and Peace, 1989–1992* (New York: G. P. Putnam's Sons, 1995), 26; Talbott, *Deadly Gambits;* Talbott, *Master of the Game;* Oberdorfer, *Turn.*

4. Talbott, *Deadly Gambits,* 262.

5. Risse-Kappen, *Zero Option;* Talbott, *Deadly Gambits;* Talbott, *Master of the Game;* Regina Cowen Karp, "U.S.-Soviet Nuclear Arms Control," *SIPRI Yearbook 1991: World Armaments and Disarmament* (New York: Oxford University Press, 1991). Also see chapter 4.

6. Talbott, *Deadly Gambits,* 342 and chapters 4 and 5.

7. Bernard Weinraub, "How Grim Ending in Iceland Followed Hard Won Gains", *NYT,* 14 October 1986, 1, 11; Oberdorfer, *Turn,* 189–205.

8. Christoph Bertram, "U.S.–Soviet Nuclear Arms Control," in *SIPRI Yearbook 1989: World Armaments and Disarmament,* ed. SIPRI (New York: Oxford University Press, 1989), 360.

9. "President Bush's Vetoes . . . A Near Perfect Record," *CQ Almanac 1992,* 6–7. In its last possible chance for an override, Congress amassed a supermajority in 1992 to reregulate cable television despite the president's objection.

10. Gorbachev, *Memoirs,* 536–42, 618–19. See also Legvold, "Revolution in Soviet Foreign Policy," 487–97; Meyer, "Sources and Prospects"; Parrott, "Soviet National Security"; J. Snyder, "Gorbachev Revolution."

11. Remnick, *Lenin's Tomb,* 219–23; Roeder, *Red Sunset,* 210–45; Brown, "Political Change."

12. Roeder, *Red Sunset;* J. Snyder, "Gorbachev Revolution."

13. Doder and Branson, *Shadows and Whispers,* 248; Hough, "Gorbachev's Endgame."

14. "Beyond Perestroyka," 322–36; Marshall Goldman, "The Effort Collapses," in *The Soviet System: From Crisis to Collapse,* ed. Alexander Dallin and Gail W. Lapidus (Boulder, CO: Westview Press, 1995), 337–48; Anders Aslund, *Gorbachev's Struggle for Economic Reform* (Ithaca, NY: Cornell University Press, 1989).

15. See the following essays in *The Soviet System: From Crisis to Collapse,* ed. Alexander Dallin and Gail W. Lapidus (Boulder, CO: Westview Press, 1995): Lapidus, "Toward the Emergence of Civil Society in the Soviet Union," 125–46; Steven Fish, "The Emergence of Independent Associations and the Transformation of Russian Political Society," 147–59; and Lapidus, "Gorbachev's Nationalities Problem," 365–75. See also Gorbachev, *Memoirs,* 569–601.

16. A prominent example of his lack of tolerance was Gorbachev's silencing of Andrei Sakharov at a session of the first Congress of People's Deputies in 1989 by turning off the microphone when the great Soviet scientist and dissident would not accede to the Party chief's request to yield the floor. Remnick, *Lenin's Tomb,* 280–81.

17. Doder and Branson, *Shadows and Whispers,* 424; Remnick, *Lenin's Tomb,* 281.

18. Gorbachev, *Memoirs,* 569–70; H. Smith, *New Russians,* 566–71.

19. Gorbachev, *Memoirs,* 570–81; Remnick, *Lenin's Tomb,* 372–75, 384–93; H. Smith, *New Russians,* 615, 617–19. See the account in *CDSP* 42, no. 52 (1991): 8.

20. For the referendum, turnout was 80.0 percent. The vote was 76.4 percent yes, 21.7 percent no; 1.9 percent of the ballots were invalid. *CDSP* 43, no. 13 (1991); H. Smith, *New Russians,* 613–14; Gorbachev, *Memoirs,* 591–93.

21. For an analysis of the electoral politics and grassroots activism in Russia, especially at that time, see Yitzhak M. Brudny, "The Dynamics of Democratic Russia, 1990–1993," *Post-Soviet Affairs* 9 (1993): 141–70; and Michael Urban, "Boris El'tsin, Democratic Russia, and the Campaign for the Russian Presidency," *Soviet Studies* 44 (1992): 187–207.

22. *CDSP* 43, no. 25 (1991): 1–4; Baker, *Politics of Diplomacy,* 470–72; Remnick, *Lenin's Tomb,* 436–37.

23. As Jerry F. Hough noted, "Mikhail Gorbachev is not merely a good politician but a great one." Hough, "Gorbachev's Endgame," 227.

24. Here, I am not arguing that START was the cause of the coup. I agree with most scholars that the putsch primarily resulted from Gorbachev's acquiescence to a union treaty that would provide for Baltic independence and significant republican autonomy. Both treaties, however, were concrete results of Gorbachev's new thinking, which the coup plotters opposed.

25. For Gorbachev's hindsight on his autonomy problems, see his *Memoirs,* 624–25.

26. The public's approval of Bush's handling of Saddam Hussein certainly helped maintain his very high ratings. Large increases in his popularity correspond to the sending of the troops to Saudi Arabia and the beginning of the war.

27. "The Inaugural Address of President Bush," *DSB* 89, no. 2145, 2.

28. Baker, *Politics of Diplomacy,* 68, 92, 143; Michael Beschloss and Strobe Talbott, *At the Highest Levels: The Inside Story of the End of the Cold War* (Boston: Little, Brown, 1993), 12–44, 166. For criticism of the Bush policy from Paul Nitze, see

Michael R. Gordon, "Reagan Arms Adviser Says Bush Is Wrong on Short-Range Missiles," *NYT,* 3 May 1989, A1, A10. Later in the year, Andrew Rosenthal wrote that "in the early months of the Bush Administration, some official questioned whether Mr. Gorbachev was really a reformer and asked whether the White House should help him." Rosenthal, "Bush–Gorbachev Proclaim a New Era for U.S.–Soviet Ties; Agree on Arms and Trade Aims; See Cold War's End," *NYT,* 4 December 1989, A1, A10.

29. "President Addresses a Joint Session of Congress, February 9, 1989," *DSB* 89, no. 2145, 3.

30. "Secretary-Designate's Confirmation Hearings, January 17, 1989, Senate Foreign Relations Committee," *DSB* 89, no. 2145, 11. Baker's memoir confirms the notion that these were not just words for public consumption. Beschloss and Talbott initially suggest that Bush's and his administration's toughness came from the desire to protect themselves from right-wing criticism. They never fully explain, however, why the president lost his fear of conservatives and ultimately changed his position on working with the Soviets.

31. "Secretary-Designate's Confirmation Hearings," Baker, "The Challenge of Change in U.S.-Soviet Relations," *DSB* 89, no. 2148, 36–39; 10; Baker, "After the NATO Summit: Challenges for the West in the World," *DSB* 89, no. 2149, 55, 58.

32. Beschloss and Talbott, *At the Highest Levels,* 27, 74, 114–16; "Secretary-Designate's Confirmation Hearings," 11.

33. Beschloss and Talbott, *At the Highest Levels,* 33–40, 69–71, 167; Rosenthal, "Bush–Gorbachev Proclaim New Era,"; Michael R. Gordon, "U.S. Shift on Arms Talks," *NYT,* 4 December 1989, A10. Also see "Bush Statement, December 3, 1989, Malta, Statement at a Joint News Conference with Gorbachev," *CQ Weekly Report,* 47, no. 49 (December 9, 1989): 3391.

34. Beschloss and Talbott, *At the Highest Levels,* 117–21.

35. Ibid., 114–17; Gordon, "Adviser Says Bush Is Wrong,"; Rosenthal, "Bush–Gorbachev Proclaim New Era."

36. Regina Cowen Karp, "U.S.–Soviet Nuclear Arms Control," *SIPRI Yearbook 1990: World Armaments and Disarmament* (New York: Oxford University Press, 1990), 439.

37. Thomas L. Friedman, "U.S.–Soviet Talks End with Progress on Arms Control," *NYT,* 24 September 1989, A1, A16.

38. Ibid.; Gordon, "Moscow Sets Aside," *NYT,* 24 September 1989, A16; Baker, *Politics of Diplomacy,* 155.

39. Baker, *Politics of Diplomacy,* 169; Beschloss and Talbott, *At the Highest Levels,* 167.

40. Gordon, "U.S. Shift."

41. Michael R. Gordon, "U.S. Invites Ideas from the Soviets on Strategic Cuts: An Administration Shift," *NYT,* 12 February 1990, A1, A11.

42. According to the plan, the first 150 American ALCM-capable bombers would be counted as having 10 missiles and the first 210 Soviet ones as having 8. U.S. bombers could really carry 20 ALCMs each, while those of the USSR were equipped for 12. Any bombers beyond the first 150 for the United States and 210 for the USSR would be counted as carrying the full number of ALCMs, 20 or 12, respectively. Because the Soviets had fewer than their allotted number of 210 bombers, they could not as easily take

advantage of the "freebies." Karp, "U.S.–Soviet Nuclear Arms Control" (1991), 384–85, 387.

43. Michael R. Gordon, "U.S. and Soviets Appear to Agree on Main Elements of Arms Treaty," *NYT,* 11 February 1990, 1; Karp, "U.S.–Soviet Nuclear Arms Control" (1991), 387–88.

44. Shevardnadze quoted in Thomas L. Friedman, "U.S. and Soviets Close to a Pact on 30% Cut in Nuclear Missiles; Agree on Chemical Arms Curbs; Baker Is Optimistic," *NYT,* 20 May 1990, 1, 18; Also see Karp, "U.S.–Soviet Nuclear Arms Control" (1991), 388, 391–93; and Michael R. Gordon, "Arms Control Process: Back on Track," *NYT,* 20 May 1990, 18.

45. Thomas L. Friedman, "U.S. and Kremlin Still Deadlocked on Arms Treaties," *NYT,* 16 March 1991, 1, 6.

46. Karp, "U.S.–Soviet Nuclear Arms Control" (1991), 385–86.

47. Ibid.; Thomas L. Friedman, "Soviets' Real Issue: Aid," *NYT,* 2 June 1991, 1, 12; Alan Riding, "U.S. and Soviets Bridge Gap on Conventional Weapons and Plan for Summit Soon," *NYT,* 4 June 1991, A8; Eric Schmitt, "Bush's Plan Cuts Battlefield Arms," *NYT,* 28 September 1991, 5.

48. Eric Schmitt, "Nuclear Treaty Next for Superpowers," *NYT,* 4 June 1991, A1, A8.

49. Friedman, "Soviets' Real Issue"; Riding, "U.S. and Soviets Bridge Gap."

50. Thomas L. Friedman, "U.S. and Soviet Union Agree on All But Technical Issue for Strategic Arms Treaty," *NYT,* 15 July 1991, A10. While the Treaty established a 6000 warhead limit, the final numbers allowed were not so neat. Special exceptions in the counting rules meant that as a result of the treaty the USSR would be left with approximately 7000 warheads and the United States would hold about 9000.

51. Thomas L. Friedman, "U.S. Arms Request Backed by Moscow," *NYT,* 9 July 1991, A1, A8; Friedman, "U.S. and Soviets Report Progress," *NYT,* 14 July 1991, A1, A8; "New Limits on Strategic Weapons," *NYT,* 17 July 1991, A7; R. W. Apple Jr., "Pact is Reached to Reduce Nuclear Arms; Bush and Gorbachev to Meet this Month; Superpower Accord Is First to Mandate Real Reductions," *NYT,* 18 July 1991, A1, A10; Friedman, "Clearing the Final Hurdles to a Strategic Arms Accord," *NYT,* 18 July 1991, A12. Ratification of START I in 1992 was not a difficult battle, despite the breakup of the Soviet Union. In fact, the Senate vote was 93–6 in favor. See "START Ratified Despite Soviet Collapse," *CQ Almanac 1992,* 513–16.

52. Beschloss and Talbott, *At Highest Levels,* 430–45; Remnick, *Lenin's Tomb,* 451–88; H. Smith, *New Russians,* 622–47; Gorbachev, *Memoirs,* 626–45.

53. Members of the State Committee for the State of Emergency included, among others, KGB Chairman Kryuchkov, Prime Minister Pavlov, Interior Minister Pugo, Defense Minister Yazov, and Vice President Yanayev. For translations of the Russian press's accounts of the coup, see *CDSP* 43, nos. 33 and 34 (1991). For how discredited the communists were after the putsch, see *CDSP* 43, no. 36 (1991).

54. Baker, *Politics of Diplomacy,* 526; Andrew Rosenthal, "Arms Plan Germinated in Back-Porch Sessions," *NYT,* 29 September 1991, 14; Michael R. Gordon, "Why U.S. Was Worried," *NYT,* 28 September 1991, 1, 5.

55. Andrew Rosenthal, "U.S. to Give Up Short-Range Nuclear Arms," *NYT,* 28 September 1991, 1, 5; Schmitt, "Bush's Plan."

56. Rosenthal, "Arms Plan Germinated."

57. Beschloss and Talbott, *At the Highest Levels,* 444–45; Michael R. Gordon, "Trust without Verifying: Arms Control by Example, Not Agreement Shatters Conventions of Cold War Treaties," *NYT,* 29 September 1991, 10.

58. Rosenthal, "U.S. to Give Up Arms"; Serge Schmemann, "Soviets Hail U.S. Arms Plan," *NYT,* 29 September 1991, 1, 10; Schmitt, "Bush's Plan."

59. Schmemann, "Soviets Hail U.S. Arms Plan," *NYT,* 29 September 1991, 10.

60. Ibid.; Rosenthal, "Arms Plan Germinated"; Schmitt, "Bush's Plan."

61. "Gorbachev's Remarks on Nuclear Arms Cuts [Excerpts]," *NYT,* 6 October 1991, 12; and four pieces by Serge Schmemann: "Soviets Hail U.S. Arms Plan"; "In Moscow, Usual Reaction to Bush Arms Plan is Muted," *NYT,* 30 September 1991, A9; "Soviets Reject Fast Reply on Arms, Saying Talks Must Be Held First," *NYT,* 1 October 1991, A1, A10; and "Gorbachev Matches U.S. on Nuclear Cuts and Goes Further on Strategic Warheads," *NYT,* 6 October 1991, 1, 12.

Chapter 7

1. While the administration has attempted to soften the goals of NATO expansion and to reassure the Russians that this alliance is not directed against their country, I still believe that NATO expansion reflects "old thinking" and an inability to reconceive security and adjust the American view of Russia. On NATO expansion, see Richard L. Kugler with Marianna V. Kozintseva, *Enlarging NATO: The Russia Factor* (Santa Monica, CA: RAND, 1996); and Craig R. Whitney, "Three Former Members of Eastern Bloc Invited Into NATO," *NYT,* 9 July 1997, A1, A8. For the "sale-of-the century" that is expected to follow expansion and benefit many American arms makers at the expense of their competitors around the world, see Jeff Gerth and Tim Weiner, "Arms Makers See Bonanza in Selling NATO Expansion," *NYT,* 29 June 1997, 1, 8. Thomas L. Friedman argues that NATO expansion was a Clinton administration policy mistake that was fueled by the hopes of appealing to Polish-American constituents in 1996 in "NATOwater," *NYT,* 19 May 1997, A15.

2. For excellent discussions of the SALT negotiations and American–Soviet relations, see Blacker and Duffy, *International Arms Control;* Henry Kissinger, *The White House Years* (Boston: Little, Brown, 1979); John Newhouse, *Cold Dawn: The Story of SALT I* (New York: Holt, Rinehart & Winston, 1973); G. Smith, *Doubletalk;* D. Caldwell, *Dynamics of Domestic Politics;* Talbott, *Endgame;* and esp. Garthoff, *Detente and Confrontation.*

3. The Soviets put great emphasis on their achieving political equality with the United States in 1972. One of their proudest achievements in détente was the signing of the Basic Principles Agreement just three days after SALT I in 1972. The Basic Principles Agreement provided a code of behavior for the two superpowers. Blacker and Duffy, *International Arms Control,* 429.

4. See Garthoff, *Detente and Confrontation,* esp. 28–73.

5. Some in the Carter administration initially believed that they could convince the Soviets to make huge cutbacks (which the United States would match) in their arsenal. The final settlement resulted from cooperative strategies on both sides but achieved much less ambitious reductions than the U.S. administration had first hoped. See Garthoff, *Detente and Confrontation,* 883–94; and Talbott, *Endgame.*

6. D. Caldwell, *Dynamics of Domestic Politics*.

7. Garthoff, *Detente and Confrontation,* 1077–86. See also D. Caldwell, *Dynamics of Domestic Politics;* and Talbott, *Endgame.*

8. George Shultz, "The INF Treaty: Strengthening U.S. Security," *DSB* 88, no. 2132, esp. 31, 39; Caspar W. Weinberger, "Arms Reductions and Deterrence," *Foreign Affairs* 66 (1988): 700–719; Davis, "Lessons of INF Treaty"; Gaddis, "Hanging Tough"; Jones, "How to Negotiate"; Haslam, *Politics of Nuclear Weapons.* For a contrary view, as expressed in their title, see Lebow and Stein, *We All Lost the Cold War.*

9. "State of Emergency Committee's Statement: 'A Mortal Danger Has Come,'" *NYT,* 20 August 1991, 13.

10. Lockwood, "Nuclear Arms Control," 549; Rotfeld, "Introduction," 1–2.

11. Lockwood, "Nuclear Arms Control," 549.

12. See Friedman, "NATOwater."

13. Lebed did not last long in the government, parting ways with the administration on the handling of Chechnya, the military, and corruption. He left in the fall and has been pursuing his own political ambitions. Many observers think that he will be one of the top candidates in 2000.

14. The presidential contest strained Russians' already limited faith in democracy. First, there were reports of irregularities in the vote counts in some districts. Second, people were not informed of Yeltsin's condition when they went to the polls for the second round. Finally, for six months after the contest, nonelected officials were making key decisions while Yeltsin recuperated.

15. While Yeltsin could regain his physical strength and be in the position to reassert himself in foreign affairs, his time is running out. The possibility derives from both the enormous power of the Russian executive and the fact that Yeltsin is only in the second year of his term. I am skeptical that Yeltsin will be able to rebuild his autonomy significantly to control policy before the onset of the next election cycle, however. Yeltsin's health is fragile, as his bout with the flu at the end of 1997 dramatically demonstrated, and few people believe that the president will be immune to illness in the future. Moreover, the Duma elections are scheduled for 1999, and while Yeltsin has eschewed joining political parties, he has not avoided involvement in past contests. Thus concerns about the parliamentary and presidential contests (Yeltsin has not definitively ruled out a third term and there is some debate on whether the Constitution precludes his running again) could become relevant in the very near future. By the middle of 1999, the election campaign will be in full swing. Under the best of conditions then, Yeltsin's time for pursuing a constructive partnership with the United States is limited (about a year) at best.

16. At this last writing in early March 1998, the president is contending with a new challenge to his position. While the allegations that Clinton had a sexual relationship with White House intern Monica Lewinsky and the possibility that the president both suborned perjury and lied in a deposition have not yet negatively affected Clinton's popularity, there is reason to wonder whether this scandal could precipitate the onset of the lame-duck phase. The American public has been willing to wait on passing judgment. If the president were to become embattled domestically, however, his ability to lead would be in jeopardy.

Here, the autonomy problems that President Reagan experienced when the story of his involvement in Iran-Contra broke are potentially instructive. A popular second term president, Reagan lost his widespread support because he was caught breaking a promise to the American people (to not trade arms for hostages) and because his popularity was so linked to his perceived truthfulness. Since a large section of the public has tended to accept the fact that Bill Clinton has problems with marital fidelity and has never viewed him as particularly honest, the people have kept an open mind. (The impressive condition of the U.S. economy as well as the tactics of the special prosecutor, Kenneth Starr, have also helped the president.) Whether Clinton will continue to be able to weather the storm of this scandal if the evidence clearly indicates his guilt is still not clear.

17. Back in 1996, a Clinton administration official, speaking on the condition of anonymity, said that "on the worry list, arms control comes in somewhere between the strength of the Mexican peso and the fight against drugs." Tyler Marshall, "Once Explosive, Arms Control is No Longer a Hot Issue," *NYT,* 18 December 1996, A16. Also see R. W. Apple Jr., "On NATO Coup, Russia's Shadow," *NYT,* 9 July 1996, A8.

18. Dunn, "New Nuclear Threats," 20–50; Klare, "Adding Fuel to Fires," 134–54; Klare, "Deadly Convergence," 170–96.

19. Robert Axelrod concluded that states facing a Prisoner's Dilemma will tend to cooperate if the "shadow of the future" is long. Axelrod, *Evolution of Cooperation;* and Axelrod and Keohane, "Achieving Cooperation," 226–54.

20. Alternatively, if ordinary people become significantly disgusted with the violence and have the power at the ballot box to remove these officials if they do not pursue peace, we may see domestic pressures pushing the various sides toward resolution. (In the United States in the 1980s, popular pressure encouraged the administration to choose cooperation.) In Northern Ireland, the former Yugoslavia, and the Middle East, some of the leaders are less dependent on voters for their positions. In addition, while often war weary, many citizens—particularly in the Middle East but also among certain groups in Northern Ireland and the Balkans—believe that "peace" is preferable.

21. Fred Barbash, "London Bombing Severely Wounds N. Ireland Peace Process," *WP,* 11 February 1996, sec. 1, p. 25; Barbash, "IRA Claims Responsibility for Bomb on London Bus," *WP,* 20 February 1996, A23.

22. Warren Hoge, "Blair Offers New Ulster Deal; Key Is Disarming Both Sides," *NYT,* 26 June 1997, A1, A7; Fred Barbash, "IRA Announces a Cease-Fire," *WP,* 20 July 1997, 22; Giles Elgood, "Protestants Resist Key Part of Northern Ireland Plan," *WP,* 23 July 1997, A20.

23. David Hoffman, "Bombings Overshadow Palestinian Parliament," *WP,* 8 March 1996, A26. Also see Serge Schmemann, "Israeli Premier Survives Vote of Confidence in Parliament," *NYT,* 25 June 1997, A5; and Yossi Klein Halevi, "The Unorthodox Politics of an Ultra-Orthodox Rebel," 6 June 1997, sec. 6, p. 59. Of course, some hawks (Menachem Begin, Anwar Sadat, and Richard Nixon) have surprised the world in becoming peacemakers. These men typically have been secure in their domestic positions and then have moved forward with an innovative approach that incorporated the recognition that the states involved in the conflict were interdependent.

24. Lizette Alvarez, "Senate Is Cool to G.I. Mission in Bosnia but Doesn't Cut Off Funds," *NYT,* 12 July 1997, 3; Chris Hedges, "As NATO Troops Patrol, Karadzic Hides in Plain Sight," 9 July 1997, A4; Hedges, "Bosnian Serbs Sink in Poverty as Their Leaders Amass Wealth," *NYT,* 7 July 1997, A3; "Embattled Bosnian Serb Leader Orders Par-

liament Dissolved," *NYT,* 4 July 1997, A3; Hedges, "Bosnian Refugees as Political Pawns," *NYT,* 27 June 1997, A6; Michael Dobbs, "Background to a Nightmare," *Washington Post National Weekly Edition,* 11–17 March 1996, 19. As this book was going to press, another part of Yugoslavia, Kosovo, was erupting in violence. Milosevic still wields enormous power there, and he does not appear to have changed his strategy toward non-Serbs. Thus, the possibility of renewed ethnic cleansing appears real. The Albanians in Kosovo will be no match for the Yugoslav forces, and Europe and NATO appear unwilling to move early to prevent the bloodshed. Whether others in the Balkans will become involved is this confrontation continues is now the subject of much speculation.

Bibliography

Books and Scholarly Articles

Allison, Graham T. *Essence of Decision: Explaining the Cuban Missile Crisis.* Boston: Little, Brown, 1971.
Allison, Graham T., and Frederic A. Morris. "Armaments and Arms Control: Exploring the Determinants of Military Weapons." In *Arms, Defense Policy, and Arms Control,* edited by Franklin A. Long and George W. Rathjens. New York: W. W. Norton, 1976.
Allyn, Bruce, James G. Blight, and David A. Welch. "Proceedings from the Moscow Conference on the Cuban Missile Crisis, January 27–28, 1989." Cambridge, MA: Center for Science and International Affairs, Harvard University, December 1989.
Ambrose, Stephen. *Eisenhower.* Vol. 2, *The President.* New York: Simon & Schuster, 1984.
Arbatov, Georgi. *The System: An Insider's Life in Soviet Politics.* New York: Times Books, 1993.
Aslund, Anders. *Gorbachev's Struggle for Economic Reform.* Ithaca, NY: Cornell University Press, 1989.
Axelrod, Robert. *The Evolution of Cooperation.* New York: Basic Books, 1984.
Axelrod, Robert, and Robert O. Keohane. "Achieving Cooperation under Anarchy: Strategies and Institutions." In *Cooperation under Anarchy,* edited by Kenneth A. Oye. Princeton, NJ: Princeton University Press, 1986.
Bacharach, Samuel B., and Edward J. Lawler. *Bargaining: Power, Tactics, and Outcomes.* Washington, DC: Jossey-Bass Publishers, 1981.
Baker, James A. III, with Thomas M. De Frank. *The Politics of Diplomacy: Revolution, War and Peace, 1989–1992.* New York: G.P. Putnam's Sons, 1995.
Ball, Desmond. *Politics and Force Levels: The Strategic Missile Program of the Kennedy Administration.* Berkeley and Los Angeles: University of California Press, 1980.
Bass, Bernard M. *Bass & Stogdill's Handbook of Leadership: Theory, Research, and Managerial Applications.* New York: Free Press, 1990.

Bechhoefer, Bernard. *Postwar Negotiations for Arms Control.* Washington, DC: Brookings Institution, 1961.
Bennett, Paul. *The Soviet Union and Arms Control: Negotiating Strategy and Tactics.* New York: Praeger, 1989.
Bertram, Christoph. "US-Soviet Nuclear Arms Control." In *SIPRI Yearbook 1989: World Armaments and Disarmament,* edited by Stockholm International Peace Research Institute. New York: Oxford University Press, 1989.
Beschloss, Michael R. *The Crisis Years: Kennedy and Khrushchev, 1960–1963.* New York: HarperCollins, 1991.
———. *May Day: Eisenhower, Khrushchev, and the U-2 Affair.* New York: Harper & Row, 1986.
Beschloss, Michael R., and Strobe Talbott. *At the Highest Levels: The Inside Story of the End of the Cold War.* Boston: Little, Brown, 1993.
"Beyond Perestroyka: The Soviet Economy in Crisis." In *The Soviet System: From Crisis to Collapse,* edited by Alexander Dallin and Gail W. Lapidus. Boulder, CO: Westview Press, 1995.
Bialer, Seweryn. *Stalin's Successors: Leadership, Stability and Change in the Soviet Union.* New York: Cambridge University Press, 1980.
Blacker, Coit, and Gloria Duffy. *International Arms Control: Issues and Agreements.* 2d ed. Stanford, CA: Stanford University Press, 1984.
Blight, James G., and David Welch, eds. *On the Brink: Americans and Soviets Reexamine the Cuban Missile Crisis.* New York: Hill & Wang, 1989.
Bovin, Aleksandr. "Novoe Myshlenie: Trebovanie Yadernogo Veka" (New Thinking: Requirement of the Nuclear Age). *Kommunist,* no. 10 (1986): 113–24.
Breslauer, George. "Evaluating Gorbachev as Leader." *Soviet Economy* 5 (1989): 299–340.
———. *Khrushchev and Brezhnev as Leaders: Building Authority in Soviet Politics.* Boston: George Allen & Unwin, 1982.
Brown, Archie. "Political Change in the Soviet Union." In *The Soviet System: From Crisis to Collapse,* rev. ed., edited by Alexander Dallin and Gail W. Lapidus. Boulder, CO: Westview Press, 1995.
Brudny, Yitzhak M. "The Dynamics of Democratic Russia, 1990–1993." *Post-Soviet Affairs* 9 (1993): 141–70.
Bull, Hedley. *The Control of the Arms Race.* New York: Praeger, 1965.
Bunce, Valerie. *Do New Leaders Make a Difference? Executive Succession and Public Policy under Capitalism and Socialism.* Princeton, NJ: Princeton University Press, 1981.
Bundy, McGeorge. "The Presidency and the Peace." *Foreign Affairs* 42 (1964): 353–65.
———. "The President's Choice: Star Wars or Arms Control." *Foreign Affairs* 63 (1984–85): 264–78.
Bundy, McGeorge, George Kennan, Robert McNamara, and Gerard Smith. "Nuclear Weapons and the Atlantic Alliance." *Foreign Affairs* 60 (1982): 754–86.

Burlatskiy, Fedor. "The Lessons of Personal Diplomacy." *Problems of Communism* 41 (special edition, 1992): 8–13.

Burns, James MacGregor. *Leadership*. New York: Harper & Row, 1978.

Caesar, James W. "The Theory of Governance of the Reagan Administration." In *The Reagan Presidency and the Governing of America,* edited by Lester M. Salamon and Michael S. Lund. Washington, DC: Urban Institute, 1984.

Caldwell, Dan. *The Dynamics of Domestic Politics and Arms Control: The SALT II Treaty Ratification Debate*. Columbia: University of South Carolina Press, 1991.

Caldwell, Lawrence. "Soviet Attitudes to SALT." *Adelphi Paper,* no. 75, London: International Institute for Strategic Studies, 1971.

Campbell, David. *Writing Security: United States Foreign Policy and the Politics of Identity*. Minneapolis: University of Minnesota Press, 1992.

Carnesale, Albert, and Richard N. Haass, eds. *Superpower Arms Control: Setting the Record Straight*. Cambridge, MA: Ballinger, 1987.

Chernoff, Fred. "Ending the Cold War: The Soviet Retreat and the US Military Build-up." *International Affairs* (London) 67, no. 1 (1991): 111–26.

Cochran, Thomas B., William M. Arkin, and Milton M. Hoenig. *Nuclear Weapons Databook*. Vol. 4. New York: Harper & Row, 1989.

Cohen, Stephen F. *Rethinking the Soviet Experience: Politics and History Since 1917*. New York: Oxford University Press, 1985.

Cohen, Stephen F., and Katrina vanden Heuvel. *Voices of Glasnost: Interviews with Gorbachev's Reformers*. New York: W. W. Norton, 1989.

Davis, Lynn E. "Lessons of the INF Treaty." *Foreign Affairs* 66 (1988): 720–34.

Dean, Arthur H. *Test Ban and Disarmament: Path of Negotiation*. New York: Harper & Row, 1966.

Dean, Jonathan. "The INF Treaty Negotiations." In *SIPRI Yearbook 1988: World Armaments and Disarmament,* edited by Stockholm International Peace Research Institute. New York: Oxford University Press, 1988.

Den Oudsten, Eymert. "Public Opinion on Peace and War." In *SIPRI Yearbook 1986: World Armaments and Disarmament,* edited by Stockholm International Peace Research Institute. New York: Oxford University Press, 1986.

Deudney, Daniel, and G. John Ikenberry. "International Sources of Soviet Change." *International Security* 16 (1991–92): 74–118.

———. "Who Won the Cold War?" *Foreign Policy,* no. 87 (1992): 123–38.

Dinerstein, Herbert, Leon Goure, and Thomas Wolfe. "U.S. Editors' Analytical Introduction." In *Soviet Military Strategy,* edited by V. D. Sokolovskii. Englewood Cliffs, NJ: Prentice Hall, 1963.

Divine, Robert A. *Blowing on the Wind: The Nuclear Test Ban Debate, 1954–60*. New York: Oxford University Press, 1978.

Dobrynin, Anatoly. *In Confidence: Moscow's Ambassador to America's Six Cold War Presidents (1962–1986)*. New York: Times Books, 1995.

———. "Za Bez'yadernyi Mir, Na Vstrechu XXI Veka" (Toward a Non-Nuclear World, On the Brink of the Twenty-first Century). *Kommunist,* no. 9 (1986): 18–31.

Doder, Dusko, and Louise Branson. *Shadows and Whispers.* New York: Random House, 1986.

Doig, Jameson W., and Erwin C. Hargrove. Introduction to *Leadership and Innovation: A Biographical Perspective on Entrepreneurs in Government,* edited by Jameson W. Doig and Erwin C. Hargrove. Baltimore: Johns Hopkins University Press, 1987.

Dunn, Lewis. "New Nuclear Threats to U.S. Security." In *New Nuclear Nations: Consequences for U.S. Policy,* edited by Robert D. Blackwill and Albert Carnesale. New York: Council on Foreign Relations, 1993.

Eisenhower, Dwight D. *Waging Peace, 1956–1961: The White House Years.* Garden City, NJ: Doubleday, 1965.

Evangelista, Matthew. "Cooperation Theory and Disarmament Negotiations in the 1950s." *World Politics* 42 (1990): 502–28.

Evans, Peter B., Harold K. Jacobson, and Robert D. Putnam, eds. *Double-Edged Diplomacy: International Bargaining and Domestic Politics.* Berkeley and Los Angeles: University of California Press, 1993.

Fish, Steven. "The Emergence of Independent Associations and the Transformation of Russian Political Society." In *The Soviet System: From Crisis to Collapse,* edited by Alexander Dallin and Gail W. Lapidus. Boulder, CO: Westview Press, 1995.

Fukuyama, Francis. *The End of History and the Last Man.* New York: Free Press, 1992.

Gaddis, John Lewis. "Hanging Tough Paid Off." *Bulletin of the Atomic Scientists* 45, no. 1 (1989): 11–14.

Gallup, George W. *The Gallup Poll: Public Opinion 1935–1971.* Vol. 2. New York: Random House, 1972.

———. *The Gallup Poll: Public Opinion 1935–1971.* Vol. 3. New York: Random House, 1972.

Gardner, John W. *On Leadership.* New York: Free Press, 1990.

Garthoff, Raymond. *Detente and Confrontation: American-Soviet Relations from Nixon to Reagan.* Rev. ed. Washington, DC: Brookings Institution, 1994.

———. *Reflections on the Cuban Missile Crisis.* Washington, DC: Brookings Institution, 1987.

———. "The Soviet SS-20 Decision." *Survival* 25, no. 3 (1983): 110–19.

Gelman, Harry. *The Brezhnev Politburo and the Decline of Detente.* Ithaca, NY: Cornell University Press, 1984.

George, Alexander. "Incentives for US-Soviet Security Cooperation and Mutual Adjustment." In *US-Soviet Security Cooperation: Achievements, Failures, and Lessons,* edited by Alexander George, Philip J. Farley, and Alexander Dallin. New York: Oxford University Press, 1988.

George, Alexander, Philip J. Farley, and Alexander Dallin, eds. *U.S.–Soviet Security Cooperation: Achievements, Failures, and Lessons.* New York: Oxford University Press, 1988.

Goldgeier, James M. *Leadership Style and Soviet Foreign Policy: Stalin, Khrushchev, Brezhnev, and Gorbachev.* Baltimore: Johns Hopkins University Press, 1994.

Goldman, Marshall. "The Effort Collapses." In *The Soviet System: From Crisis to Collapse,* edited by Alexander Dallin and Gail W. Lapidus. Boulder, CO: Westview Press, 1995.

Gorbachev, Mikhail. *Memoirs.* New York: Doubleday, 1995.

———. *Perestroika: New Thinking for Our Country and the World.* New York: Harper & Row, 1987.

Gourevitch, Peter. "The Second Image Reversed: The International Sources of Domestic Politics." *International Organization* 32 (1978): 881–911.

Gowa, Joanne. "Anarchy, Egoism, and Third Images: *The Evolution of Cooperation* and International Relations." *International Organization* 40 (1986): 167–86.

Greenhalgh, Leonard, and Deborah I. Chapman. "Joint Decision Making: The Inseparability of Relationships and Negotiation." In *Negotiation as a Social Process,* edited by Roderick M. Kramer and David M. Messick. Thousand Oaks, CA: Sage Publications, 1995.

Greenstein, Fred I., ed. *The Reagan Presidency: An Early Assessment.* Baltimore: Johns Hopkins University Press, 1983.

Grieco, Joseph. "Anarchy and the Limits of Cooperation: A Realist Critique of the Newest Liberal Institutionalism." *International Organization* 42 (1988): 485–508.

Griffith, William E. *The Sino-Soviet Rift.* Cambridge: MIT Press, 1964.

Griffiths, Franklyn. "The Sources of American Conduct: Soviet Perspectives and their Policy Implications." *International Security* 9 (1984): 3–50.

Gruliow, Leo, ed., *Current Soviet Policies III: The Documentary Record of the Extraordinary 21st Congress of the CPSU.* New York: Columbia University Press, 1960.

Gustafson, Thane, and Dawn Mann, "Gorbachev's First Year: Building Power and Authority." *Problems of Communism* 35, no. 3 (1986): 1–19.

———. "Gorbachev's Next Gamble." *Problems of Communism* 36, no. 4 (1987): 1–20.

Haig, Alexander. *Caveat: Realism, Reagan, and Foreign Policy.* New York: Macmillan, 1984.

Halperin, Morton. *Bureaucratic Politics and Foreign Policy.* Washington, DC: Brookings Institution, 1974.

———. "The Gaither Committee and the Policy Process." *World Politics* 13 (1961): 360–84.

Haslam, Jonathan. *The Soviet Union and the Politics of Nuclear Weapons in Europe, 1969–1987.* Ithaca, NY: Cornell University Press, 1990.

Heller, Mikhail, and Aleksandr M. Nekrich. *Utopia in Power: The History of the Soviet Union From 1917 to the Present.* New York: Summit Books, 1986.

Herman, Robert G. "Identity, Norms, and National Security: The Soviet Foreign Policy Revolution and the End of the Cold War." In *The Culture of National Security: Norms and Identity in World Politics,* edited by Peter J. Katzenstein. New York: Columbia University Press, 1996.

Herrmann, Richard K. *Perceptions and Behavior in Soviet Foreign Policy.* Pittsburgh: University of Pittsburgh Press, 1985.

Herspring, Dale. "On Perestroyka: Gorbachev, Yazov, and the Military." *Problems of Communism* 36, no. 4 (1987): 99–107.

Hilsman, Roger. *To Move a Nation: The Politics of Foreign Policy in the Administration of John F. Kennedy.* Garden City, NJ: Doubleday, 1967.

Holloway, David. "State, Society, and the Military." In *The Soviet System in Crisis,* edited by Alexander Dallin and Gail W. Lapidus. Boulder, CO: Westview Press, 1991.

Holzman, Franklyn D. "Politics and Guesswork: CIA and DIA Estimates of Soviet Military Spending." *International Security* 14, no. 2 (fall 1989): 101–31.

Horelick, Arnold, and Myron Rush. *Strategic Power and Soviet Foreign Policy.* Chicago: University of Chicago Press, 1966.

Hough, Jerry. "Andropov's First Year." *Problems of Communism* 32, no. 6 (1983): 49–64.

———. "Gorbachev Consolidating Power." *Problems of Communism* 36, no. 4 (1987): 21–43.

———. "Gorbachev's Endgame." In *The Soviet System in Crisis,* edited by Alexander Dallin and Gail W. Lapidus. Boulder, CO: Westview Press, 1991.

———. *Opening up the Soviet Economy.* Washington, DC: Brookings Institution, 1987.

———. *Russia and the West: Gorbachev and the Politics of Reform.* New York: Simon & Schuster, 1988.

Hough, Jerry, and Merle Fainsod. *How the Soviet Union Is Governed.* Cambridge: Harvard University Press, 1979.

Ikle, Fred Charles. *How Nations Negotiate.* New York: Harper & Row, 1964.

Jervis, Robert. "Cooperation under the Security Dilemma." *World Politics* 30 (1978): 167–214.

———. *Perception and Misperception in World Politics.* Princeton, NJ: Princeton University Press, 1976.

Jones, David T. "How to Negotiate with Gorbachev's Team." *Orbis* 33 (1989): 357–73.

Jonsson, Christer. *Soviet Bargaining Behavior: The Nuclear Test Ban Case.* New York: Columbia University Press, 1979.

Karp, Regina Cowen. "The START Treaty and the Future of Strategic Nuclear Arms Control." In *SIPRI Yearbook 1992: World Armaments and Disarmament,* edited by Stockholm International Peace Research Institute. New York: Oxford University Press.

———. "U.S.–Soviet Nuclear Arms Control." In *SIPRI Yearbook 1990: World Armaments and Disarmament,* edited by Stockholm International Peace Research Institute. New York: Oxford University Press, 1990.

———. "U.S.–Soviet Nuclear Arms Control." In *SIPRI Yearbook 1991: World Armaments and Disarmament,* edited by Stockholm International Peace Research Institute. New York: Oxford University Press, 1991.

Katzenstein, Peter J., ed. *The Culture of National Security: Norms and Identity in World Politics.* New York: Columbia University Press, 1996.

"Kennedy-Khrushchev Correspondence," *Problems of Communism* 41 (special edition, 1992): 30–120.

Kennedy, John F. *Strategy of Peace,* edited by Allan Nevins. New York: Harper & Brothers, 1960.

Keohane, Robert O. *After Hegemony: Cooperation and Discord in the World Political Economy.* Princeton, NJ: Princeton University Press, 1984.

Keohane, Robert O., and Joseph S. Nye. *Power and Interdependence: World Politics in Transition.* Boston: Little, Brown, 1977.

Khrushchev, N. S. *Khrushchev Remembers.* Vol. 1. Translated and edited by Strobe Talbott. Boston: Little, Brown, 1970.

———. *Khrushchev Remembers: The Last Testament.* Vol. 2. Translated and edited by Strobe Talbott. Boston: Little, Brown, 1974.

———. "Report to the XX Party Congress, February 14, 1956." In *The International Situation and Soviet Foreign Policy: Reports of Soviet Leaders,* edited by Myron Rush. Columbus, OH: Charles E. Merrill, 1970.

Killian, James R., Jr. *Sputnik, Scientists, and Eisenhower: A Memoir of the First Special Assistant to the President for Science and Technology.* Cambridge: MIT Press, 1977.

Kissinger, Henry. *The White House Years.* Boston: Little, Brown, 1979.

Klare, Michael. "Adding Fuel to Fires: The Conventional Arms Trade in the 1990s." In *World Security: Challenges for a New Century,* 2d ed., edited by Michael Klare and Dan Thomas. New York: St. Martin's Press, 1994.

———. "Deadly Convergence: The Arms Trade, Nuclear/Chemical/Missile Proliferation, and Regional Conflict in the 1990s." In *World Security: Trends and Challenges at Century's End,* edited by Michael Klare and Dan Thomas. New York: St. Martin's Press, 1991.

———. "Redefining Security: The New Global Schisms." *Current History* 95 (1996): 353–58.

Klotz, Audie J. *Norms in International Relations: The Struggle against Apartheid.* Ithaca, NY: Cornell University Press, 1995.

Knopf, Jeffrey W. "Beyond Two-Level Games: Domestic-International Interaction in the Intermediate Range Nuclear Forces Negotiations." *International Organization* 47 (1993): 599–628.

Korb, Lawrence J. "The 1991 Defense Budget." In *Setting National Priorities: Policy for the Nineties,* edited by Henry J. Aaron. Washington, DC: Brookings Institution, 1990.

Krasner, Stephen. "Are Bureaucracies Important? (or Allison Wonderland)." *Foreign Policy,* no. 7 (1972): 165–79.

———. "Structural Causes and Regime Consequences: Regimes as Intervening Variables." In *International Regimes,* edited by Stephen Krasner. Ithaca, NY: Cornell University Press, 1983.

Kugler, Richard L., with Marianna V. Kozintseva. *Enlarging NATO: The Russia Factor.* Santa Monica, CA: RAND, 1996.

Kurth, James. "Why We Buy the Weapons We Do." *Foreign Policy,* no. 11 (1973): 33–56.

Ladd, Everett Carll. "The Reagan Phenomenon and Public Attitudes Toward Government." In *The Reagan Presidency and the Governing of America,* edited by Lester M. Salamon and Michael S. Lund. Washington, DC: Urban Institute, 1984.

Lapidus, Gail W. "Gorbachev's Nationalities Problem." In *The Soviet System: From Crisis to Collapse,* edited by Alexander Dallin and Gail W. Lapidus. Boulder, CO: Westview Press, 1995.

———. "Toward the Emergence of Civil Society in the Soviet Union." In *The Soviet System: From Crisis to Collapse,* edited by Alexander Dallin and Gail W. Lapidus. Boulder, CO: Westview Press, 1995.

Larson, Deborah Welch. "Crisis Prevention and the Austrian State Treaty." *International Organization* 41 (1987): 27–60.

———. *Origins of Containment: A Psychological Explanation.* Princeton, NJ: Princeton University Press, 1985.

Lebow, Richard Ned. *Between Peace and War: The Nature of International Crisis.* Baltimore: Johns Hopkins University Press, 1981.

Lebow, Richard Ned, and Janice Gross Stein. *We All Lost the Cold War.* Baltimore: Johns Hopkins University Press, 1994.

Legvold, Robert. "The Revolution in Soviet Foreign Policy." In *The Soviet System in Crisis,* edited by Alexander Dallin and Gail W. Lapidus. Boulder, CO: Westview Press, 1991.

Lepingwell, John W. R. "START II and the Politics of Arms Control in Russia." *International Security* 20 (1995): 63–91.

Ligachev, Yegor. *Inside Gorbachev's Kremlin: The Memoirs of Yegor Ligachev.* Translated by Catherine A. Fitzpatrick, Michele A. Berdy, and Dobrochna Dyrcz-Freeman. New York: Pantheon, 1993.

Linden, Carl A. *Khrushchev and the Soviet Leadership, 1957–1964.* Baltimore: Johns Hopkins Press, 1966.

Lockwood, Dunbar. "Nuclear Arms Control." In *SIPRI Yearbook 1993: World Armaments and Disarmament,* edited by Stockholm International Peace Research Institute. New York: Oxford University Press, 1993.

Long, Franklin, and George Rathjens, eds. *Arms Defense Policy and Arms Control.* New York: W. W. Norton, 1976.

Lowi, Theodore J. "American Business, Public Policy, Case Studies and Political Theory." *World Politics* 16 (1964): 677–715.

———. *The End of Liberalism: The Second Republic of the United States.* 2d ed. New York: W. W. Norton, 1979.

———. *The Personal President: Power Invested, Promise Unfulfilled.* Ithaca, NY: Cornell University Press, 1985.

———. "The Public Philosophy: Interest-Group Liberalism." *American Political Science Review* 61 (1967): 5–21.

———. "Ronald Reagan—Revolutionary?" In *The Reagan Presidency and the Governing of America,* edited by Lester M. Salamon and Michael S. Lund. Washington, DC: Urban Institute, 1984.

Lynn-Jones, Sean M., and Steven E. Miller, eds. *Global Dangers: Changing Dimensions of International Security.* Cambridge: MIT Press, 1995.

MccGwire, Michael. *Military Objectives in Soviet Foreign Policy.* Washington, DC: Brookings Institution, 1987.

Mearsheimer, John J. "Assessing the Conventional Balance: The 3:1 Rule and its Critics." *International Security* 13 (1989): 54–89.

———. "Nuclear Weapons and Deterrence in Europe." *International Security* 9 (1984–85): 19–46.

Melanson, Richard A. "The Foundations of Eisenhower's Foreign Policy: Continuity, Community, and Consensus." In *Reevaluating Eisenhower: American Foreign Policy in the 1950s,* edited by Richard A. Melanson and David Mayers. Urbana: University of Illinois Press, 1987.

Meyer, Stephen M. "The Sources and Prospects of Gorbachev's New Political Thinking on Security." *International Security* 13 (1988): 124–63.

———. "Soviet Theater Nuclear Forces." *Adelphi Papers,* no. 187. London: International Institute for Strategic Studies, 1983.

———. "Soviet Theater Nuclear Forces." *Adelphi Papers,* no. 188. London: International Institute for Strategic Studies, 1984.

Milner, Helen. "International Theories of Cooperation among Nations: Strengths and Weaknesses." *World Politics* 44 (1992): 466–96.

Moravcsik, Andrew. "Introduction: Integrating International and Domestic Theories of International Bargaining." In *Double-Edged Diplomacy: International Bargaining and Domestic Politics,* edited by Peter B. Evans, Harold K. Jacobson, and Robert D. Putnam. Berkeley and Los Angeles: University of California Press, 1993.

Morgenthau, Hans. *Politics among Nations: The Struggle for Power and Peace.* 5th ed. New York: Knopf, 1973.

National Conference of Catholic Bishops. *A Pastoral Letter on War and Peace.* Washington, DC: United States Catholic Conference, 1983.

Neustadt, Richard. *Presidential Power: The Politics of Leadership from FDR to Reagan.* New York: Free Press, 1990.

Newhouse, John. *Cold Dawn: The Story of SALT I.* New York: Holt, Rinehart & Winston, 1973.

Newnham, Randall E. "Gorbachev and the Soviet Military: A Chronology." In *Gorbachev and His Generals: The Reform of Soviet Military Doctrine,* edited by William C. Green and Theodore Karasik. Boulder, CO: Westview Press, 1989.

Nincic, Miroslav. "U.S. Soviet Policy and the Electoral Connection." *World Politics* 42 (1990): 370–96.

Norris, Robert S., Richard W. Fieldhouse, Thomas B. Cochran, and William M. Arkin. "Nuclear Weapons." In *SIPRI Yearbook 1991: World Armaments and Disarmament,* edited by Stockholm International Peace Research Institute. New York: Oxford University Press, 1991.

Nye, Joseph S. Jr., "Nuclear Learning and U.S.–Soviet Security Regimes." *International Organization* 41 (1987): 371–402.

Oberdorfer, Don. *The Turn From the Cold War to a New Era.* New York: Touchstone, 1992.

Onuf, Nicholas Greenwood. *World of Our Making: Rules and Rule in Social Theory and International Relations.* Columbia: University of South Carolina Press, 1989.

Oye, Kenneth A. "Explaining Cooperation under Anarchy." In *Cooperation under Anarchy,* edited by Kenneth A. Oye. Princeton, NJ: Princeton University Press, 1986.

Parrott, Bruce. "Soviet National Security under Gorbachev." *Problems of Communism* 37, no. 6 (1988): 1–36.

Pope, Ronald. *Soviet Views on the Cuban Missile Crisis: Myth and Reality in Foreign Policy Analysis.* Washington, DC: University Press of America, 1982.

Posen, Barry. "Measuring the European Conventional Balance: Coping with Complexity in Threat Assessment." *International Security* 9 (1984–85): 47–88.

President's Commission on Strategic Forces. *Report of the President's Commission on Strategic Forces.* Washington, DC: GPO, April 11, 1983.

Pruitt, Dean. "Strategy in Negotiation." In *International Negotiation: Analysis, Approaches, Issues,* edited by Victor Kremenyuk. San Francisco: Jossey-Bass, 1991.

Putnam, Robert D. "Diplomacy and Domestic Politics: The Logic of Two Level Games." *International Organization* 42 (1988): 427–60.

Quandt, William B. "The Electoral Cycle and the Conduct of American Foreign Policy." In *American Foreign Policy,* 3d ed., edited by C. W. Kegley, Jr. and E. R. Wittkopf. New York: St. Martin's Press, 1987.

Raiffa, Howard. *The Art and Science of Negotiation.* Cambridge: Belknap Press of Harvard University Press, 1982.

Remnick, David. *Lenin's Tomb: The Last Days of the Soviet Empire.* New York: Vintage Books, 1994.

Richter, James G. *Khrushchev's Double Bind: International Pressures and Domestic Coalition Politics.* Baltimore: Johns Hopkins University Press, 1994.

Risse-Kappen, Thomas. "Did 'Peace Through Strength' End the Cold War?" *International Security* 16 (1991): 162–88.

———. "Public Opinion, Domestic Structure, and Foreign Policy in Liberal Democracies." *World Politics* 43 (1991): 479–512.

———. *The Zero Option: INF, West Germany, and Arms Control.* Boulder, CO: Westview Press, 1988.

Rockefeller Brothers Fund. *Prospect for America: The Rockefeller Panel Reports.* Garden City, NJ: Doubleday, 1961.

Roeder, Philip. "Do New Soviet Leaders Really Make a Difference? Rethinking the 'Succession Connection' Hypothesis." *American Political Science Review* 79 (1984): 958–76.

———. *Red Sunset: The Failure of Soviet Politics.* Princeton, NJ: Princeton University Press, 1993.

Romm, Joseph J. *Defining National Security: The Nonmilitary Aspects.* New York: Council on Foreign Relations Press, 1993.

Rosenau, James N. *Domestic Sources of Foreign Policy.* New York: Free Press, 1965.

Rotfeld, Adam Daniel. "Introduction: Parameters of Change." In *SIPRI Yearbook 1993: World Armaments and Disarmament,* edited by Stockholm International Peace Research Institute. New York: Oxford University Press, 1993.

Rush, Myron. "Guns over Growth in Soviet Policy." *International Security* 7 (1982–83): 167–79.

———. *How Communist States Change Their Rulers.* Ithaca, NY: Cornell University Press, 1974.

———. *Political Succession in the USSR.* New York: Columbia University Press, 1968.

———. *The Rise of Khrushchev.* Washington, DC: Public Affairs Press, 1958.

———. "The Soviet Military Build-up and the Coming Succession." *International Security* 5 (1981): 168–85.

———. "Succeeding Brezhnev." *Problems of Communism* 32, no. 1 (1983): 2–7.

Russett, Bruce. *Controlling the Sword: The Democratic Governance of National Security.* Cambridge: Harvard University Press, 1990.

Sagan, Carl. "Nuclear War and Climatic Catastrophe: Some Policy Implications." *Foreign Affairs* 62 (1983–84): 257–92.

Salamon, Lester M., and Michael S. Lund. "Governance in the Reagan Era: An Overview." In *The Reagan Presidency and the Governing of America,* edited by Lester M. Salamon and Michael S. Lund. Washington, DC: Urban Institute Press, 1984.

Schell, Jonathan. *The Fate of the Earth.* New York: Alfred A. Knopf, 1982.

Schelling, Thomas. *Arms and Influence.* New Haven, CT: Yale University Press, 1966.

———. *The Strategy of Conflict.* Cambridge: Harvard University Press, 1960.

Schelling, Thomas, and Morton Halperin. *Strategy and Arms Control.* New York: Twentieth Century Fund, 1961.

Schlesinger, Arthur M. *A Thousand Days: John F. Kennedy in the White House.* Boston: Houghton Mifflin, 1965.

———. "Onward and Upward from the Missile Crisis." *Problems of Communism* 41 (special edition, 1992): 5–7.

Schmidt, Helmut. "The 1977 Alastair Buchan Memorial Lecture." *Survival* 20 (1978): 2–10.

Schnapper, M. B., ed. *New Frontiers of the Kennedy Administration: The Texts of the Task Force Reports Prepared for the President.* Washington, DC: Public Affairs Press, 1961.

Schwartz, David. *NATO's Nuclear Dilemmas.* Washington, DC: Brookings Institution, 1983.

Seaborg, Glenn. *Kennedy, Khrushchev, and the Test Ban.* Berkeley and Los Angeles: University of California Press, 1981.

Shevardnadze, Eduard. *The Future Belongs to Freedom.* Translated by Catherine A. Fitzpatrick. New York: Free Press, 1991.

Shulman, Marshall. "SALT and the Soviet Union." In *SALT: The Moscow Agreements and Beyond,* edited by Mason Willrich and John B. Rhinelander. New York: Free Press, 1974.

Skowronek, Stephen. *The Politics Presidents Make: Leadership from John Adams to George Bush.* Cambridge: Belknap Press of Harvard University Press, 1993.

Smith, Gerard. *Doubletalk: The Story of the First Strategic Arms Limitation Talks.* Garden City, NJ: Doubleday, 1980.

Smith, Hedrick. *The New Russians.* New York: Avon Books, 1991.

Snyder, Glenn Herald, and Paul Diesing. *Conflict among Nations: Bargaining and Decision-Making in International Crises.* Princeton, NJ: Princeton University Press, 1977.

Snyder, Jack. "East-West Bargaining over Germany: The Search for Synergy in a Two-Level Game." In *Double-Edged Diplomacy: International Bargaining and Domestic Politics,* edited by Peter B. Evans, Harold K. Jacobson, and Robert D. Putnam. Berkeley and Los Angeles: University of California Press, 1993.

———. "The Gorbachev Revolution: A Waning of Soviet Expansionism?" *International Security* 12 (1987–88): 93–131.

———. *The Myths of Empire: Domestic Politics and International Ambition.* Ithaca, NY: Cornell University Press, 1991.

Sorensen, Theodore C. *Kennedy.* New York: Harper & Row, 1965.

Stein, Arthur. *Why Nations Cooperate: Circumstance and Choice in International Relations.* Ithaca, NY: Cornell University Press, 1990.

Stein, Janice Gross, ed. *Getting to the Table: The Processes of International Prenegotiation.* Baltimore: Johns Hopkins University Press, 1989.

———. "The Political Economy of Security Agreements: The Linked Costs of Failure at Camp David." In *Double-Edged Diplomacy: International Bargaining and Domestic Politics,* edited by Peter B. Evans, Harold K. Jacobson, and Robert D. Putnam. Berkeley and Los Angeles: University of California Press, 1993.

Steinberg, Dmitri. "The Soviet Defence Burden: Estimating Hidden Defence Costs." *Soviet Studies* 44 (1992): 237–63.

Steinbruner, John, and Barry Carter. "Organizational and Political Dimensions of Strategic Posture: The Problems of Reform." In *Arms, Defense Policy, and Arms Control,* edited by Franklin A. Long and George W. Rathjens. New York: W. W. Norton, 1976.

Talbott, Strobe. *Deadly Gambits: The Reagan Administration and the Stalemate in Nuclear Arms Control.* New York: Vintage Books, 1985.

———. *Endgame: The Inside Story of SALT II.* New York: Harper & Row, 1979.

———. *The Master of the Game: Paul Nitze and the Nuclear Peace.* New York: Alfred A. Knopf, 1988.

Tatu, Michel. *Power in the Kremlin: From Khrushchev to Kosygin.* Translated by Helen Katel. New York: Viking Press, 1970.

Taubman, William. "The Correspondence: Khrushchev's Motives and his Views of Kennedy." *Problems of Communism* 41 (special edition, 1992): 14–18.

Tichy, Noel M., and Mary Anne Devanna. *The Transformational Leader.* New York: Wiley, 1990.

Tompson, William J. "The Fall of Nikita Khrushchev." *Soviet Studies* 43 (1991): 1101–21.

Turco, R. P., D. B. Toon, T. P. Ackerman, J. B. Pollack, and Carl Sagan. "Nuclear Winter: Global Consequences of Nuclear Explosions." *Science,* no. 222: 1283–92.

Ulam, Adam. *Expansion and Coexistence: The History of Soviet Foreign Policy, 1917–1967.* New York: Praeger, 1968.

United States Arms Control and Disarmament Agency. *Arms Control and Disarmament Agreements: Text and Histories of Negotiations.* Washington, DC: United States Arms Control and Disarmament Agency, 1980.

United States Senate. *Hearings before the Committee on Foreign Relations, United States Senate, 100th Congress, 2nd Session on The Treaty Between the United States of America and the Union of Soviet Socialist Republics on the Elimination of their Intermediate and Shorter-Range Missiles.*

Urban, Michael. Boris El'tsin, Democratic Russia, and the Campaign for the Russian Presidency. *Soviet Studies* 44 (1992): 187–207.

Walt, Stephen M. "Alliance Formation and the Balance of World Power." *International Security* 9 (1985): 3–41.

———. *The Origins of Alliances.* Ithaca, NY: Cornell University Press, 1987.

Waltz, Kenneth. *Theory of International Politics.* Reading, MA: Addison-Wesley, 1979.

Weber, Steve. *Cooperation and Discord in U.S.–Soviet Arms Control.* Princeton, NJ: Princeton University Press, 1991.

Weinberger, Caspar. *Fighting for Peace: Seven Critical Years in the Pentagon.* New York: Warner Books, 1990.

———. "Arms Reductions and Deterrence." *Foreign Affairs* 66 (1988): 700–719.

Wendt, Alexander E. "The Agent-Structure Problem in International Relations Theory." *International Organization* 41 (1987): 341–70.

———. "Anarchy Is What States Make of It: The Social Construction of Power Politics." *International Organization* 46 (1992): 391–425.

———. "Constructing International Politics." *International Security* 20 (1995): 71–81.

Wohlforth, William Curti. *The Elusive Balance: Power and Perceptions During the Cold War.* Ithaca, NY: Cornell University Press, 1993.

———. "Realism and the End of the Cold War." *International Security* 19 (1994–95): 91–129.

Young, Oran R. "Political Leadership and Regime Formation: On the Development of Institutions in International Society." *International Organization* 45 (1991): 281–308.

Zartman, I. William. "The Structure of Negotiation." In *International Negotiation: Analysis, Approaches, Issues,* edited by Victor Kremenyuk. San Francisco: Jossey-Bass, 1991.

Zubok, Vladislav, and Constantine Pleshakov. *Inside the Kremlin's Cold War: From Stalin to Khrushchev.* Cambridge: Harvard University Press, 1996.

"1994 Convention Update: *New Agenda of World Politics.*" *International Studies Newsletter* nos. 2 & 3 (1993): 1–4.

Periodicals and Yearbooks [abbreviations]

Congressional Quarterly Almanac [*CQ Almanac*]. Washington, DC: Congressional Quarterly Press.

Congressional Quarterly Weekly [*CQ Weekly*]. Washington, DC: Congressional Quarterly Press.

Current Digest of the Soviet Press [*CDSP*]. Columbus, OH: American Association for the Advancement of Slavic Studies.

Gallup Report, name changed in 1989 to *Gallup Poll Monthly.*

International Institute for Strategic Studies [IISS]. *The Military Balance.* London: International Institute for Strategic Studies.

Kommunist.

New York Times [*NYT*].

Pravda.

SShA: Ekonomika, Politika, Ideologiya [SShA].

United States Arms Control and Disarmament Agency. *Documents on Disarmament* [*DoD*]. Washington, DC: US Government Printing Office (after 1961).

United States Department of State Bulletin [*DSB*], renamed in 1989 *United States Department of State Dispatch* [*DSD*].

United States Disarmament Administration. *Documents on Disarmament* [*DoD*]. Washington, DC: US Government Printing Office (prior to 1961).

———. *Geneva Conference on the Discontinuance of Nuclear Weapons Tests: History and Analysis of Negotiations.* Washington, DC: Department of State Publication 7258, 1961. [*Geneva Conference*].

Washington Post [*WP*]

Archival Materials [abbreviations]

    Dwight D. Eisenhower Library, Abilene, KS [DDEL]
      Ann C. Whitman File [ACWF]
        Dulles-Herter Series [DHS]
        Dwight D. Eisenhower Series [DDES]
        National Security Council Series [NSCS]
      White House Office Files [WHOF]
        Office of the Special Assistant for National Security Affairs: Records, 1952–61 [OSA NSA], NSC Series [NSCS]
        Office of the Special Assistant for Science and Technology [OSAST]
    "Memorandum of Conference with the President" [MCP]

    John F. Kennedy Library, Dorchester, MA [JFKL]
      President's Office Files [POF]
        Subjects Series, Disarmament Subseries
        Special Correspondence Series
        Departments and Agencies Subseries, United States Information Agency [USIA]
      National Security Files [NSF]
        Countries Subseries—USSR
        Nuclear Weapons Subseries
        Meetings and Memoranda
        Meetings with the President Series

    W. Averell Harriman Papers, Library of Congress, Washington, DC [WAH Papers]
      Special Files, Public Service, 1915–81 Series, Trips and Missions Subseries

Index

Accommodation
  as bargaining strategy, 4–5
  Gorbachev's strategy, 90, 95
Accommodation, Soviet
  in bargaining (1989–91), 116
  of Gorbachev in INF talks (1987), 100, 107, 117
  policy after Reykjavik, 105
  at Reykjavik (1986), 95
  in START negotiations (1989), 120
Adelman, Kenneth, 107
Afghanistan
  Soviet invasion of, 82
Air-launched cruise missiles (ALCMs), 126
Andropov, Yuri, 66, 69, 80, 81
  autonomy of (1980s), 70
Anti-Ballistic Missile (ABM)
  research under LTBT, 62
Anti-Ballistic Missile (ABM) Treaty
  from SALT I negotiations, 140
Arbatov, Georgi, 91
Arms control
  concerns related to Reagan's position on, 87–88
  effect of leader's autonomy on approach to, xvi
  Eighteen Nation Disarmament Committee (ENDC) talks, 56
  future U.S.-Russian agenda, 144
  INF Treaty as success for, 107–10
  negotiations deadlock (1983), 81, 83
  policy of Kennedy administration, 52
  potential (1998), 145
  potential in post–Cold War world, xx
  Reagan's position in second term, 99
  Reykjavik meeting (1986), 95
  as seen by domestic politics analysts, 2
  Soviet agenda at Reykjavik (1986), 103
  Soviet attitude (1985), 89–90
  states' choice of strategy, 7–10
  U.S. attitude (1985), 87–89
  U.S. attitudes toward (1957–58), 36–37
  U.S.-USSR achievements beyond START, 136–37
  U.S.-USSR agreement to resume talks (1985), 89
Arms Control and Disarmament Agency (ACDA), United States, 46, 52
Autonomy
  of Andropov and Brezhnev (1980s), 70
  of Bush (1989–91), 116, 131
  of Carter, 142
  of Clinton, 145
  of Eisenhower, 23, 25–27, 35, 43, 138
  to explain arms control initiatives, 47

207

208   Index

Autonomy (*continued*)
  of Gorbachev (1985–87), 90–93, 95, 106, 109
  of Gorbachev (1989–91), 116–20, 123, 126. 129, 131
  of Khrushchev, 22–25, 41, 48
  of leader, xvi, 138–39
  in leadership model, 15–19
  of Reagan, 71, 77, 87, 96, 98–100, 110
  when leaders lack, 138
  of Yeltsin, 144

Baker, Howard, 88
Baker, James A. III, 122, 124–25, 127
Ballistic missiles
  anti-ballistic missiles, 62
  ICBMs, 30, 35, 116
  Soviet SS-20s, 79, 81
Bargaining
  bargaining game, xvi
  determinants of negotiation strategy, 6–10
  interstate, 18
  transactional and transformational, 18–19
Bargaining strategy
  accommodation as, 4–5, 116
  of Bush during START talks, 116–17
  cooperation as, 4–5
  to explain states' behavior, 4–5
  factors in determining, xv
  Gorbachev's cooperative, 95
  in leadership model, 15–19
  obfuscation as, 4–5
  predomination, 4–5
  SALT II talks, 142
  Soviet new thinking, 94, 109
  Soviet Union at Reykjavik (1986), 95
  of U.S. and USSR at INF negotiations (1980s), 77–83
  U.S.-USSR (1958–91), 134–35

  U.S.-USSR at INF talks (1985–87), 100–107
Berlin Wall, 54
Bessmertnykh, Aleksandr, 127
Brezhnev, Leonid, 66, 68
  autonomy of (1980s), 70
  illness and death of, 69, 80
  position on intermediate-range nuclear missiles, 78
Bundy, McGeorge, 51
Burt, Richard, 127
Bush, George
  approval rating (1989–91), 120–21
  autonomy of (1989–91), 116, 131
  bargaining strategies during START negotiations (1989–91), 116–17
  recognition of U.S.-USSR interdependence, 137
  role in START negotiations, 114
  transactional strategies of, 137
Bush administration
  seeing Soviet Union as threat, 122
  START decision making, 114

Carter, Jimmy
  autonomy of, 142
  Comprehensive Proposal (1977), 78
  INF talks begin in administration of, 65
  loses election (1980), 68, 70–71
  U.S. foreign policy toward Soviet Union under, 82
Chernenko, Konstantin, 90–91, 101
China
  relations with Soviet Union under terms of LTBT, 63
  response to Soviet removal of Cuban missiles, 58–59
Clinton, Bill
  autonomy of, 145
Clinton administration
  foreign policy options, 145
  transactional leadership approach, 138

Cold War
    culture of, 137–38
    factors leading to demise of, xix
    security issues during, 7
    superpower relationship during, 8
    uncertainty with end of, xix–xx
Communist Party of the Soviet Union (CPSU), 15
Comprehensive Proposal (1977), 78
Concessions
    of Soviets to conclude START agreement, 113
    of Soviets related to INF (1987), 105–7
    of Soviets at Reykjavik INF talks (1986), 103–4
    by Soviets in START negotiations, 124–25
    U.S.-USSR at Geneva Conference (1961), 54
Congress of People's Deputies (CPD), 14–15
Conventional Forces in Europe (CFE) treaty, 126–27
Convention on the Prohibition of the Development, Production, Stockpiling and Use of Chemical Weapons and Their Destruction, 143–44
Cooperation strategy
    of Brezhnev, 140–41
    of Bush during START negotiations (1989–91), 117, 123–25, 130–31
    of Eisenhower, 29–36, 39–40
    forced by domestic pressure, 138
    of Gorbachev, 90
    of Kennedy, 63–64
    of Khrushchev, 46, 51, 53, 58–59, 62–64
    of Reagan, 69
    shift of Soviet Union in INF talks to (1986), 102–3, 109
    of Soviet Union at Reykjavik (1986), 104, 109
    of United States (1961–62), 52–53
Cooperative strategy
    of Eisenhower in test ban negotiations, 29–36, 43
    of Gorbachev in INF talks (1986), 100
    of Nixon in negotiations with Soviets, 140
CPD. *See* Congress of People's Deputies (CPD)
Cruise missiles
    ground-launched, 68, 79
    START agreements on air- and submarine-launched, 126
Cuban Missile Crisis, 46, 48
    Kennedy's handling of, 64
    outcome of, 58
    Soviet strategy after, 51, 53, 62–64

Dean, Arthur, 57
Defense spending
    during Reagan administration, 76–77
    of Soviet Union (1975–91), 111–13
    See also Strategic Defense Initiative (SDI)
Détente
    effect of, 70
    Nixon as author of, 66, 141–42
    positions in USSR on (1980s), 69–70
    Reagan administration rejection of, 69, 71, 74–77
    Reagan's conception of, 76
    Soviet view of, 70
Dictate policy, 5, 10
Domestic politics
    in analysis of INF negotiations, 65–67
    framework of, 1–2
    Soviet INF choices related to, 86–90
    in Soviet Union (1980s), 69–70
    U.S. INF choices related to, 87–90
Dulles, John Foster, 29, 31, 33–34

Eighteen Nation Disarmament Committee (ENDC), 56
Eisenhower, Dwight D.
  autonomy of, 23, 25–27
  consideration of U.S.-USSR test ban, 30–37
  effect of U-2 incident on autonomy of, 138
  erosion of autonomy (1960), 35
  handling of U-2 incident, 28–29, 40–42, 47
  moderate autonomy, 43
  strategy of cooperation, 29–36, 39–40
  in test ban negotiations, 23
  test ban policy of, 42–43
  transactional strategies of, 137
ENDC. *See* Eighteen Nation Disarmament Committee (ENDC)

Foreign policy
  effect of failure on leader's autonomy, 138–39
Foreign policy, U.S.
  after Soviet invasion of Afghanistan, 82
  Bush administration review of, 122
  concerns related to Reagan's, 87–88
  Reagan administration intent to revamp, 71, 74–77
Foster, William, 52

Gaffney, Frank, 107
Geneva Conference on the Discontinuance of Nuclear Weapons Tests, 53–54
Geneva System, 38, 42
Gilpatric, Roswell, 55
Glasnost
  Gorbachev's introduction of, 91–93
  new phase (1987), 95
Gorbachev, Mikhail
  accommodation strategy at Reykjavik arms control talks, 95
  after Soviet coup, 114–15
  approval rating (1990), 118–19
  assessment of U.S. intent related to INF, 109
  autonomy (1985–87), 90–93, 95, 106, 109
  autonomy of (1989–91), 116–20, 123, 126, 129, 131
  cooperation and accommodation strategies, 90
  offer to eliminate most intermediate- and short-range missiles (1987), 105–6
  Party reform and replacement of officials, 91–92, 96, 109
  perestroika, glasnost, democratization, and new thinking, 91–94
  promulgation of Sinatra Doctrine, 139
  proposes Congress of People's Deputies, 14–15
  recogntion of U.S.-USSR interdependence, 137
  role in concluding START agreement, 113–14
  selection as general secretary (1985), 90–91
  as Soviet leader, 87
  strategies based on his domestic autonomy, 109
  strategies in renewed INF talks (1985), 101–3
  strategy at Reykjavik (1986), 103–4
Grenada (1983), xxii–xxiii
Grishin, V. V., 91
Gromyko, Andrei, 60, 81, 89
  agreement related to resumption of arms control talks, 89
  at INF negotiations, 81
  support for Gorbachev, 90–91
  on weapons inspections, 60
Ground-launched cruise missiles (GLCMs), 68, 79

Harriman, Averell, 60
Herter, Christian, 39

INF. *See* Intermediate-range nuclear forces (INF)
Information, asymmetric
  Khrushchev's use of, 36–42, 62
Intercontinental ballistic missiles (ICBMs)
  in early START negotiations, 116
  projections of U.S.-USSR balance in, 35
  successful Soviet test (1957), 30
Intermediate-range missiles
  in INF talks (1985), 101–2, 115
Intermediate-range nuclear forces (INF)
  impasse (1983), 81, 83
  lack of superpower agreement on, 82
  NATO's decision to modernize (1979), 68
  opening of talks (1980), 77
  Reagan's strategy of cooperation related to (1983), 82–83
  Soviet choices related to, 86–87
  Soviet efforts to prevent deployment, 80
  Soviet placement and aiming of, 67
  Soviet position at Reykjavik (1986), 103
  Soviet-U.S. negotiations, 65–66, 68
  talks (1981), 78
  U.S.-USSR agreement to eliminate, 90
Intermediate-range nuclear forces (INF) talks
  Gorbachev's autonomy during, 92
  Gorbachev's role in, 90
  U.S.-USSR bargaining strategies (1985–87), 100–107
  U.S.-USSR positions at opening (1985), 101–2
Intermediate-range Nuclear Forces (INF) Treaty (1987)
  factors contributing to conclusion of, 107–10

  signing of, 85
  U.S. advantages under, 107
Iran-Contra affair, 96–98, 105

Kennedy, John F.
  campaign for LTBT ratification, 60–61
  cooperative strategy of, 46–47, 63–64
  handling of Cuban Missile Crisis, 64
  perception of Soviet Union, 52
  popular support for, 49–50
  position on military power, 51–52
  strategy to gain public support, 60
  transactional strategies of, 137
  weapons limitation policy, 46
Keohane, Robert, 4–5
Khrushchev, Nikita
  advocates test ban treaty, 46
  autonomy of, 23–25
  confidence of, 51
  dismissal of, 58
  domestic autonomy (1950s), 41
  growing control and influence, 47–48
  levels of autonomy (1961–62), 48
  perception of Eisenhower, 25, 28, 42
  perception of Kennedy, 49, 51
  shift to strategy of cooperation (1963), 46, 51, 53, 58–59, 62–64
  strategy of predomination, 27–29, 39, 42
  in test ban negotiations, 22–23
  transactional strategies of, 137
  visit to United States and United Nations (1960), 47
Kohl, Helmut, 106
Korb, Lawrence, 76
Kozlov, Frol, 45–46
Kvitsinsky, Yuli, 78, 79, 81

Leaders
  with autonomy, xxiv
  determinants of autonomy of, xvi
  impact of autonomy on, 138–39

Leaders (*continued*)
  in Soviet Union, 13–18
  taking transformational approach, xvi–xvii
Leadership
  of Gorbachev, 87
  problems of Soviet Union (1985), 90
  transactional, xvi, 17–19, 138–39
  transformational, 17–19
Leadership model
  of adversarial bargaining, 3
  components to reach national bargaining strategy, 15–18
  development of, xx–xxi
  elements of, xv
  predictions of, 152n. 8
  testing validity of, xvii
Lebed, Aleksandr, 144
Ligachev, Yegor, 90–92
Limited Test Ban Treaty (LTBT)
  domestic politics model of decision making for, 47–49
  effect on Soviet-Sino relations (1963), 63
  Kennedy administration campaign for, 61–62
  leadership model prediction related to, 52–62
  ratification (1963), 45
  ratification process in United States, 60–61

Macmillan, Harold, 59
Malenkov, Georgi, 24
Malinovsky, R., 28
Maneuverable Re-entry Vehicle (MARV) technology, 79
McCloy, John, 53
Missiles. *See* Anti-Ballistic Missile (ABM); Ballistic missiles; Cruise missiles; Cuban Missile Crisis; Intermediate-range missiles
Multiple independently targetable reentry vehicles (MIRVs), 67

Neustadt, Richard, 48
New thinking
  concept of, 94–95, 109, 117
  Gorbachev retreats from (1990), 119
  Gorbachev's campaign for, 91–94
  Gorbachev's commitment to, 117
  Gorbachev's use of, 108–9
Nitze, Paul, 78, 79, 81
Nixon, Richard, 66, 140, 141
North Atlantic Treaty Organization (NATO)
  deployments in Europe (1980s), 68, 115
  nuclear systems, 68
  proposal for nuclear missile deployment in Europe, 67–68
Nuclear Planning Group, 77
Nuclear tests
  of Soviet Union (1961), 54–55
  of United States (1961), 55
Nuclear weapons
  failed test ban negotiations (1950s), 21–23, 44
  Khrushchev's confidence based on, 27
  proposal for U.S. missiles in Europe, 67–68
  resumed test ban negotiations (1961), 45
  superpower capabilities and experience, 21–22
  testing of (1945–60), 21
  U.S. decision to stockpile, 29–30
  U.S. internal debate related to, 30–36
Nunn, Sam, 98

Obfuscation
  as bargaining strategy, 4–5
On-site inspections (OSIs)
  Soviet offer to accept (1962), 59

U.S. requirements for comprehensive ban, 60
VELA detection as alternative to, 57

Pavlov, V. S., 119
Peace movements, Western Europe and United States (1980s), 82
Perle, Richard, 106
Pershing II, 79
Predomination strategy
   as bargaining strategy, 4–5
   of Bush during START negotiations (1989–91), 116–17, 123, 130
   of Khrushchev, 27–29
   of Reagan (1985–86), 110
   of Soviets (1961–62), 52–53
   of Soviet Union in renewed INF talks (1985–86), 100–102
   of United States at Reykjavik (1986), 104
   of United States in renewed INF talks (1985–86), 103
Public opinion
   Soviet efforts in Western Europe to sway, 80
Putnam, Robert, 10–11

Reagan, Ronald, 65, 66
   approval ratings in first term, 72–75, 80
   approval ratings in second term, 96–98
   assessment of Soviets (1985), 109–10
   autonomy of, 71, 77, 87, 96, 98–100, 110
   cooperation strategy (1983), 69
   cooperative strategy (1983, 1987), 77, 81–83, 96, 100
   effect of weakness of, 82
   negotiating position in INF talks, 71
   platform and election of, 68–71
   policy toward USSR (1984), 87–88
   position on elimination of intermediate-range nuclear missiles, 78
   position on SDI development, 89
   predomination strategy (1981–82), 69, 77
   predomination strategy (1985), 89
   at Reykjavik arms control talks (1986), 95
   strategies based in his domestic autonomy, 110
   transactional strategies of, 137
   view of Soviet Union as an enemy, 69, 89, 99
Reagan administration
   defense spending during, 76–77
   dual-track decision, 77
   foreign policy toward Soviet Union, 82
   position on START talks, 83
   strategy at Reykjavik (1986), 104
Realist model, xviii–xix
Realist position
   in international relations, 1–2
   on nuclear testing, 21
   related to military power (1983), 170–71n. 1
Rowny, Ed, 106

SALT. *See* Strategic Arms Limitation Talks (SALT)
Schmidt, Helmut, 67, 106
SDI. *See* Strategic Defense Initiative (SDI)
Seaborg, Glenn, 55
Security issues
   assessment on, xv
   Clinton administration policy, 138
   components of, 7–8
   Gorbachev's approach to, 109
   Kennedy's conception of, 52
   post–Cold War, xx
   post–World War II, 1

214   Index

Security issues (*continued*)
  Reagan's position related to, 89
  of Soviet new thinking, 94–95, 109, 117
Self-adjustment strategy, 5–6, 10
Shevardnadze, Eduard, 91, 124–26
Shultz, George
  agreeing to resume arms control talks, 89
  at Reykjavik arms control talks (1986), 95
  on Soviet tactics, 99
SLCMs. *See* Submarine-launched cruise missiles (SLCMs)
Soviet Union
  bargaining at Reykjavik (1986), 95
  Brezhnev way, 70
  choices related to INF, 86–87
  coup (1991), 128, 131, 137
  demands and rejection of concessions at Geneva Conference (1961), 53–54
  determinants of executive autonomy, 13–18
  dictate policy, 5
  in INF negotiations, 65–66, 68
  interest in limited test ban treaty, 60
  Kennedy's perception of, 52
  Kennedy's strategy to cooperate with, 63–64
  position in INF negotiations, 82
  power position under START I, 111–12
  predomination strategy at ENDC, 56
  predomination strategy in INF negotiations, 70, 83
  Reagan administration assessment of, 99
  relations with China under terms of LTBT, 63
  role in Cuban Missile Crisis, 58
  in U.S. foreign policy (1981), 71, 74–77
Space systems
  in INF talks (1985), 101, 115
  Soviet position at Reykjavik (1986), 103
Sputnik satellite, Soviet, 30, 43
START. *See* Strategic Arms Reduction Talks (START)
Strategic Arms Limitation Talks (SALT)
  abandoned (1982), 115
  Nixon as author of process, 66
Strategic Arms Limitation Talks (SALT I)
  ABM Treaty and interim agreement from, 140–41
  nuclear parity coded in, 67, 142
  U.S.-USSR complementary strategies, 141–42
Strategic Arms Limitation Talks (SALT II)
  agreements of, 140
  motivations and bargains of leaders in, 142
  not ratified, 154n. 6
Strategic Arms Reduction Talks (START)
  first U.S.-USSR accord (1991), 111
  Reagan administration position on (1983), 83
Strategic Arms Reduction Talks (START I)
  Bush's position in negotiations (1991), 120–22
  last phase (1989–91), 123
  post-Reykjavik positions, 116
  potential treaty framework created at Reykjavik (1986), 115–16
Strategic Arms Reduction Talks (START II)
  completion of, 143
  failure to ratify, xv

Strategic Arms Reduction Talks (START III), 144
Strategic Defense Initiative (SDI)
    Congress restrains development of, 88, 98, 105
    Gorbachev seeks assurances related to, 106
    Reagan's position related to (1985), 89, 99–100
Strategic power
    U.S.-USSR balance (1972–87), 85–86
    U.S-USSR balance (1980–90), 112
Submarine-launched cruise missiles (SLCMs), 126

Test ban
    approval of partial treaty, 2
    Eisenhower considers U.S.-USSR, 36
    Eisenhower's policy, 42–43
    negotiations for treaty (1961), 52
    U.S. goal of partial, 39, 60
    U.S. internal debate related to, 30–36
    U.S. proposal for threshold (1959), 40
    U.S. requirements for comprehensive, 60
Test ban negotiations
    Eisenhower during (1958–60), 25–27
    Soviet and U.S. strategies (1958–60), 36–41
Test control system
    Geneva System, 38, 42
    U.S. idea to implement (1958–60), 36–37
Tomahawk missiles (GLCMs), 79
Tower Commission (1987), 105

Transactional strategies
    of Kennedy, 137
    of Khrushchev, 137
    of leaders, xvi

U-2 incident
    effect on Soviet domestic policy, 42, 139
    effect on test ban negotiations, 23, 25, 28–29, 40–41, 43–44, 47, 138
United States
    concessions at Geneva Conference (1961), 54
    determinants of executive autonomy, 11–13
    dictate policy, 5
    in INF negotiations, 65–66, 68
    military force buildup in Europe (1961), 54
U.S. Congress
    Republican Mainstream Committee, 88
    restrictions on defense spending, 88, 98, 105
USSR. *See* Soviet Union

VELA seismic research project, 57

Walk-in-the-Woods formula, 83, 79–81
Weinberger, Caspar, 77, 106

Yakovlev, Aleksandr, 91
Yeltsin, Boris
    autonomy of, 144
    erosion of confidence in, xix–xx
    weakened by domestic conflict, 138

Zhukov, 24